T0331956

Disrupted Development in the Congo

CRITICAL FRONTIERS OF THEORY, RESEARCH, AND POLICY IN INTERNATIONAL DEVELOPMENT STUDIES

Series Editors

Andrew Fischer, Naomi Hossain, Briony Jones, Alfredo Saad Filho, Benjamin Selwyn, and Fiona Tregenna

The contemporary world is characterized by massive wealth alongside widespread poverty, inequality, and environmental destruction—all bound up through class, race, and gender dynamics of inequality and oppression. *Critical Frontiers of Theory, Research, and Policy in International Development Studies*, the official book series of the Development Studies Association of the UK, was established to contribute to critical thinking about local, national, and global processes of structural transformation. The series publishes cutting-edge monographs that promote critical development studies as an interdisciplinary and applied field and shape the theory, practice, and teaching of international development for a new generation of scholars, students, and practitioners. As the series evolves, we wish to publish a diverse and inclusive range of authors whose work engages in critical, multidisciplinary, decolonial, and methodologically plural development studies.

RECENTLY PUBLISHED IN THE SERIES

Politics and the Urban Frontier
Transformation and Divergence in Late Urbanizing East Africa
Tom Goodfellow

The Many Faces of Socioeconomic Change
John Toye

The Power of Proximate Peers
Reconfiguring South–South Cooperation for Equitable Urban Development
Gabriella Y. Carolini

They Eat Our Sweat
Transport Labor, Corruption, and Everyday Survival in Urban Nigeria
Daniel Agbiboa

Philanthropy and the Development of Modern India
In the Name of Nation
Arun Kumar

Disrupted Development in the Congo

The Fragile Foundations of the African Mining Consensus

Ben Radley

OXFORD
UNIVERSITY PRESS

OXFORD
UNIVERSITY PRESS

Great Clarendon Street, Oxford, OX2 6DP,
United Kingdom

Oxford University Press is a department of the University of Oxford.
It furthers the University's objective of excellence in research, scholarship,
and education by publishing worldwide. Oxford is a registered trade mark of
Oxford University Press in the UK and in certain other countries

Published in the United States of America by Oxford University Press
198 Madison Avenue, New York, NY 10016, United States of America

British Library Cataloguing in Publication Data

Data available

Library of Congress Control Number: 2023941060

ISBN 9780192849052

DOI: 10.1093/oso/9780192849052.001.0001

Printed and bound in the UK by
Clays Ltd, Elcograf S.p.A.

Acknowledgements

First and foremost, I would like to thank the many Congolese who gave their time, energy, and support to my research. Of those I am able to mention, special thanks must go to Father Gabriel Mushagalusa Buhendwa and Phillipe Dunia, Yvette Bujiriri, and their children, all of whom provided me with generous hospitality during my research. Both South Kivu residences quickly became homes away from my home in Kinshasa and hold many fond memories.

Thank you to Andrew Fischer, whose conversation and writings provided a continual source of inspiration and insight for my work. This book has benefited enormously from his attentive reading of much of the material. A special thank you must also go to the wonderfully gifted Elie Lunanga, my research assistant during much of my fieldwork and who, any day now, will be finishing his doctorate at the University of Antwerp. A bright future for a sharp, young mind lies ahead. To everyone at the *Centre d'expertise en gestion minière* (CEGEMI) at the Catholic University of Bukavu, I would like to express my thanks and gratitude for your input and encouragement over the years, in particular to Sara Geenen and Gabriel Kamundala.

Others I would like to thank for their interest in and support of this project at various moments are Marie-Rose Bashwira, Zacharie Bulakali, Enrico Carisch, Mihika Chatterjee, Tom de Herdt, Bettina Engels, Barbara Harriss-White, Sudeep Jain, Eric Kajemba, Cynthia Kamwengo, Remy Kasindi, Sarah Katz-Lavigne, Janvier Kilosho Buraye, Serge Lammens, Amir Lebdioui, Wim Marivoet, Stefaan Marysse, Lonjezo Masikini, Antoine Mbala, Kate Meagher, Jefferson Mok, Duncan Money, Francine Iragi Mukotanyi, Léonide Mupepele, Crispin Mutwedu, James Putzel, Keith Slack, Soraya Aziz Souleymane, Théodore Trefon, Claudine Tshimanga, Boris Verbrugge, and Christoph Vogel.

Finally, thank you to the Leverhulme Trust, Deutsche Gesellschaft für Internationale Zusammenarbeit (GIZ), and CEGEMI for their funding, without which the completion of this book would not have been possible.

Contents

List of figures

List of tables

List of acronyms

AfDB	African Development Bank
APEF	*Action pour la promotion de l'enfant et la femme*
ATS	Allterrain Services
ASM	artisanal and small-scale mining
AU	African Union
CAR	Central African Republic
CCALU	*Comité des creuseurs artisanaux de Luhwindja*
CEEC	*Centre d'expertise, evaluation et certification*
CEGEMI	*Centre d'expertise en gestion menière*
CEPAL	United Nations Economic Commission for Latin America
CFL	*Chemins de fer du Congo Supérieur aux Grands Lacs*
CIFA	Canada Investment Fund for Africa
CIPEC	Intergovernmental Council of Copper Exporting Countries
CODELU	*Comité de développement de Luhwindja*
DGDA	*Direction générale des douanes et accises*
DGI	*Direction générale des impôts*
DGRAD	*Direction génerale des recettes administratives, domaniales, judiciaires et de participation*
DOM	domestic-owned mining
DRC	Democratic Republic of the Congo
EITI	Extractive Industries Transparency Initiative
ESTMA	Extractive Sector Transparency Measures Act
FAO	Food and Agriculture Organization
FARDC	*Forces armées de la République Démocratique du Congo*
FDI	foreign direct investment
FEC	*Fédération des entreprises du Congo*
FOM	foreign-owned mining
FPI	*Fonds de promotion de l'industrie*
GDP	gross national product
GECAMINES	*Société générale Congolaise des minerais*
GFCF	gross fixed capital formation
GNI	gross national income
GVC	global value chain
IMF	International Monetary Fund
LDCs	least-developed countries
LIC	low-income country
LMICs	low- and middle-income countries
LSM	large-scale mining
MGL	*Société minière des Grands Lacs*

NGO	non-governmental organization
OECD	Organisation for Economic Co-operation and Development
SAP	structural adjustment programme
SGS	*Société générale de surveillance*
SOE	state-owned enterprise
SOMICO	*Société minière du Congo*
SOMINKI	*Société minière et industrielle du Kivu*
TNC	transnational corporation
TSE	Toronto Stock Exchange
UAE	United Arab Emirates
UHLU	*Union des habitants de Luchiga*
UMHK	*Union minière de Haut Katanga*
UNCTAD	United Nations Conference on Trade and Development
UNDP	United Nations Development Programme
UNECA	United Nations Economic Commission for Africa
UNIDO	United Nations Industrial Development Organization
ZEA	*zone d'exploitation artisanale*

Note to the reader

The Democratic Republic of the Congo (DRC) was renamed the Republic of Zaire from 1971 to 1997. Zaire, Zairian, and Zaires (the currency) are used when unavoidable, but otherwise and for the purpose of fluidity, the DRC, Congolese, and Congolese francs are used throughout. All translations from French texts, documents, and interviews are my own.

Epigraph

One of the most conspicuous deficiencies of general economic theory, from the point of view of the periphery, is its false sense of universality.

Raúl Prebisch (1950)

1
Disrupted development in the Congo

In July 2010, then US President Barack Obama signed into law the Dodd–Frank Wall Street Reform and Consumer Protection Act, drafted in response to the North Atlantic financial crisis of 2007–2008. Buried deep down in the Act's miscellaneous provisions, on page 839 of the 849-page document, was Section 1502, whose last-minute insertion into the Act was the outcome of a US campaign to sever the link between mining and conflict in the eastern Democratic Republic of the Congo (DRC). The campaign was informed by a series of reports highlighting the involvement of armed groups in mineral production and trade to finance their activities in the region.

The legislation required companies registered on the US stock market to report on an annual basis whether they had sourced tin, tantalum, tungsten, or gold from the eastern DRC or neighbouring countries and, if so, whether those minerals had financed conflict. Its passing was celebrated by US campaigners as a significant milestone in the struggle to help end the conflict. By preventing armed group profiteering from the local mineral trade, campaigners hoped, their capacity to wage conflict would be reduced.

At the time the legislation was passed, there was no way for US corporations such as Apple and Intel, or their European and Asian suppliers, to determine the origin of minerals sourced from the DRC or whether they had financed conflict. Consequently, rather than expose themselves to reputational risk or economic sanctions, most international buyers withdrew from the region.

A few months later, in September 2010, then DRC President Joseph Kabila announced a six-month suspension of all mining activities in the eastern provinces of North Kivu, South Kivu, and Maniema. This decision, without historical precedent, was motivated by two factors: first, the need to respond to the international attention generated by the passing of Dodd–Frank, second, as a furtherance of national strategy to industrialize mining in a part of the country where production was characterized by low levels of capital intensity (Sematumba 2011).

Disrupted Development in the Congo. Ben Radley, Oxford University Press. © Ben Radley (2023).
DOI: 10.1093/oso/9780192849052.003.0001

The hardship generated by the presidential ban was severe and widespread. With few willing buyers once the suspension was lifted in March 2011 due to Dodd–Frank, it was also sustained. Mining was the most important source of employment in the region after agriculture, with several hundred thousand workers active in the sector (Geenen and Radley 2014). As documented by local research centre the Pole Institute at the time, the situation was characterized by the mass unemployment of miners, declining farmer incomes, parents unable to pay school fees, and the absence of basic food products such as sugar and salt in rural areas (Tegera 2011). To regain access to global markets, local miners had to await the arrival of mineral certification systems (and many continue to wait today, more than ten years on). These systems would, in theory, allow for the origin and conflict-free status of minerals sourced from the region to be determined.

Over time, the need for certification systems was strengthened by the passing of similar legislation and policy elsewhere. The Organisation for Economic Co-operation and Development (OECD) and the United Nations (UN) developed corporate guidelines for sourcing natural resources in high-risk areas such as the eastern DRC. In February 2012, the Congolese government ratified the OECD guidelines into national law. On 5 March 2014, the European Union introduced a voluntary 'conflict minerals' regulation scheme for all member states.[1]

Foreign mining corporations, on the other hand, could more easily fulfil the requirements of Dodd–Frank. The logic went that as mining corporations tightly control the export of their product from the point of extraction to when it leaves the country, armed groups cannot extort profit from industrial production. Consequently, when the Canadian corporation Banro arrived in South Kivu province and began commercial production at its flagship Twangiza gold mine in September 2012 (forcibly displacing several thousand villagers and local miners from the land), US campaigners welcomed the development, and the mining firm was permitted to export its gold to international markets. As Bafilemba and Lezhnev (2015: 3) declared, writing for US advocacy organization the Enough Project, 'gold mines in South Kivu that were previously occupied by rebels are now certified conflict-free mines operated by the Canadian company Banro. The gold from those mines does not go to armed groups any longer.' For the Enough Project and others involved in the campaign, Banro's arrival signalled a further marker of progress in efforts to bring peace and development to the region.

---

[1] Similar logics are now repeating themselves ten years on as North American and Western European countries concerned with child labour and other human rights abuses connected to the local mining of Congolese cobalt, a critical energy transition metal, seek comparable remedies.

The passing of Dodd–Frank in July 2010 to the beginning of industrial gold production at Banro's Twangiza mine in September 2012 marked a tumultuous two-year period of eastern Congolese mining history. For local Congolese miners, certification schemes—however dubious in achieving their intended aims (Radley and Vogel 2015; Vogel 2022)—eventually trickled in, and buyers slowly returned. Yet, Banro's acquisition of research and exploitation permits, stretching across South Kivu's most valuable gold deposits, signalled the beginning of a shift towards a foreign corporate-led model of mining-based development not seen in the region since the collapse of industrial mining in the late 1990s following the onset of the First Congo War.

1.1 Aims and contributions

This book, first and foremost, is an attempt to better understand how the shift in South Kivu from a locally based mining economy towards a foreign-owned model, signalled by Banro's arrival, has interacted with and influenced economic development and conflict trajectories in the province. While much of the book focuses on the period 2010 to 2019, covering the rise and fall of Banro, this is supplemented by travelling through the history, social relations, and economic organization of mining in South Kivu. This journey covers its colonial origins in the 1900s and the emergence of an alternative network of mining production and trade from around the 1950s, to the final decline of Belgian-owned mining in the 1990s and the sector's privatization, deregulation, and liberalization in the early 2000s, through to more recent efforts, from the mid-2010s onwards, to redress the perceived excesses of this earlier reform.

In addition, the book locates the dynamics observed in South Kivu in their broader national and regional context, which, over the past few decades, have similarly been characterized by a shift towards foreign corporate-led industrial mining. Since the turn of the century, and as discussed in more detail in Chapter 2, the DRC has been one of seventeen mineral-rich, low-income countries (LICs) in Africa to have undergone a process of World Bank-financed mining-sector reform, resulting in the ceding of resource sovereignty to transnational corporations (TNCs) within a process of foreign-led mining (re)industrialization.[2] This process has been sustained

---

[2] The term '(re)industrialization' is used when referring to this group as, for some countries, the process involves a reindustrialization of formerly declining or stagnant industrial mining sectors, such as in the DRC, while others are new to the process.

by an African Mining Consensus (hereafter, Consensus) uniting international financial institutions, African governments, development agencies, and various strands of the academic literature.

The country grouping is derived from the twenty-four African LICs listed in the World Bank's fiscal year 2020 country classifications by income level, defined as countries with a gross national income (GNI) per capita of $1,025 or less.[3] Each country was categorized as having either 'insignificant', 'modest', or 'high' levels of metals and mineral wealth.[4] Those with high levels of wealth comprise the mineral-rich African LIC group (Table 1.1).

The purpose of relating the case of the DRC to this country group is not to make abstract, universalizing claims that deny or dismiss the variety of individual countries' internal dynamics. The institutional political economy of each country, alongside the agency deployed by different groups and actors within it and the composition of its metal and mineral endowments, will be critical in determining the developmental effects of foreign-led mining (re)industrialization in specific settings.

Acknowledging this variation, the aim is twofold: first, to make grounded claims which generalize by detailing how the case of the DRC problematizes significant theoretical assumptions within the Consensus concerning the anticipated transformative impact of foreign-led mining (re)industrialization in an African LIC setting;[5] second, to foreground a set of structural constraints facing African LICs as they pursue forms of mining-led industrialization, however devised, in the shape of price volatility, enclavity, and low

Table 1.1 African LIC metal and mineral wealth

Insignificant or modest	High
Benin, Burundi, Gambia, Guinea-Bissau, Rwanda, Somalia, South Sudan	Burkina Faso, Central African Republic (CAR), Chad, DRC, Eritrea, Ethiopia, Guinea, Liberia, Madagascar, Malawi, Mali, Mozambique, Niger, Sierra Leone, Tanzania, Togo, Uganda

Sources: Author classification based on the World Bank's fiscal year 2020 country classifications by income level, US Geological Survey country reports (https://www.usgs.gov/centers/nmic/africa-and-middle-east#sl, accessed 12 August 2021), and the Artisanal and Small-Scale Mining Knowledge Sharing Archive (http://artisanalmining.org/Inventory, accessed 8 August 2021).

[3] Use of the dollar sign refers to US dollars throughout, unless otherwise stated.
[4] The categorization is based on a qualitative reading of US Geological Survey country reports combined with a quantitative appraisal of the Artisanal and Small-Scale Mining Knowledge Sharing Archive's database. The former provides detailed information on country-level metal and mineral reserves. The latter collates published data to estimate the country-level number of miners engaged in labour-intensive forms of mining, which serves as a good proxy for metal and mineral reserves.
[5] This follows Cornish's (2020) conceptualization of generalization as a communicative and dialogical process, where generalizability is not categorically asserted but left for the epistemic community of readers to determine.

labour absorption. These constraints, observed in the DRC, are theorized as generalizable to other mineral-rich African LICs based upon the group's peripheral position in the global economy, unable to control demand for their commodity exports (heightening their exposure to price volatility), at comparably low levels of industrial development (heightening their exposure to enclavity), and with abundant supplies of labour (heightening their need for high levels of labour absorption). By drawing attention to these structural impediments, the book hopes to highlight the challenges facing African LICs as they pursue peripheral forms of mining-based development and how these might best be confronted.

The idea of peripherality has come in for much criticism by post-development and decoloniality scholars as well as, more recently, by mainstream development studies academics keen to disassociate themselves from what they see as a colonial project and for whom twenty-first-century convergence through the 'rise of the South' has challenged the intellectual and moral relevance of this analytical framing (see, e.g., Horner and Hulme 2019). The North–South binary, they contend, is based upon a simplified, antiquated, and derogatory bifurcation of the world into centres and peripheries. Given these critiques, it is worth briefly stating how the term is understood in this book and why it is used.

Peripheries and centres are never static but are constantly in flux over the long run. From the tenth to the twelfth centuries, Europe was part of the global periphery, with Asia and the Middle East holding the centre (Amin 2011). The emergence of capitalism in Western Europe and its uneven spread globally through imperialist expansion and colonial conquest placed the near entirety of the global South—Asia, Africa, and Latin America—in a subordinate position within a new world order.[6] By the mid-twentieth century, the global centres of wealth and power were firmly located in Western Europe and North America.

There is no doubting that the world has experienced profound change over the past several decades, in particular the rise of China and East Asia more broadly. Notwithstanding these changes, contemporary structuralists have drawn attention to the continued monopoly of technology and capital flows in the global North and the resultant technological and industrial subordination of countries and regions in the periphery of the capitalist world economy (Ocampo et al. 2009; Montes 2014; Akyüz 2017). The highly uneven distribution of COVID-19 vaccines in the wake of the 2020 pandemic—determined by which nations had the required manufacturing capacity and which had

---

[6] While the exact timing and origins of the emergence of capitalism are debated, there is broad agreement that it took place in Western Europe at some point between the thirteenth and eighteenth centuries.

the most influence over the institutions of international governance (such as to uphold intellectual property rights)—provides a modern exemplar of how peripherality plays out in the global economy and at what human cost.

Despite the critiques mounted around the concept, then, this book adopts the position that:

> It is nonetheless still useful to frame the contemporary challenges of develop-
> ment in terms of peripherality. The concept reflects certain common asymmetries
> and constraints that continue to structure the lagging and subordination of the
> global South in the current world order, even despite the monumental changes
> and variations, and without denying the importance of Southern agency.
>
> (Fischer 2015: 704)

By 'force of example' (Flyvbjerg 2006), the book hopes to demonstrate the continued relevance of peripherality for understanding the specificity of development challenges in African LICs, the various mechanisms through which North–South (or centre–periphery) inequalities continue to be sustained and reproduced, and how different groups resist and seek to transform their conditions by forging alternative paths of social and economic change.

By returning to, and adapting, some of the classic critiques of peripheral development, the book also aims to challenge the academic and development industry wave of African resource optimism for TNC-led mining (re)industrialization that so heavily characterized the 2000s and 2010s and appears to live on unabated in the 2020s, driven this time round by the mineral and metal intensity of the hoped-for global transition to low-carbon economies and societies in the coming decades (a point I return to at more length in the concluding Chapter 8).

In addition, the book offers a reframing of how we—as development studies scholars, social scientists, policymakers, and practitioners—write, think about, and discuss African mining, away from a focus on artisanal, small-scale, or large-scale and towards distinguishing more clearly between different forms based on capital intensity and ownership. The habitual discursive framing contrasts 'artisanal and small-scale mining' (ASM) with 'large-scale mining' (LSM) or, more simply still, artisanal mining with industrial mining.

Pierre (2020: 87) has argued that, in the African context, the use of artisanal falls into a racial vernacular of development that 'thrives on the construction of a notion of fundamental African racial difference (and white Western normativity) while rendering the unequal institutional and material relations of resource extraction [. . .] through terms that sediment cultural narratives of this presumed African inferiority'. A cursory scan of the literature on African mining makes this apparent. Artisanal mining and miners are frequently labelled as 'primitive', 'simplified', 'basic', 'inefficient', 'rudimentary', and 'unproductive' and industrial mining as 'efficient', 'modern', 'complex', and 'productive'. A similar framing can be observed in the description of state-owned African mining enterprises, typically cast as inefficient, mismanaged, and corrupt.

This vernacular, in turn, feeds into an underlying teleology in which the backward and inefficient techniques of African miners, or corrupt and mismanaged state-owned African enterprises, should be replaced by more modern, complex, and efficient forms of production and technology embodied by the foreign mining corporation.[7] This teleology has, no doubt, contributed to and helped sustain the African Mining Consensus, discussed in more detail in section 1.2, which adheres to this line of thinking. However, the teleology fails to account for the potential developmental advantages of African artisanal mining or, conversely, why industrial mining in this setting might be undesirable. It dismisses greater relative labour intensity as inefficient and unproductive and deems ownership and choices of technology unimportant in favour of prioritizing rapid productivity growth by advancing to the technological frontier of heavily industrialized mining as quickly as possible.

As will be shown in this book, both perspectives are problematic. To the first, labour-intensive production can be highly valuable in a context of widespread unemployment and rapidly growing populations, especially when it generates higher wages than those available in the surrounding economy. To the second, operating under foreign ownership at the technological frontier can shift the distribution of value generated by productive activity away from domestic groups and towards overseas firms, directors, and shareholders.

For these reasons, this book replaces the ASM/artisanal-LSM/industrial framing with descriptors based on ownership—domestic-owned mining (DOM) and foreign-owned mining (FOM)—and the relative capital or labour intensity underpinning production (Figure 1.1). Ownership, here, is understood in the traditional Marxist sense of ownership over the means of production coupled with the developmentalist understanding of strategic ownership and control over a firm or industry.

Within this schema, most social science mining books from the past decade or so have tended to focus exclusively on either capital-intensive FOM or labour-intensive DOM. With the notable exception of Verbrugge and Geenen (2020), few existing publications provide a framework that allows for an

---

[7] See Engels (2022) for a more in-depth discussion along a similar line of analysis.

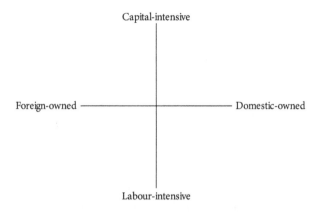

Figure 1.1 Forms of mining production
Source: Author creation.

investigation into how these two interact and with what developmental consequences, along with an elucidation of the variation that exists between the
two poles, from labour-intensive FOM to more capital-intensive, industrializing forms of DOM. This book attempts to offer such a perspective.

Through this framework, the book aims to engage and contribute to
the broad literature on global value chains (GVCs), which, over the past
decade or so, has helped to generate great enthusiasm around the econom-
ically transformative potential of TNC-led mining (re)industrialization in
Africa.[8] GVC analysis was mainstreamed by the development industry in the
2010s as a central focus of contemporary development efforts in the global
South (Werner et al. 2014). The literature is primarily concerned with the
institutional and regulatory contexts in which domestic firms in low- and
middle-income countries (LMICs) can integrate into and 'upgrade' within
TNC-led GVCs to higher value-added activities, both in mining and other
sectors and industries (Gereffi et al. 2005; Gereffi 2014).[9]

In the African commodities sector, GVC scholarship has provided much
insight into how, and in what contexts, policy interventions can strengthen
(or undermine) the position of domestic firms in global mining value chains.
It has been generally uncritical, though, of the underlying assumption that
African governments should focus on integrating domestic firms and actors

---

[8] I follow Suwandi (2015) here by taking the position that the GVC, global production network, and
global commodity chain approaches are reasonably overlapping as the terms are used interchangeably,
and so GVC is used to encompass all three.

[9] The literature on African mining is heavily clustered among high- and middle-income countries such
as South Africa, Nigeria, Sudan, Zambia, and Ghana. This even though low-income countries comprise
more than half of the national economies on the continent.

into, and 'upgrading' them (moving to higher value-added activities) within, a model of capital-intensive FOM.[10] The book challenges this assumption by drawing attention to the developmental potential of pre-existing forms of labour-intensive DOM and a consideration of how TNC arrival can marginalize and disrupt these forms of mining, leading to an intensification of local conflict rather than its reduction or resolution.

In so doing, this book extends the conventional mining GVC analytical framework to incorporate a wider consideration of not only how value is created and distributed in mining GVCs but also from where (and whom) it is transferred within this process, what use is made of the value by those who capture it, and with what effects on social relations, economic development, and conflict. Here, the book connects to an emergent area of research on African resource nationalism (Jacob and Pederson 2018; Kinyonde and Huggins 2019; Pederson et al. 2019), which takes a more critical view of capital-intensive FOM and gives greater analytical space to the developmental role of labour-intensive, DOM alternatives.

Finally, the book conceptualizes economic development as a process achieved through increasing labour productivity (measured as the output per unit of labour time) and sustained by capital accumulation (Fischer 2014:14).[11] Usually, such economic development encompasses a transformative process, commonly referred to as structural transformation, in which productive resources move from low-productivity to higher-productivity sectors and activities. By relating mining to this specific understanding of economic development as structural transformation, the book connects to and complements non-extractive industry literatures, in particular those on developmental states and industrial policy, which share a common interest in studying transformative processes of social and economic development and—for the more critical strands—the various forms of polarization, marginalization, and exclusion to which these processes inevitably give rise (Cramer et al. 2020).

The book's contribution here is in drawing attention to the role of African capitalists, a neglected group in scholarship on African statism and industrial policy (Behuria 2019). A recent body of work attempting to correct this imbalance has focused on large African corporations and conglomerates, or Diversified Business Groups (Behuria 2019; Andreoni and Sial 2020; Itaman and Wolf 2021). The book builds on and expands this line of enquiry by focusing, in contrast, on 'capitalism from below' (Byres 1996).

---

[10] The work of Hilson and Ovadia (2020) provides a notable exception.
[11] Capital accumulation refers here, in the Marxian sense, to the accumulation of the produced means of production, such as machines and infrastructure.

It does so through the analytical primacy given to the rural emergence of a Congolese capitalist class via their engagement with labour-intensive DOM and the struggles they face operating on the margins of a mining landscape dominated by foreign corporations, whose presence has been facilitated and legitimized by proponents of the African Mining Consensus.

1.2 The African Mining Consensus

The African Mining Consensus is not without its dissenters. It is contested, refuted, and resisted, both on the ground and by policymakers and scholars. The Consensus is also not hegemonic in the Gramscian sense that its realization has been achieved through consent rather than coercion. As will become clear in this book, and as others have illustrated (Engels and Dietz 2017), coercion has been a central guiding tenet. The contention is that, in recent decades, the Consensus has been the dominant discourse and conceptual framework nourishing and directing mining strategy and policy on the continent.

Theoretically, the Consensus is founded on the premise that African countries should leverage their comparative advantage in metals and minerals to drive productivity growth and that the resultant distribution of value from these productivity gains will stimulate the structural transformation of local and national African economies. For this, state-owned enterprises (SOEs) and local forms of labour-intensive mining are both deemed unsuitable. The former is characterized as corrupt and mismanaged and the latter as an inefficient, low-productivity, subsistence activity with links to conflict financing. The Consensus holds, instead, that mining (re)industrialization should be led by the superior expertise and efficiency of foreign corporations.

The World Bank (1992) laid the early groundwork for this position in its landmark 1992 report, *A Strategy for African Mining*. In the report, the decline and stagnation of capital-intensive DOM in the 1970s and 1980s was explained by 'inward-looking, import-substitution economic policies and state ownership and control of productive facilities' (World Bank 1992: 9). Labour-intensive DOM was brandished as 'illegal' and 'inefficient' and as 'having brought problems of law and order, safety, environmental degradation, and the loss of potential government revenue' (World Bank 1992: 42). Instead, African governments were told, with no lack of clarity, 'The private sector should take the lead. Private investors should own and operate mines' (World Bank 1992: xiii). Managed in this way, the report continued, the African mining sector 'can provide important benefits in terms of exports, foreign exchange earnings, and tax receipts to support economic recovery and growth in Africa' (World Bank 1992: x). The state's role was to privatize SOEs as soon as possible, as a signal to investors that they intended to pursue a foreign corporate-led mining strategy. Nearly thirty years on, the Bank remains wedded to the idea that capital-intensive FOM can form 'growth poles' on the continent (World Bank 2010; Hilson 2019).

Economic and social science scholarship has provided some support to this position, arguing that, if properly managed, capital-intensive FOM can drive sustainable development (Botin 2009; Richards 2009; Addison and Roe 2018). This includes in the DRC, where Garrett and Lintzer (2010: 419), assessing whether TNC-led copper and cobalt industrialization can drive growth and development in the country, concluded with 'a cautious yes'. De Putter and Decrée (2013: 60–61) argued that, under the right conditions, a corporate-owned industrial mining sector can benefit 'all Congolese'.[12]

African and international development agencies have adopted a similar position. The African Development Bank's (AfDB) flagship 2013 report, *Structural Transformation and Natural Resources*, argued that 'Africa must work on its strengths. The continent has a strong comparative advantage in natural resources, either in the form of energy, minerals, or agriculture. These can be the drivers of structural transformation through linkages, employment, revenue, and foreign investment' (AfDB 2013: 112–113). Similarly, in the foreword to the 2012 report *Promoting Industrial Diversification in Resource Intensive Economies*, the Director-General of the United Nations Industrial Development Organization (UNIDO) commented:

> The ongoing boom in commodity prices offers numerous opportunities for resource-rich low- and middle-income countries in sub-Saharan Africa and Central Asia. For one, commodity producers—both governments and firms—have gained access to growing financial surpluses which, in turn, provide funds for investment in industrial diversification to complement the resources sector. Both the direct and indirect income generated by the commodities sector furthermore has the potential to spur industrial development through the establishment of a domestic market and the generation of new export opportunities which facilitate employment creation and economic growth.
>
> (UNIDO 2012: 7)

---

[12] The doctoral thesis of Dr Augustin Matata Ponyo (2017)—who served under President Joseph Kabila as minister of finance (2010–2012) and the prime minister (2012–2016)—went further still, arguing that mining reindustrialization was central to the period of macroeconomic recovery and stability after the end of the Congo Wars in 2002.

African governments have embraced a similar logic and, often working in close collaboration with the World Bank, have reformed their policy and regulatory frameworks accordingly (as described in greater depth in Chapter 2). While the African Mining Vision, adopted by African Heads of State at the 2009 African Union (AU) summit, was part of a push to assert greater national resource sovereignty on the continent, implementation has been poor (Graham 2022; Maphanga 2022). The reality at the national level has remained a model of mining-based industrialization which prescribes a central role to foreign corporations. Even the African Mining Vision itself, while departing from the World Bank by advocating various forms of state intervention to develop stronger linkages with other sectors of the economy, adheres to the general Consensus vision of capital-intensive FOM as a potentially 'viable component of an integrated and sustainable growth and development strategy for Africa' (AU 2009: 5).

In developing this position, African governments and development agencies have been influenced and guided by a body of GVC scholarship which has been optimistic about the potential for capital-intensive FOM to drive broader-based processes of structural transformation and industrialization on the continent. In the early 2010s, two of the most influential commodity-focused GVC policy papers were published, arguing that 'the enclave mentality to diversification in low-income [African] economies is an anachronism' (Kaplinsky et al. 2011: 29), and in the right conditions, TNC-led mining in African LICs can 'provide a considerable impetus to industrialization' (Morris et al. 2012: 414). This was because:

> The global mining industry has [. . .] undergone a radical restructuring of its historically dominant production model. Mines have moved away from a high level of vertical integration towards outsourcing almost every stage in the mining process to independent firms. This incorporates not only the provision of equipment and capital goods, as well as inputs such as chemicals, but also key knowledge services.
>
> **(Kaplinsky et al. 2011: 15)**

Inspired by these papers, and GVC analysis more broadly, much of the scholarly and development industry literature on African mining throughout the remainder of the decade focused on whether, and how, African states can make better use of local content and localization policies to strengthen the position of domestic firms and the contribution of capital-intensive FOM to economic development and industrialization (Bloch and Owusu 2012; UNIDO 2012; AfDB 2013, 2016; Esteves et al. 2013; Farole and Winkler

2014; World Bank 2015; Hansen et al. 2016; Ovadia 2016; Ramdoo 2016; UNDP 2016; Dziwornu 2018).[13]

Governments have been less enthusiastic about labour-intensive DOM. This has primarily been because of its perceived low productivity and inefficiency, as initially stated by the World Bank in its 1992 report, limiting its desirability as a poverty-alleviating, transformative development strategy. The following depiction from the African Mining Vision is typical:

> Working from a low capital and asset base, most ASM activities are of a rudimentary nature, with little mechanization (shovels, hoes, picks, and wheelbarrows are the tools commonly used). Where there is mechanization, equipment and techniques are inefficient and hazardous to the environment and to the miners. In consequence, productivity, ore recovery and yields are low and income remains at subsistence level. This hinders re-capitalization and upgrading of mining operations and keeps small-scale miners in a vicious cycle of poverty.
>
> **(AU 2009: 27)**

Due to this kind of framing, labour-intensive DOM has been peripheral to mining development strategies on the continent. While policy frameworks have acknowledged its existence and importance to rural livelihoods, these same frameworks have tended 'to constrain rather than encourage artisanal mining' (Bryceson and Jønsson 2014: 19). This can be seen most clearly in the procedurally complex, bureaucratically burdensome, and financially costly demands made of African miners to formalize and legalize their activity (Banchirigah and Hilson 2010).

In the DRC, for example, Congolese miners must work in officially recognized *zones d'exploitation artisanale* (ZEA)—artisanal exploitation zones. Within these zones, miners must self-organize into cooperatives, apply for individual exploitation cards, and comply with security and environmental regulations, with each requirement carrying a sizeable financial cost (Geenen and Radley 2014). Progress has been slow. In South Kivu, as of 2017, only seven ZEAs covering an area of 250 square kilometres had been established. This contrasts sharply with the 16,000 square kilometres covered by foreign-owned mineral research and exploitation permits that same year.[14] At the national level, in the early 2010s, the concessions owned by

---

[13] Local content refers to the local procurement of goods and services, while localization is intended as a broader concept, which incorporates an additional focus on firm capacity, skills training, and industrial development.

[14] South Kivu Provincial Ministry of Mines mining permit data set, 2017.

foreign gold mining corporations covered 83 per cent of the DRC's known gold reserves (Mupepele 2012).

The result for African miners, illustrated by Geenen (2014: 279) in the case of the DRC, is a formalization process that 'criminalizes everyone who does not comply with the regulations' and dispossesses those 'who do not and cannot obtain an official title, often to the advantage of actors with more financial capital, such as industrial companies'. The criminalization of African miners, cast by policy frameworks as illegally encroaching on a concession once it has been assigned to a corporation, paved the way for their forced displacement (a phenomenon discussed at more length in section 2.3).

An additional reason for marginalizing labour-intensive DOM in favour of capital-intensive FOM has been the belief that while the former contributes to conflict, the latter can help to alleviate it. Since the turn of the century, academics, Western advocacy organizations, and UN reports have drawn attention to the relationship in Africa between labour-intensive DOM and conflict. This body of work has taken theoretical inspiration from the scholarship of Collier and Hoeffler (2002), who argued that contemporary conflict was motivated more by potential profits in easy-to-access natural resources than by social or political grievance.

This literature has had two waves. The first wave was focused on labour-intensive diamond mining in West Africa, depicted as 'blood diamonds' (Lujala et al. 2005; Olsson 2006; Rodgers 2006). As with the work of Collier and Hoeffler, it was predominantly based around economic modelling and econometrics. The second wave focused on 'conflict minerals' in Central Africa, with particular attention on the DRC but also neighbouring Burundi, Rwanda, and Uganda (Cuvelier and Raeymaekers 2002; Garrett and Mitchell 2009; Global Witness 2009; Rustad et al. 2016).

One of the arguments made in this literature is that, as touched upon in the chapter opening, TNC-led supply-chain management prevents armed group profiteering from production, alleviating conflict intensity. The economist Ola Olsson (2006), the principal early proponent of this line of thought, observed that Botswana and Namibia achieved better development outcomes and witnessed lower levels of conflict from diamond production than Angola, the DRC, and Sierra Leone. Olsson interpreted these divergent outcomes as due to the presence of the industrial diamond transnational De Beers in the former group compared to the presence of local mining (and the absence of De Beers, or a foreign corporate counterpart) in the latter group.

A similar logic can be found in the 'conflict minerals' literature, which has drawn attention to the fact that 'rebel groups compete [over natural resources] to extract maximum commercial and material benefits' (Cuvelier and Raeymaekers 2002: 5). Local forms of mining thus finance conflict, and an alternative is required. The alternative, as with diamonds in West Africa, is to be found in the foreign mining corporation, whose efficient supply-chain management 'can help limit revenues for armed actors operating in the informal market' (Bafilemba and Lezhnev 2015: 3). In this way, this literature conjoins itself with the other strands reviewed in this section to bolster belief in the developmental preference for, and potential of, capital-intensive FOM in the African periphery.

1.3 Recentring the periphery

In establishing the Consensus position around the model of mining (re)industrialization that ought to be pursued in Africa, proponents have tended to misrepresent or disregard some of the classic critiques mounted by a group of pioneering early development economists. These critiques focused on the specific challenges and constraints faced by income-poor peripheral countries seeking development through deeper integration with the global capitalist economy. Returning to these earlier critiques provides helpful lenses with which to explore, with some adaptation, several axes of tension within the ongoing process of TNC-led mining (re)industrialization in African LICs that are overlooked by the absent or simplistic representation of these critiques by Consensus proponents.

The first tension derives from the Consensus's abandonment of the concept of peripherality itself, originally developed by a group of structuralist economists in the 1940s and 1950s, most notably by Raul Prebisch (1950) and his colleagues at the UN Economic Commission for Latin America (CEPAL). The centre–periphery framework arising out of Prebisch's seminal formulation—a framing which had been prefigured by the work of earlier scholars in the Black Radical Tradition, such as Du Bois (Edwards 2020)—drew attention to the structural constraints faced by countries in the periphery that were distinct from but linked to those faced in the industrialized centre and that risked undermining peripheral development.

By abandoning this framework, Consensus proponents cleared the way to point to historical instances of resource-based industrialization and structural transformation during the early stages of capitalist development in today's industrialized countries as refuting the basis of early structuralist insights. The cases of Australia, Belgium, Britain, Canada, Finland, France, Germany, Norway, Spain, Sweden, and the United States are commonly cited by scholars and development agencies alike as evidence that—contra the critiques of Prebisch and other development economists of his time—commodity production has driven transformative and sustained economic development, including higher wages, through the stimulation of domestic manufacturing and industry (Blomstrom and Kokko 2007; Wright and Czelusta 2007; Domenech 2008; AU 2009; Kaplinsky et al. 2011; UNECA 2011; Morris et al. 2012; Calvo et al. 2019).

Citing historical examples of resource-driven economic development in today's industrialized countries as evidence to invalidate early structuralist thought and dismiss the relevance of peripherality misses the key insight of this lineage. Neither Prebisch nor his CEPAL colleagues denied that resource exploitation might have been a contributing factor to the industrialization and economic transformation of Northern economies. This was neither the focus nor interest of their critique but rather their starting point. Precisely because of the successful industrialization of these economies, CEPAL structuralists were concerned with the specificity of twentieth-century resource exploitation in non-industrialized Latin America, which, Prebisch and his contemporaries contended, led to a polarizing spread of productivity in these countries, in contrast to the growth experience of the industrial centres, where productivity had spread more evenly and widely throughout domestic economies.

According to Prebisch (1950), this disparity was because of the enclaved nature of peripheral resource extraction, dependent upon capital and technology emanating from, and developed in, the centre, which, once received by the periphery, created externally oriented production structures disarticulated from domestic economies, unlike the more strongly articulated economies of early industrializing countries. Here, articulation implies embeddedness with, and connection to, the surrounding local or national economy, while disarticulation implies dis-embeddedness and disconnection. As a result, peripheral capitalist economies were prone to experiencing declining terms of trade, macroeconomic instability, and the marginalization of local populations (Fischer 2015: 705).

The work begun by the early CEPAL structuralists was continued and expanded by a new generation of Latin American economists and political economists, or dependency theorists, who developed a line of critique centred around the idea that the outcomes of peripheral development were dependent upon (but not determined by) development in the industrialized centre (Cardoso 1977; Cardoso and Faletto 1979; Furtado 1983). Working within this tradition, the pioneering work of the Chilean Osvaldo Sunkel and Constantine Vaitsos (Greek by origin, Colombian by adoption) leads us to a second axis of tension within the process of TNC-led mining (re)industrialization in African LICs.

Sunkel (1972, 1973) and Vaitsos (1973) were among the first to highlight the contradictions of a model of Latin American development delivering high growth rates but predicated on the dominance of foreign direct investment (FDI) in key industries. Their critique centred on the effects of TNC structures of ownership and control, which entailed a massive penetration of foreign subsidiaries into Latin American economies. This allowed TNCs to exert control over value flows and induced dramatic socio-political consequences—including (à la Prebisch) widening inequality—by instigating fundamental changes in the ownership patterns, social structures, and political systems associated with production (Sunkel 1972).[15] In these ways, the heavy presence of FDI in key sectors of the economy might represent a deepening of, rather than a departure from, the condition of dependency.[16]

The work of the Egyptian Marxian economist Samir Amin further develops this issue around the potentially deleterious effects of FDI dominance in key industries and leads us to a third axis of tension for investigation. Having developed a similar line of dependency thought to his Latin American contemporaries of the 1970s, Amin (1990) proposed 'delinking' as a strategic model to promote autonomous development in the periphery. The strategy centred around breaking from the demands imposed by the external global economy and reorienting strategy and policy towards serving domestic demand and promoting popular development (grounded in an understanding of the needs and interests of workers and peasants) (Kvangraven et al. 2021). A core pillar of the model was the capacity for the 'technological absorption and ingenuity' required to drive transformative and sustained processes of auto-centred development (Amin 1990: 60).

Picking up on Amin's work, and writing in the late 1970s and 1980s, Egyptian economists Fawzy Mansour and Mohamed Dowidar, and the Tunisian agronomist and dependency theorist Slaheddine el-Amami, raised the importance of grounding the technological component of Amin's 'delinking' project in the selection of 'appropriate technology' (Ajl 2021). Central to this was the pursuit of a combination of technological transfer and local innovation rather than a fixation of the former at the expense of the latter

---

[15] This Latin American scholarship quickly travelled to Africa, where, in the DRC, for example, French translations of the work of Prebisch, Sunkel, Furtado, Cardoso, and others were circulated, debated, and adapted by a group of Congolese academics from the mid-1970s onwards (Tshibambe 2018).

[16] Working in the tradition of Caribbean dependency thought, Jamaican Norman Girvan (1970) similarly found the penetration of vertically integrated foreign firm subsidiaries in 1960s mineral-exporting economies to significantly undermine the creation of linkages, the dissemination of technology, and the domestic reinvestment of profits in other industries.

(Ajl 2021: 90). Transfer without innovation, it was held, would inevitably lead to technological dependence, deepening rather than overcoming the constraints of peripheral development. Local control over technological choices, they argued, was a prerequisite for internally articulated development. If pursued along these lines, Amami contended, technology and knowledge systems within a given industry provided the bases for 'accumulation from below, a widened internal market, [and] staunching the bleeding-out of value' (Ajl 2021: 93).

Here, we are brought full circle back to the 1960s and 1970s Latin American (and Indian) debates around 'choice of technique' (Boianovsky 2013) and 'tecnologia social' (Pozzebon and Fontenell 2018). Within these debates, in a similar vein to the African literature on 'appropriate technology', were those—including CEPAL members—who contended that high capital intensity in labour-abundant peripheries was undesirable at the early stages of industrialization and that low capital intensity should form a guiding principle to development planning in this context. Such a position stands at odds with Consensus prescriptions, which give short shrift to the notion and potential value of low capital-intensity production, preferring instead rapid advancement to the technological frontier through capital-intensive FOM.

Working at the same time as Prebisch and his CEPAL contemporaries, albeit outside of these structuralist and dependency lineages, the Saint Lucian classical economist Arthur Lewis (1954) was also engaged with thinking through the specific challenges and constraints related to the condition of peripheral development. Here, his open economy model of economic growth with unlimited supplies of labour provides a fourth and final axis of tension for investigation. In the model, and in a similar vein to Prebisch, Lewis theorizes the relationship between productivity and wages in the global periphery, as distinct from its historical evolution in the industrialized centres. Pursuing the question of why Caribbean commercial crops were so cheap, despite their high productivity, Lewis argued that wages in this industry are set according to the productivity of what he called 'subsistence sectors' rather than in capitalist export sectors. As a result, he contended, the benefits of increasing productivity in capitalist export sectors accrue to Northern importers, via lower prices, and not to the workers.

Transposed to African LICs today, Lewis's model suggests that industrial miner wages will be set in the 'subsistence sectors' of the surrounding informal economy, not according to the productivity of the formal export sector. Under these conditions, unless the productivity of subsistence producers or the overall availability of employment are simultaneously increased, wages and general living standards will not improve. Lewis's theorization questions if and how the value created by productivity is captured in peripheral settings and to what extent workers in the periphery benefit from productivity gains via increased wages. By so doing, Lewis leads us to a fourth axis of tension for further investigation by complicating the Consensus assumption that capital-intensive FOM can drive broader processes of consumption-led economic growth and structural change by raising wages among the local population.

More recent changes in the global economy indicate that the analytical frameworks advanced by these pioneering groups of Latin American and African economists and dependency theorists retain their relevance at the onset of the 2020s. The productivity gap between OECD countries and LICs in 2010 was more than five times greater than the gap in the nineteenth century between the Netherlands and the United Kingdom and the first round of late industrializers, such as Finland and Japan (UNCTAD 2010). Further, the recent growth of East Asian economies has shrunk the industrialization space for African LICs, while more liberal trade rules and deregulated capital markets have limited the room for industrial and trade policies (Storm 2015).

The era of structural adjustment and globalization of the 1980s and 1990s, conjoined with the generalized abandonment of projects of national development that so heavily populated the immediate post-colonial era of the 1960s and 1970s, have made the actual dependence of Southern—and especially (but not just) African—economies more acute than previously (Girvan 2006). Foreign direct investment and TNC activity has expanded to levels far beyond those of the 1970s.[17] Through this expansion, TNCs have gained considerable power in relation to the state. The now commonplace use by corporations of investor–state dispute settlements to sue governments for taking actions that threaten their profits provides a case in point. Highlighting the challenge of overcoming modern peripherality, only three of the original thirty-six least-developed countries (LDCs) in Africa have graduated from their status since the list's inception in 1971: Botswana (in 1994), Cape Verde (in 2007), and Equatorial Guinea (in 2017).

To render an analysis of peripheral development fit for the contemporary context, however, the growth of financialization must be incorporated into the framework. Financialization refers to the increasing dominance, since around the 1970s, of the sphere of circulation over the sphere of production, creating new processes of surplus extraction from the periphery to the capitalist financial centres (Newman 2012). Financialization tends to reduce

---

[17] The value of global FDI stock has risen from 7.8 per cent of global gross domestic product in 1967 to 67.2 per cent in 2014 (Dunning and Lundan 2008; UNCTAD 2015). The number of TNCs globally rose from around 7,000 in 1969 to more than 100,000 in 2012 (Ietto-Gillies 2013).

overall levels of accumulation of real capital and to prioritize shareholder value over other values (Fine 2008).

In the context of the growing financialization of commodity markets, metals and minerals 'have become attractive for portfolio diversification and hedging' (Sensoy et al. 2015: 159). By contributing to the further redirecting of monetary value from productive centres in the periphery to predominantly Northern centres of non-productive financial capital, financialization might exert downward pressure on TNC profits, alleviated in turn by squeezing the value accruing to domestic governments, firms, and labour further down the chain. This fifth and final axis of tension is the corollary of the global mining industry restructuring away from vertical integration observed by scholars of African commodity GVCs but absent in their analyses. While potentially providing opportunities for productive and service sectors in the periphery at the lower levels of the chain, it might also direct value at the upper levels into non-productive, financial activities located primarily in financial capitalist centres.

At their core, the critiques of peripheral development reviewed here are preoccupied with four central issues: how and by whom productivity is created in the periphery; how the resultant value generated is distributed between and within different groups; what use these different groups make of the value accruing to them; and the resultant effects of these processes on social relations and structural transformation in the periphery, with a particular focus on TNC strategies of ownership and control. The major lines of argument put forward in this book are based on an analysis of these four issues in relation to mining-led development in South Kivu province of the eastern DRC.

The remainder of this book pursues these lines of investigation in the context of mining reindustrialization in South Kivu province of the eastern DRC, beginning by locating this case within its historical, national, and regional context.

1.4 The argument

Through a detailed case study of mining reindustrialization in South Kivu, the book offers an extended investigation into the solidity of the theoretical foundations underlying the African Mining Consensus by asking how Banro's entry into South Kivu's mining economy has influenced processes of economic development and conflict trajectories in the province. Pursuing this line of enquiry, the main empirical argument advanced by the book is that mining reindustrialization was, in fact, already underway in South Kivu, independent of TNC tutelage. A locally led process of mining mechanization was contributing to several of the outcomes theorized by Consensus proponents of capital-intensive FOM, including increased productivity via capital formation and raised local wages. Furthermore, a high proportion of the end value of labour-intensive DOM was being retained and distributed domestically, overseen by an emerging capitalist class investing in productive accumulation, including in non-mining sectors. TNC entry into South Kivu has disrupted this process, replacing it with a foreign-managed, externally oriented, and enclaved mining economy that has reproduced (and, in some cases, accentuated) historically rooted forms of peripheral marginalization, polarization, and conflict.

Drawing from the empirical evidence presented, the central assumption underlying the Consensus that modern corporations will be more efficient and effective at leading structurally transformative processes of mining-based development than the SOEs that preceded them, or existing local alternatives, is challenged. Foreign corporations in South Kivu have been prone to mismanagement, inefficiencies, and rent-seeking and implicated in fuelling conflict and violence. In addition, structural impediments to the transformative effects of mining industrialization in the form of price volatility, enclavity, and low labour absorption occur irrespective of ownership and management structures.

Within the confines of these constraints, and in light of the levels of overseas surplus extraction and domestic marginalization associated with capital-intensive FOM, a shift to domestic-owned forms of mining-based development—and, in particular but not just, efforts to mechanize labour-intensive forms of local mining—would better meet the needs of African LIC economies for rising productivity, labour absorption, and the domestic retention of the value generated by productive activity than the currently dominant but disconnected and disruptive TNC-led industrial model.

More broadly, based on the evidence presented, the wisdom of the continued deference shown to FDI as the driver par excellence of development in African LIC settings is questioned. Such deference overlooks two key tendencies of TNCs operating in peripheral economies, as seen through the case of South Kivu: first, the tendency to marginalize domestic firms and emergent capitalist classes, groups observed historically as central to the process of late industrialization and structural transformation (Evans 1995; Singh and Ovadia 2018); second, the tendency to retain strict control over value flows, the value of most of which is redirected to overseas shareholders, senior company directors, and firms at the expense of the domestic reinvestment required to productively absorb rapidly growing labour forces. Considering these observed tendencies, TNC dominance in key industries might be less a means to overcome African peripherality than an explanatory cause. This has state business and industrial policy implications for the pursuit of economic development in the global periphery at a time of increasing TNC expansion and infiltration into societies and economies across the continent.

1.5 Outline of the book and methods

Following this introductory chapter, Chapter 2 charts the return and spread of the transnational mining corporation across a wider group of African LICs than was the case during the colonial period. It is organized in three sections, each corresponding to a separate stage of the process that facilitated this trend. The first stage involved a diagnosis of the economic challenges faced by African economies in the late 1970s as due to misguided state intervention and government corruption. During the second stage, the International Monetary Fund (IMF) and the World Bank advocated for, financed, and, in many instances, directly oversaw the liberalization, privatization, and deregulation of African LIC mining sectors. The third stage required criminalizing African miners engaged in labour-intensive production and, if required, forcibly displacing them to make way for the construction of capital-intensive, foreign-owned mines.

In Chapters 3–5, the book turns its attention to an in-depth investigation of foreign-owned mining in South Kivu, both historically across the twentieth century and more recently in the 2010s. Each of the three chapters gravitates around a separate structural constraint to mining-based development in an African LIC setting: price volatility (Chapter 3), enclavity (Chapter 4), and low labour absorption (Chapter 5). Chapter 3 analyses how the supposed superiority of capital-intensive FOM has unravelled in South Kivu not once but twice, the first time during the latter half of the twentieth century and, more recently, under Banro in the 2010s. The evidence presented suggests that foreign-owned mining corporations are no less vulnerable to mismanagement, firm inefficiencies, and volatile prices than their state-owned counterparts. In the case of capital-intensive FOM, the developmental impact of this vulnerability has been exacerbated through a high degree of overseas surplus extraction, the costs of which, in the case of Banro, have been borne domestically by the Congolese state and Congolese firms and labour.

Chapter 4 investigates the degree of articulation between the Congolese economy and the manufacture and provision of goods, equipment, and capital infrastructure to FOM in South Kivu during the twentieth century and how the turn to corporate outsourcing since the 2000s has affected this articulation. Based on the findings presented, it is argued that the greatly advanced technological frontier of mining in the twenty-first century has led to a heightened level of disarticulation and alienation between Banro's Twangiza mine and the surrounding Congolese economy compared to earlier eras of FOM in South Kivu.

In Chapter 5, it is shown how FOM in South Kivu has demonstrated a historical tendency to deliver low and stagnant wages to most workers while delivering high wages to a narrow managerial group. Meanwhile, the industry turn to outsourcing has—by expanding labour informality and entrenching spatial separation between workers—weakened the collective strength of workers at Twangiza to resist and transform their conditions. Together with a low level of labour absorption and the external orientation of most of the managerial stratum, who consume and invest their wages outside of the DRC, the ability of wages derived from capital-intensive FOM to stimulate economic development in South Kivu has been limited. Taking the evidence presented across Chapters 3–5 together bears out many of the concerns raised by the critiques of peripheral development reviewed in section 1.3.

Chapters 6 and 7 explore the developmental potential of a locally led alternative to the foreign-owned model in the form of labour-intensive DOM, alongside a consideration of how Banro's entry into South Kivu has interacted with and influenced this pre-existing mining economy. Chapter 6 demonstrates how labour-intensive DOM in South Kivu has been a site of dynamic domestic accumulation through technological assimilation and innovation, capital formation, and productive investments outside of mining. Moreover, the capital–labour social relation underpinning labour-intensive DOM in South Kivu has delivered higher wages to workers than those available in the surrounding economy, while facilitating the emergence of a capitalist class of dynamic and prosperous rural Congolese.

Chapter 7 reveals how labour-intensive DOM has been subjected to processes of displacement, subversion, and suppression following Banro's arrival. This, in turn, has given rise to new forms of protest, violence, and killings as different groups of local actors have sought to resist their new-found marginality. Chapter 8 concludes by reflecting on the implications of the findings, including what scope there might be for the social forces driving labour-intensive DOM to emerge as a viable alternative to capital-intensive FOM in the coming years and decades, both in and beyond South Kivu.

Most of the data collection was undertaken between May 2016 and August 2017, at which point I was living in the capital city of Kinshasa and travelling regularly to South Kivu. This was informed more generally by my work and research on the DRC's mining sector since 2011, when I first moved to the country (based initially in Bukavu, South Kivu), some of which is drawn on directly in the book. The research was further aided by continuing to reside in the country until early 2019. This allowed me to follow up on certain strands and missing pieces of data, as well as sharing and discussing my findings with academic and local communities in South Kivu and Kinshasa.

Data was mostly collected across four main sites: Luhwindja (home to Banro's Twangiza mine and the adjacent labour-intensive Kadumwa mine), Kamituga (home to one of Banro's major concessions and a historically important mining town in the region), South Kivu's provincial capital city of Bukavu (where Banro had a regional office and Congolese gold traders operate and export their merchandise), and Kinshasa (mostly for archival research). Much of my time, around six months, was spent in Luhwindja with my research assistant Elie Lunanga. This included a two-week stay inside the compound of the Twangiza mine itself towards the end of the research.[18] The approach in Luhwindja was predominantly ethnographic, involving a combination of direct and participant observation, conversations, and informal interviews. French fluency and conversant Swahili allowed me to hold most of these exchanges directly. When the Swahili eluded my grasp or the local language of Shi was preferred by participants, Elie provided invaluable support with translation.

While it was difficult to keep track of every interaction, insights to the research problem were generated by speaking with or interviewing at least 408 people across these different sites, predominantly those in mining (both past and present) but also farmers, herders, teachers, hospital workers, priests, police, military, civil servants, and government authorities. A range of other methodologies were employed, including archival research, the collection of corporate documentation, labour and subcontractor surveys, and the creation of financial and production logbooks with local miners and gold traders.

---

[18] To counter the widely held belief locally that I worked for Banro, I made every effort to distance myself from, and maintain my neutrality with, the corporation. This included, for example, declining Banro's offer to drive us to and from Luhwindja (from Bukavu) and to lodge and transport us around while there. Instead, we travelled on local buses, lodged at the local Franciscan parish, and got around by foot or taxi motorbikes. As my on-site presence at Twangiza would no doubt have aroused further suspicion, I delayed this visit until the end of the fieldwork period.

2

The return and spread of the transnational mining corporation in the African periphery

In the 1960s, African governments used their newfound independence to assert sovereignty over their mineral resources, often through direct state ownership. This marked a reversal of their prior colonial exploitation by European mining corporations. Over the course of the past forty years, the pendulum has swung back the other way. By the close of the 2010s, transnational mining corporations had once again become the dominant force assuming ownership and management of industrial mining projects across a greater number of African low-income countries (LICs) than during the colonial period.

The aim of this chapter is to historically situate the case of mining in South Kivu within this broader context. It is organized in three sections, each corresponding to a separate stage of the process that led us from 'there' to 'here'. The first stage involved a diagnosis of the economic challenges faced by African economies from the mid-1970s as due to misguided state intervention and government corruption. This involved ignoring or downplaying the post-independence progress made up to this period and the weight of external shocks in bringing about a rapid reversal of fortunes.

Based on this diagnosis, during the second stage, the International Monetary Fund (IMF) and the World Bank advocated for, financed, and, in many instances, directly oversaw the liberalization, privatization, and deregulation of African LIC mining sectors. Supported by a commodity supercycle, this facilitated the significant growth of resource-seeking, inward foreign direct investment (FDI) flows from the 1990s onwards across the country group. As will be shown, at the onset of the 2020s, African LICs are more heavily dependent upon FDI as a source of development financing than ever before, and this dependence is greater relative to other country groups and regions.

Disrupted Development in the Congo. Ben Radley, Oxford University Press. © Ben Radley (2023).
DOI: 10.1093/oso/9780192849052.003.0002

The third stage required confronting the inconvenient reality that many of the deposits targeted by incoming mining transnational corporations (TNCs) were already occupied by African miners involved in labour-intensive forms of production. This obstacle was dealt with by criminalizing these miners and, if required, forcibly displacing them to make way for the construction of capital-intensive mines. With this hurdle overcome, mining TNCs could turn their attention to the business of ramping up production.

As noted in section 1.1, the analytical focus on low-income African countries is not intended to imply a homogeneity of experience across the country group or to downplay each country's internal dynamics, which will be critical in determining the developmental effects of foreign-owned mining (FOM) (re)industrialization. Indeed, the uneven pace with which FOM (re)industrialization has taken place across the country group since the 1980s is emphasized throughout the chapter. The intention here is rather to foreground the justification for their collective grouping by highlighting the commonalities of their shared trajectory, in particular the uniformity of World Bank-financed mining-sector reform, the resultant ceding of resource sovereignty to foreign corporations, and the marginalization of both state-owned enterprises (SOEs) and African miners within this process.

2.1 Stage one: Blame the African state

During the colonial period, a handful of African LICs produced and exported metals and minerals to European markets: the Democratic Republic of the Congo (DRC), Guinea, Liberia, Sierra Leone, Tanzania, and Uganda.[1] Most African LIC mineral deposits remained unknown to foreign capital at this time, particularly in West Africa (Amin 1972). Where mining sectors were established, they were disarticulated from pre-existing economies, functioning as economic enclaves through which a substantial proportion of profits were repatriated to mother companies overseas (Ghai 1972). In the DRC, for example, between 1924 and 1949 shareholders of *Société minière des Grands Lacs* (MGL, Great Lakes Mining Company), the Belgian mining firm that held a monopoly on production in the east of the country, received an eighteen-fold return on their original investment of 377.4 million Belgian francs.[2]

The wave of political independence from European colonial rule, beginning in the mid-1950s, ushered in a period of resource-based national

---

[1] British Geological Survey World Mineral Production Yearbooks.
[2] MGL Annual Reports, 1924–1950.

developmentalism, including the pursuit of African socialism in several countries. This was based on the recognition that during the colonial period, Africa's natural resources had been exploited by European mining corporations to the benefit of their directors, shareholders, and general populations (by virtue of low prices). For these resources to serve the national interest of African countries, economies, and peoples, it was held that—along with other areas of the economy, including the financial sector—external control and ownership had to be reduced. Buoyed by the long commodity boom of the 1950s, and the spirit of events such as the 1955 Bandung Conference and the 1958 All African People's Conference, there was a general commitment by African governments and states to wrest the control and management of their natural resource wealth back from the hands of their former colonizers (Hormeku-Ajei and Goetz 2022).

In the DRC, the first step was taken under the presidency of Joseph-Désiré Mobutu with the Bakajika Law of June 1966, which—in an attack on the contentious 1960 Belgian law giving colonial Congolese corporations Belgian nationality just a few weeks before Independence—required all foreign-based companies whose main activities were in the DRC to establish their headquarters in the DRC by the end of the year. The government failed to reach an agreement on the nationality of the largest and Belgian-owned colonial mining subsidiary, *Union minière de Haut Katanga* (UMHK)—Haut Katanga Mining Union. So, on 31 December 1966, the Mobutu administration announced its decision to expropriate UMHK and transfer its assets to a new company, *Société générale Congolaise des minerais* (Gécamines, the Congolese General Company of Minerals), which was to eventually become 100 per cent state-owned. The policy of increasing state participation in the productive economy continued in other sectors. By 1970, the Congolese public sector controlled 40 per cent of national value added (Young and Turner 1985: 68–69).

Efforts elsewhere were similarly ambitious, such as Kenneth Kaunda's Zambian-led initiative of the Intergovernmental Council of Copper Exporting Countries (CIPEC) and Julius Nyerere's nationalist ban on extractives, 'aimed at keeping resources in the soil until the nation could develop the productive forces to manage extractives for national development' (Greco 2020: 512). The early results were impressive. In the DRC and Zambia, copper production increased steadily between 1960 and 1974—across the inaugural years of the CIPEC—from around 300,000 to 500,000 tonnes and 500,000 to 700,000 tonnes, respectively.[3]

---

[3] British Geological Survey World Mineral Production Yearbooks.

In the DRC, this contributed to a tripling of state revenue from $190 million in 1967 to $630 million in 1970 (World Bank 1970). A national health system numbering 500,000 employees was established, seen as a model for primary health care in the global South. The education system was nationalized, achieving 92 per cent primary school enrolment and increased access to the secondary and tertiary sectors (Putzel et al. 2008). Across Africa, manufacturing value-added grew at a rate of 7.5 per cent annually between 1960 and 1975 (Mkandawire 1988: 13). Primary school enrolments increased from 41 per cent of the eligible population to 68 per cent between 1965 and the mid-1980s (Mkandawire and Soludo 1999: 16).

This period culminated in May 1974 with the United Nations (UN) adoption of a Declaration and Programme of Action on the Establishment of a New International Economic Order. This declaration and programme 'set out principles for equality between nations, including sovereignty over natural resources and an equitable relationship between the producers and consumers of raw materials' (Money et al. 2020: 589). Rather than usher in a new international economic order, however, the period during which this declaration was signed was to prove a stark reminder of the solidity of the old order and the difficulty of pursuing peripheral development in a global capitalist economy.

The declaration was inaugurated at a time when the oil price was beginning to rise and demand for African exports beginning to diminish due to recession in the global North, leading to a decrease in commodity prices. In the DRC and Zambia, the copper price crashed from $1.40 per pound in April 1974 to $0.53 per pound in early 1975 and stagnated thereafter. Around the same time, from 1973 to 1977, the cost of oil imports quadrupled (Young and Turner 1985: 307). Coupled with rising inflation globally during this period, the effect of these price shifts on government revenue would have been even greater in real terms. In addition, as African government loan repayments became due, interest rates on the loans began to rise as the United States sought to control inflation through monetary policy. Previously rising mining production levels stagnated or dropped, growth slowed, and debt grew across the continent, reducing the foreign exchange available to purchase the imports needed to further industrialization. Between 1980 and 1988, 25 African countries rescheduled their debts 105 times (Cheru 1992). In the DRC, copper and cobalt exports decreased sharply, eventually collapsing by the early 1990s.

Of course, external shocks were not the sole cause of the reversal. Internal dynamics had a critical role to play, most notably perhaps the 'socially rootless' nature of industrialization efforts in Africa (Mkandawire 1988: 18). In the DRC, external shocks unmasked the failures and limitations of Mobutu's nation state-building project. Nationalization measures undertaken in 1973 and 1974 to provide an emerging politico-commercial class of senior state bureaucrats with access to productive capital—known as Zairianization—were poorly planned and implemented and went badly awry. Agriculture had been neglected, receiving less than 1 per cent of state expenditure from 1968 to 1972, and the Congolese manufacturing sector was in decline (World Bank 1973, 1975).

Yet, a consideration of the impact of external shocks, alongside recognition of the progress made by newly independent African governments in the short time frame up until this juncture, was largely missing from influential publications in the 1980s seeking to understand the causes of African economic stagnation from the mid-1970s onwards. Instead, misguided African state intervention and government corruption were put forward as primary causal explanations, to the exclusion of other factors. Championed largely by Africanists based in North American universities (such as Robert Bates (1981) and Eliot Berg, author of the World Bank (1981) report *Accelerated Development in Sub-Saharan Africa: A Plan for Action*), this line of thinking was immediately embraced by the IMF and the World Bank (Mkandawire and Soludo 1999). Toye (1994) has theorized that the appeal of the diagnosis lay in its apparent offering of a development panacea: by locating the state as the single source of economic failure, this failure could then be easily overcome by removing the state from the development process.

In the DRC, World Bank reports from the 1980s show how ingrained this view was at the time. In one, the Bank (1984: 12) argued that the country's economic decline was due to 'a long series of inadequate economic and financial decisions. Nothing in the past decade has had a more lasting and devastating effect on the economy than the Zairianization and Nationalization measures of 1973 and 1974.' The following year, the Bank (1985: 4) argued that 'the largely inefficient parastatal sector has inflicted high opportunity costs on the Zairian economy and exacerbated internal and external imbalances'.

There is no doubting that the ill-conceived nationalization policies of the 1970s, and in particular the Zairianization measures, held some responsibility for the DRC's economic difficulties during this period. Yet, such factors ought to be weighed in consideration with the impact of external shocks— which began for the DRC with the copper price crash in 1974—and the achievements made by the Mobutu administration up until this point. Such a weighting exercise is absent from both reports.

Offering a regional perspective, the seminal work of Mkandawire and Soludo (1999: 39) on the causes of the mid-1970s decline in African economic performance is worth citing at length:

> Our intention here is not to rationalize, let alone ignore the infamous misman-agement of economies by African governments. Rather, the point is to emphasize that successful adjustment will be elusive unless Africa's vulnerability to external factors is recognised. Such a recognition will serve in rethinking the form and con-tent of Africa's structural transformation. Failure to account for such factors, even as one corrects for internal policy errors, can frustrate attempts at change and condemn them to involuntary reversal.

By downplaying the external and foregrounding the internal, the result is an analysis and diagnosis that lays the blame firmly on the state management and ownership structures underpinning national developmentalist ambitions in the 1960s and early 1970s, to the exclusion of shocks and trends in the global economy.

With governments across the global South in debt distress, and with lit-tle or no access to international capital markets during this period, both the IMF and the Bank grew significantly in influence, formulating a set of policies that came to be known as the Washington Consensus (Williamson 1993). The policies revolved around a neoliberal menu of fiscal discipline, reducing public expenditure, import liberalization, FDI liberalization, the privatization of SOEs, and the general deregulation of economic activities. 'Getting the prices right' was the central tenet, and the state was perceived as a price-distorting obstacle to this goal. The doctrine was implemented across Africa by the World Bank—and IMF-financed structural adjustment programmes (SAPs), geared towards currency devaluation, trade liberal-ization, reducing the role of the state, and eliminating subsidies. Between 1980 and 1991, while the number of SAPs implemented by each coun-try varied, all seventeen mineral-rich, African LICs underwent some form of structural adjustment (Mosley and Weeks 1993).[4] Crucially, most SAPs also had a focus on increasing primary commodity exports, but this time around—to correct for the perceived failures of the recent past—under new management.

---

[4] Accounting for the fact that during this period, Eritrea had yet to gain independence from Ethiopia.

2.2 Stage two: Roll out the corporation

It was in this political and ideological context that, alongside and, in some cases, through the implementation of SAPs, the World Bank set about financing and overseeing the deregulation, privatization, and liberalization of the African mining industry. As Hormeku-Ajei and Goetz (2022: 12) have summarized, 'at the onset of neoliberalism the World Bank told African governments to abandon any notion to use mineral resources to serve social priorities or developmental priorities and give up the running and management of minerals and mineral wealth to transnational companies'. Towards this end, between 1980 and 2021, the Bank provided around $1.1 billion in mining-sector grants and loans to fifteen mineral-rich African LICs (all except for Chad and Eritrea), of which more than $300 million was still active in 2021.[5] The country-level distribution of this financing is listed in Figure 2.1 and shows that more than 50 per cent of the total amount was distributed to just five countries: Mozambique, the DRC, Guinea, Niger, and Tanzania.

The concentration of grant and loan value in just a few countries, however, masks a high level of uniformity in the regulatory and institutional reform prescribed by the Bank across the country group. The Bank's vision for

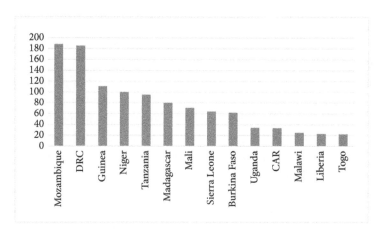

Figure 2.1 World Bank mining grants and loans to mineral-rich African LICs, 1980–2021 (millions of USD)

Source: Author calculations based on data from the World Bank Projects & Operations Database, http://projects.worldbank.org/en/projects-operations/projects-home (accessed 9 August 2021).

---

[5] These figures do not include grants and loans provided for energy and infrastructure projects, which are often directly related to mining industry development.

reform is most succinctly presented in its 1992 guiding document, *Strategy for African Mining*:

> The private sector should take the lead. Private investors should own and oper-
> ate mines. The government should promote private investment, establish policies
> and regulations, supervise implementation of established policies, and monitor
> the private companies. Existing state mining companies should be privatized at
> the earliest opportunity to improve productivity of the operations and to give a
> clear signal to investors with respect to the government's intention to follow a
> private-sector-based strategy.
>
> **(World Bank 1992: xiii)**

Prior to the rise of China as an alternative source of resource-linked finance, and with many African countries still unable to access international capital markets, the Bank was able to exert significant influence through these grants and loans to implement its strategic vision for how mining should be organized and managed.

In the African LIC mining policies that followed, state regulation was sanctioned only insofar as securing FDI and upholding the sanctity of private property (Bush 2010). Tanzania's 1997 policy, for example, was geared to the pursuit of a model of 'private sector-led mineral development, while the major roles of the government are regulating, promoting, and facilitating' (EITI 2011: 10), a far cry from the nationalist ban on extractives of the Nyerere era.

In the DRC, where the World Bank has provided \$185 million in loans to oversee mining-sector reform, staff from the Bank worked in close collaboration with a Congolese committee on the drafting of the mining law. Blaming mining-sector decline on poor governance under the Mobutu administration, reform was driven by the World Bank's maxim that 'Zaire must be less, but better governed' (World Bank 1994, cited in Mazalto 2008: 57). The eventual 2002 Mining Code moved to privatize state-owned mining enterprises and attract fresh FDI by offering a generously liberal fiscal regime, including tax holidays and exemptions and low royalty rates.[6] This included the eventual privatization of the country's two largest SOEs, Gécamines (as previously noted) and the diamond producer *Société minière de Bakwanga*—Bakwanga Mining Company.

Campbell (2008: 369) has shown how the experience of loan-recipient African countries during the 1990s and 2000s was 'a cumulative process

---

[6] Much later, in 2015, the IMF DRC head of mission would comment, 'the 2002 Mining Code is too generous, so much so that the state captures very little in the end' (cited in Lukusa 2016: 156).

of reform leading to several generations of increasingly liberalized mining regimes'. By the end of the 2000s, African LIC governments had reduced or eliminated state participation in mining enterprises, provided a wide range of fiscal and tax incentives to encourage FDI, liberalized exchange controls and exchange rate policy, and enshrined investment-protection assurances (UNECA 2011: 17).

Despite some modifications during the 2010s (with increasing emphasis on environmental regulation, social provisions, and transparency, reflected through the emergence of discourses around 'corporate social responsibility' and 'sustainable mining'), the Bank's underlying logic that African mining should follow the model of capital-intensive FOM held fast (Hilson 2019). In 2021, the Bank had ongoing mining reform programmes in the seven mineral-rich African LICs of Niger ($100 million), Guinea ($65 million), Mozambique ($50 million), Mali ($40 million), Sierra Leone ($20 million), Togo ($15 million), and CAR ($10 million). Each programme was focused, in whole or in part, on institutional and regulatory change within a general framework giving overall priority to capital-intensive FOM.

Recent mining code and policy revisions led by African LIC governments, such as Tanzania, the DRC, Sierra Leone, and Malawi, have sought to redress the liberal excesses of earlier eras. These revisions have taken inspiration from the Africa Mining Vision (AU 2009), a framework developed in 2009 to deepen the linkages between FOM and national economies and strengthen government capacity to negotiate with and leverage developmental benefits from foreign mining corporations (as discussed in section 1.2). In 2018, for example, the DRC passed a new mining code which raised royalty rates, introduced a super-profits tax, and increased government participation in industrial projects from five per cent to ten per cent.

The global mining industry, and some scholarship (Andreasson 2015; Pederson et al. 2019), has been quick to herald this as a new era of resource nationalism. Yet, recent policy reform has sought only to regulate more tightly, rather than challenge and overturn, the dominant model of capital-intensive FOM industrialization on the continent. This remains a far cry from the earlier era of 1960s and 1970s resource sovereignty to which the discourse on resource nationalism alludes (Greco 2020).

With the regulatory framework overhauled, foreign investment was freed to seek out fresh opportunities. Mining exploration in Africa increased from 4 per cent of total mineral exploration expenditure worldwide in 1991 to 17.5 per cent in 1998, and overall mining investment in Africa doubled between 1990 and 1997 (Pegg 2006). The start of a commodity supercycle in 1999 gave fresh impetus to this activity. In 2004, the $15 billion invested in mining in

Africa represented 15 per cent of the total of mining investment worldwide, up from 5 per cent in the mid-1980s and putting the region third globally, behind Latin America and Oceania (UNCTAD 2005). From 2002 to 2012, a period spanning most of the supercycle, mineral exploration spending in Africa rose by more than 700 per cent, reaching $3.1 billion in 2012 (Wilburn and Stanley 2013).

Gold was the major attraction, with the gold price increasing by a factor of six from $279 per troy ounce in 2000 to $1,669 per troy ounce in 2012.[7] Alongside Banro in South Kivu, for example, the Australian explorer Vector Resources, Canadian TNC Monument Mining, US-listed Panex Resources, and UK-listed ARC Minerals together invested tens of millions of dollars in advanced gold exploration programmes in the 2000s and early 2010s.

In 2007, the United Nations Conference on Trade and Development (UNCTAD) noted that:

> the sweeping changes in African LDCs' mining policy in the 1980s and 1990s were aimed at attracting FDI and increasing exports, in which they have been successful. Total FDI inflows into African LDCs rose fourfold from an annual average of $1.7 billion in the 1990s to $6.8 billion in 2000 to 2005 [. . .] the bulk of which was directed to mineral extractive industries.
>
> **(UNCTAD 2007: 35)**

In 2012, FDI inflows to LDCs grew robustly by 20 per cent to a record level of $26 billion and were highly concentrated in several African countries (UNCTAD 2013: xviii). In 2014, total FDI inflows to LDCs reached $23 billion and remained 'concentrated in a small number of mineral-rich economies', with African LICs among three of the top five LDC FDI recipients (UNCTAD 2015: 78–81).[8] The scale of the trend was such that, by the mid-2010s, for many African LICs, the mining sector had become 'one of the most crucial sources of investment and income in their economies' (Farole and Winkler 2014: 117). In the DRC, FDI inflows increased by a factor of seventeen between 2002 and 2012, from $188 million to $3.3 billion.[9] Across the same period, FDI stocks rose from $907 million to $22.5 billion or from 10 per cent to 59 per cent of gross domestic product (GDP). The fresh investment was almost exclusively focused on mining (Englebert 2014).

---

[7] World Gold Council, http://www.gold.org/goldhub/data/gold-prices (accessed 13 August 2021).

[8] The top five countries were Mozambique ($4.9 billion), Zambia ($2.5 billion), the DRC ($2.1 billion), Tanzania ($2.1 billion), and Equatorial Guinea ($1.9 billion).

[9] UNCTADstat database.

Looking at the aggregate level of inward FDI flows to mineral-rich African LICs from 1970 to 2019 confirms this picture (Figure 2.2). Total FDI inflows to the group were low and stable during the 1970s and 1980s, at an annual average of just $0.2 billion, increasing only slightly to $0.6 billion in the 1990s. Hereafter, they grew to an annual average of $3.9 billion in the 2000s and $13.9 billion in the 2010s. Notably, inward flows have declined following a 2012 peak of $17.8 billion. This peak year coincided with the end of the supercycle, further supporting the notion that much of the prior increase was primarily resource-seeking. This underscores the vulnerability of this type of investment and activity to world price fluctuations, a point taken up for closer examination in Chapter 3.

Despite this post-supercycle drop, inward flows throughout the 2010s were still significantly greater than those experienced during any year of the previous decade (at $11.5 billion in 2019, for example, compared to the $7.9 billion peak for the 2000s in 2008). At $46 billion, FDI inflows to Africa in 2019 (the year prior to the COVID-19 pandemic outbreak) were comparable to the annual average of the preceding ten years of around $50 billion, driven by 'the continuation of resource-seeking investments' (UNCTAD 2019: 3). An important factor here is the significant demand generated for several minerals and metals deemed critical for the global transition from fossil fuels to renewable energy, many of which are found in abundance on the continent (see section 2.3 and Chapter 8 for further discussion of this point).

Table 2.1 presents data disaggregated by country on the size and importance of FDI inflows to mineral-rich African LIC economies since the 1990s,

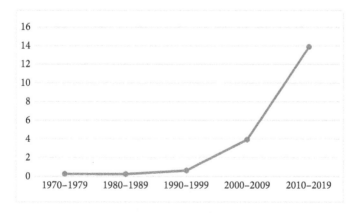

Figure 2.2 Annual inward FDI flows to mineral-rich African LICs, period averages (billions of current USD)

Source: Author calculations based on data from UNCTAD and UNCTADstat.

Table 2.1 Select indicators on annual inward FDI flows to mineral-rich African LICs, period averages (millions of current USD)

Country	Value			FDI flows As % of GDP			As % of GFCF		
	1990–1999	2000–2009	2010–2019	1990–1999	2000–2009	2010–2019	1990–1999	2000–2009	2010–2019
Mozambique	92	366	3,696	2.0	4.4	24.7	14.7	31.9	94.0
Ethiopia	69	311	2,101	0.9	2.9	3.2	4.9	11.2	9.2
DRC	3	591	1,919	0.0	4.0	6.0	1.6	35.1	31.0
Tanzania	121	603	1,388	1.2	3.1	3.1	5.3	11.9	9.4
Uganda	80	440	929	1.2	3.5	3.6	5.6	13.5	13.8
Niger	10	141	662	0.3	2.2	6.8	3.4	9.7	23.5
Liberia	72	130	517	10.2	17.0	28.6	14.6	83.0	101.3
Madagascar	19	421	502	0.5	4.9	4.3	4.3	18.4	21.2
Guinea	20	123	452	0.4	2.2	5.5	3.5	10.6	20.8
Mali	24	199	397	0.9	3.2	2.9	3.2	16.9	16.0
Sierra Leone	3	54	382	0.4	3.1	10.3	4.5	33.0	47.2
Chad	22	282	321	1.3	10.4	2.8	10.4	28.0	14.8
Burkina Faso	7	71	246	0.3	1.0	1.8	1.3	5.9	9.1
Malawi	13	76	161	0.5	1.8	2.6	3.9	12.2	20.6
Togo	14	53	141	0.8	2.5	3.6	7.0	15.5	13.4
Eritrea	77	38	55	9.7	2.3	1.5	30.5	14.4	17.1
CAR	1	30	23	0.2	1.7	1.1	2.0	16.4	8.0
Country Group	602	3,918	13,891	1.5	4.1	6.6	7.8	21.6	27.7
Country Group (minus Liberia)				0.9	3.3	5.2	5.6	17.8	23.1
Africa				1.1	2.6	2.2	5.4	11.6	10.0
Developing economies				1.9	2.9	2.3	7.7	10.8	7.6
World				1.3	2.3	2.1	5.6	9.9	8.6

Notes: GFCF = gross fixed capital formation.
Source: Author calculations based on data from UNCTAD and UNCTADstat.

when inflows first began to noticeably increase.[10] Three stylized trends emerge from the data. First, there is a high level of FDI concentration in just a few countries. For the most recent period of 2010–2019, 55 per cent of total FDI went to just three countries (Mozambique, Ethiopia, and the DRC) and 72 per cent to just five countries (the addition of Ethiopia and Uganda).

Second, FDI concentration has been coupled with significant growth across all countries except for Eritrea. While the countries located towards the bottom of Table 2.1 received the lowest absolute levels of inward FDI flows between 2010 and 2019, they experienced pronounced increases in these flows since the turn of the century, much of which was mineral-seeking. In Madagascar, for example, 74 per cent of total FDI inflows between 2007 and 2011 went to the country's mining sector (EITI 2015: 61). Throughout the 2010s, FDI to Burkina Faso, Guinea, Malawi, and Mali was driven by a gold boom. The significant levels of country-level FDI growth across the group indicate the presence of nascent and emerging forms of capital-intensive FOM across a broader range of African countries than is often implied by the 'concentration' narrative. Indeed, as highlighted above, it is in several of these lower-placed countries that, in 2021, the World Bank had active mining-sector reform programmes.

Third (and, again, apart from Eritrea), while in the 1990s the importance of FDI relative to mineral-rich African LIC GDP and gross fixed capital formation (GFCF) was comparable to Africa, to developing economies, and globally, by the 2010s, FDI had become a significantly more important component of mineral-rich African LIC economies than in these other groupings. In other words, FDI growth since the 1990s has altered the composition of these economies, which have become increasingly dependent upon FDI as a source of development financing, and this level of dependence is greater today relative to other country groups and regions.[11]

While not undermining the overall nature and direction of the trends observed, it should be noted that a sizeable portion of the significantly increased inward FDI flows to the country group is motivated by non-mining interests. In Mozambique and Uganda, for example (two of the top five countries in terms of total FDI inflows during the 2010–2019 period), FDI has been primarily targeting oil and gas.

---

[10] Due to rounding, values and percentages in Table 2.1 and throughout the book do not necessarily add to totals.

[11] The Burundian economist Ndikumana (2015: 6) has pointed out that 'although the volume of private capital flows into [Africa] has increased substantially over the past two decades, the continent's share in global financial flows remains small'. Yet, given the level of absolute increase in FDI inflows documented, FDI is nevertheless a more important component of mineral-rich African LIC economies than was the case during the previous century.

It should also be acknowledged that foreign capital is not the only source of mining investment to the country group. It is, nonetheless, the dominant source. In 2014, seven countries from the group submitted mining project ownership data to the Extractive Industries Transparency Initiative (EITI).[12] The data is not comprehensive as mining companies reported on a voluntary basis and many failed to do so. Nevertheless, of the 180 mining firms that did report, 159 (or 89 per cent) were foreign-owned TNC subsidiaries. Moreover, nearly all the reporting domestic firms were SOEs holding minority stakes in foreign-owned projects, such as Gécamines in the DRC.

To summarize, by the 2010s, the earlier post-independence model of national ownership and control over natural resources had given way to a new era in which mineral-seeking FDI had grown dramatically. This, in turn, led to the en masse arrival of mining TNCs to establish a new model of capital-intensive FOM across the African periphery.

2.3 Stage three: Displace African miners

One final stage was required before transnational corporations could move front and centre. This involved dealing with the on-the-ground reality that, for many incoming TNCs, their prized deposits were already occupied by African miners involved in a wide range of labour-intensive forms of mining. Most commonly associated with gold and diamonds, labour-intensive African mining is also involved in the production of silver, copper, cobalt, tin, tantalum, iron ore, aluminium, tungsten, wolframite, phosphates, precious and semi-precious stones, and rare earth minerals, among others. Globally, labour-intensive mining has been estimated to contribute up to 30 per cent of total cobalt production, 25 per cent for tin, tantalum, and diamonds, 20 per cent for gold, and 80 per cent for sapphires (Fritz et al. 2018; World Bank 2020).

In 1989, the World Bank (1992) estimated the annual value of labour-intensive gold and diamond production in Africa at $1 billion, produced by an estimated one million miners. This included a consideration of gold production in thirteen of the seventeen mineral-rich African LICs, which, as a group, comprised around 80 per cent of the estimated production value across the continent. The size of labour-intensive domestic-owned mining (DOM) in mineral-rich African LIC economies by the 2010s can be

---

[12] The submitting countries were Burkina Faso, DRC, Ethiopia, Madagascar, Mali, Tanzania, and Togo. The status 'foreign owned' was assigned if a non-national entity owned more than 50 per cent of the company equity.

estimated by looking at the number of miners engaged in this form of production by country and their percentage composition of the rural population (Table 2.2). Due to the largely informal and undocumented nature of this mining, numbers are highly approximate, yet nonetheless offer some sense of scale.

With an estimated total of around 7 million miners across the country group, representing around 3 per cent of the rural population, the general picture confirms Hilson's (2009: 1) observation that labour-intensive DOM has established itself as 'an economic mainstay in rural sub-Saharan Africa'. Factoring in secondary economies, supply chains, and dependents, the number of people directly and indirectly connected to the sector is greater still.

The growth in labour-intensive DOM since the 1980s has been driven by three factors. First, the crisis of African agriculture (Bernstein 2007), reflected in low agricultural productivity, declining farm sizes, and rising populations, has led to an increasingly important role for off-farm employment (Alobo Loison 2015).[13] Second, and often overlooked, 'much of the poverty driving people to [labour-intensive DOM] appears, at least in the case of sub-Saharan Africa, to have been created by reforms' (Banchirigah 2006: 167).

Table 2.2 Labour-intensive DOM in mineral-rich African LICs

Country	Number of miners		Country	Number of miners	
	Total	As a % of rural population		Total	As a % of rural population
Burkina Faso	150,000	1.2	Malawi	40,000	0.3
CAR	200,000	6.8	Mali	500,000	4.7
Chad	146,000	1.3	Mozambique	200,000	1
DRC	2,000,000	4.5	Niger	291,000	1.8
Eritrea	400,000	10	Sierra Leone	300,000	7.7
Ethiopia	728,000	0.9	Tanzania	1,000,000	2.7
Guinea	250,000	3.2	Togo	17,000	0.4
Liberia	125,000	5.5	Uganda	300,000	0.9
Madagascar	500,000	3.1			
TOTAL/AVERAGE				7,147,000	2.9

Source: The Artisanal and Small-Sale Mining Knowledge Sharing Archive, http://artisanalmining.org/ Inventory (accessed 13 August 2021).

[13] This dynamic is captured by Bryceson's 'deagrarianisation' (1996) or 'depeasantisation' (1999) thesis, which documents the gravitation made by rural Africans into off-farm employment as a result of multiple economic, social, and political pressures from the 1970s onwards.

The decline of state-led developmentalism and the collapse of welfare provisioning under the weight of structural adjustment during the 1980s exerted significant strain on the productive and reproductive capacity of rural African households. Third, rising commodity prices, especially during the supercycle of 1999–2012, pulled people towards the sector, where (as demonstrated in section 6.2) there were often higher wages and profits to be made than locally available alternatives.

Despite the sector's importance to rural employment and income across the country group, African miners engaged in various forms of labour-intensive DOM have been forcibly displaced from their sites to make way for the construction of corporate-led industrial mines. Often financed by the incoming TNCs themselves, and echoing violent colonial practices of the past, displacement has frequently taken place as government military-led 'sweeps':

> AngloGold-Ashanti, for example, which has operations in Ghana, Guinea, Tanzania, Mali, Namibia and South Africa, and exploration sites in the Democratic Republic of Congo, has made it no secret that actions taken to forcibly remove illegal miners from company concessions are, in the view of their officers, well justified [. . .] Companies such as Barrick Gold, which operates the Bulyanhulu Mine in Northwest Tanzania, and Anvil Mining, the majority owner of the Kulu Project in the Democratic Republic of Congo, also regularly call upon local security forces to remove illegal artisanal miners from concessions.
>
> **(Banchirigah and Hilson 2010: 166)**

In 2017, 70,000 miners were forcibly displaced by Ugandan military and police in Mubende to make way for a Canadian-listed mining corporation. Speaking to local media shortly after the displacement, Edwards Katto, a Director at the Ugandan Ministry of Energy and Mineral Development, said:

> Those people [Ugandan miners] still joking should style up. Now, I'm not only a director [in the Ministry] but also a commander of the Minerals Protection Unit of the Uganda Police Force. So, those illegal artisanal miners still behaving like those in Mubende [who were evicted], they should pack and vacate the mines, otherwise, my police force will them help to pack.
>
> **(AllAfrica 2017)**

This statement speaks well to the general regard held for African miners within the process of capital-intensive FOM (re)industrialization. While not strictly analogous, these dynamics recall Marx's description of primitive accumulation or Harvey's (2004: 74) reconceptualization of this as a continuous process of accumulation by dispossession, involving 'the com-modification and privatization of land and the forceful expulsion of peasant populations, conversion of various forms of property rights into exclusive pri-vate property rights, [and] suppression of rights to the commons'. Displaced and removed from the best deposits, African miners are restricted to working in less productive areas (Luning 2008).

With African miners out of the way, the arrival of TNCs to lead African LIC mining economies has resulted in production and revenue increases across much of the country group since the 2000s. Looking at production trends in major metal and mineral commodities from 2000 to 2020, Table 2.3 indicates rising production in ten of the seventeen mineral-rich African LICs.

In the DRC, copper production grew from 33,000 tonnes in 2000 to more than one million tonnes in 2020 and gold production from 0.1 tonnes to 40 tonnes across the same period. By 2013, the total estimated annual value of mining output in the DRC was $10.2 billion, or more than 50 per cent of GDP (Englebert 2014). In Liberia and Sierra Leone, iron ore production has soared, as has bauxite in Guinea, mica and nickel in Madagascar, and phosphates in Tanzania.

The largest increase across the group has been in gold. Of the ten countries listed, seven have experienced significant production increases in the 2000s and 2010s, rising as a group from 63 tonnes in 2000 to 336 tonnes in 2020.

Table 2.3 Mineral-rich African LIC metal and mineral production, select years (tonnes)

Country	Commodity	2000	2005	2010	2015	2020
Burkina Faso	Gold	0.6	1.3	23.5	36.5	62.4
DRC	Copper	33,000	97,500	378,300	1,039,007	1,023,687
	Gold	0.1	7.2	10	38	40
Ethiopia	Gold	3.2	3.7	6	9.4	7.5
Guinea	Bauxite	17,991,900	19,237,300	16,427,300	20,905,000	87,766,199
	Gold	15.7	25.1	24.8	21.5	91.8
Liberia	Iron Ore	–	–	386,968	5,748,520	4,874,409
Madagascar	Mica	67	546	2,069	16,634	70,000
	Nickel	0	0	5,695	47,271	42,105
Mali	Gold	28.7	49.2	44.3	46.5	65
Sierra Leone	Bauxite	0	0	1,089,131	1,435,195	1,301,584
	Iron Ore	0	0	339,330	5,247,688	6,576,576
Tanzania	Gold	15.1	47.3	39.5	43.3	55.5
	Phosphates	5,100	7,096	17,180	23,000	28,376
Togo	Gold	0	6.1	10.4	15.6	14

Source: British Geological Survey World Mineral Production Yearbooks.

In the DRC, along with Banro, the rise in gold production has been driven by the Kibali project in Haut-Uélé province, led by a joint venture between the Canadian TNC Randgold Resources and the South African TNC AngloGold Ashanti.

Taken together, the FDI and production data indicate that, at the onset of the 2020s, a general process of FOM (re)industrialization is underway across the country group, although in a non-uniform manner. While the process is well advanced in Burkina Faso, the DRC, Guinea, Mali, and Tanzania, it is less visible in the Central African Republic (CAR), Chad, Eritrea, Malawi, Mozambique, Niger, and Uganda, with Ethiopia, Liberia, Madagascar, Sierra Leone, and Togo occupying the middle ground. Yet, even in countries where the process is apparently less advanced, the journey is nonetheless underway.

Eritrea, the most inactive country in the group by the metrics of World Bank-financed reform and FDI inflows, has attracted fourteen mining and exploration firms from Australia, Bermuda, Canada, China, Libya, the United Arab Emirates and the United Kingdom (Mayer Brown 2015) and holds aspirations to develop its economy through TNC-led gold, copper, zinc, and potash mining projects (Blair 2016). In CAR and Niger, the World Bank launched mining-sector reform projects in 2018 and 2020, respectively, with a focus on improving foreign investor attractiveness in both cases. With significant deposits of critical energy transition minerals and metals, Madagascar (cobalt and rare earths), Malawi (rare earths), Mozambique (bauxite and rare earths), Sierra Leone (bauxite and iron ore), Togo (iron ore), and Uganda (iron ore) are all targets of current investment.[14]

The three-stage process detailed in this chapter raises three central issues: first, the cogency, as per the IMF and the World Bank, of attributing the economic difficulties faced by African governments from the mid-1970s as due to state inefficiencies, mismanagement, and corruption, while downplaying the weight of external shocks and trends; second, and relatedly, whether the now ascendant foreign-controlled form of mining industrialization—in place across a far wider spread of African LICs than was the case during the colonial period—can go beyond delivering GDP growth to drive the transformative processes of economic development that the earlier era failed to deliver; third, the developmental implications of the displacement of labour-intensive forms of DOM to make way for incoming TNCs seeking to establish capital-intensive forms of FOM across the continent.

Each of these issues is taken up for investigation in the remainder of the book, beginning in Chapter 3 with a focus on the first: the notion, central to

---

[14] US Geological Survey country reports.

the African Mining Consensus, that state ownership and management structures explain the decline of industrial production on the continent from the mid-1970s onwards. Evidence of superior foreign firm efficiency and management would provide support to this Consensus position. As Chapter 3 demonstrates through the case of South Kivu, however, foreign mining corporations are just as vulnerable to firm inefficiencies, mismanagement, and the vagaries of volatile prices as the state-led model they were promoted to replace.

3

Foreign mining corporations on trial

By the 2010s, the view that state mismanagement and inefficiencies under-lay the Democratic Republic of the Congo's (DRC) economic malaise had become so commonplace as to permeate nearly all thinking about develop-ment in the country. In an opening speech to an international conference on natural resource management in 2012, then finance minister Matata Ponyo asserted that the DRC's failure to benefit from its natural resource wealth 'was largely due to bad governance' (Marysse and Tshimanga 2013: 23). The Congolese economist Gaston Lukusa's (2016: 56) book on economic development in the DRC from 2007 to 2016 was guided by the thesis that 'for many years now, bad governance has been at the origin of the crises experienced by the DRC'. For the prominent US scholar of the DRC Pierre Englebert (2014: 16), two decades of structural adjustment and neoliberal reform had not been enough: 'what is also generally needed is a disengage-ment of the state from the economy and society [. . .] There can be little hope for more accountable economic governance and genuine development without a general deflation of its role.'

The aim of this chapter is to challenge this line of thinking and ques-tion the wisdom underpinning the African Mining Consensus of moving from capital-intensive domestic-owned mining (DOM) to foreign-owned mining (FOM) based on a belief in the superior efficiency of the lat-ter. By charting the rise and fall in South Kivu of Belgian-owned *Société minière et industrielle du Kivu* (SOMINKI)—the Kivu Mining and Indus-trial Company (1976–1997)—and Canadian-owned Banro (1995–2019), its main line of argument is that foreign-owned and managed mining corpo-rations are no less vulnerable to mismanagement, firm inefficiencies, and volatile prices than their state-owned counterparts. Indeed, the model of capital-intensive FOM promoted by Consensus proponents might be more damaging to prospects of transformative mining-based development in the African periphery than domestic-owned alternatives. This is due to its ten-dency, as seen in the case of South Kivu, to prioritize overseas surplus

Disrupted Development in the Congo. Ben Radley, Oxford University Press. © Ben Radley (2023).
DOI: 10.1093/oso/9780192849052.003.0003

extraction, redirecting value to directors and shareholders located in global centres of financial wealth at the expense of productive capacity and to the detriment of the Congolese state and Congolese firms and labour.

3.1 SOMINKI (1976–1997)

The DRC gained its independence from Belgian colonial rule on 30 June 1960. Up until this point, formal mining in South Kivu had been wholly owned and operated by Belgian firms. Following the creation of the *Société manière des Grands Lacs* (MGL) in 1923 as a mining subsidiary, owned by the Belgian industrialist Baron Empain's *Groupe Empain* (Empain Group) through until the 1970s, all mining operations in the Kivu region were run by the subsidiaries of private Belgian corporations, most of which were connected to the Empain family (Empain Group n.d.). It wasn't until 1974 that, as part of President Mobutu's nationalization efforts, the DRC government began to negotiate increased state participation in South Kivu's formal mining sector.

Negotiations were protracted, ending two years later in 1976 with the merger of MGL, Cobelmin, and Symetain (along with six associated subsidiaries) into SOMINKI. It has often been wrongly assumed that SOMINKI was state-owned. Carisch (2014: 2010) has called the Belgian firm 'Congo's second largest state-owned gold mining company', and the Congolese civil society organization *Observatoire gouvernance et paix* (Governance and Peace Observatory) (OGP 2010: 30) referred to it as 'a public enterprise'. Kamundala et al. (2015: 169) listed SOMINKI as one of 'the large foreign mining companies in the four mining provinces [that] became state-owned societies' following nationalization in 1973.

Yet, like its predecessor MGL, SOMINKI was never state owned. From the 1970s until its final demise in the 1990s, SOMINKI was a majority Belgian-owned and managed subsidiary in which the state only ever held a 28 per cent stake. The remaining 72 per cent was held by COGEMIN, a Belgium-based subsidiary of the Empain Group. SOMINKI avoided, then, the nationalization of mining that took place in other mineral-rich Congolese provinces such as Katanga and Kasaï. In so doing, it became the largest foreign-owned mining company in the DRC at the time and the only one (foreign or state-owned) operating in the Kivu region.[1]

SOMINKI's primary export was tin, alongside gold and, in smaller quantities, wolframite and monazite. Shortly after the merger, in the early 1980s,

---

[1] Personal memoires of Serge Lammens, former SOMINKI director; interview with former SOMINKI supervisor, Bukavu, 6 September 2016; Ministry of Mines SOMINKI meeting minutes, Kinshasa, 1991.

SOMINKI's shareholders, encouraged by a rising tin price since 1975, made investments to modernize tin production, as easily exploitable tin and gold deposits had become increasingly scarce. Share capital in SOMINKI increased from 6 million Zaires in 1978 to 125 million Zaires by 1985.[2] A fresh investment plan was developed for the period 1984–1987, totalling 560 million Belgian francs (equivalent to around $24 million at today's prices), of which 303 million had been invested by the end of the first quarter of 1985.[3] The total investments made in the first half of the 1980s stabilized and then increased previously declining tin output, which grew from 2,593 tonnes in 1980 to 3,806 tonnes in 1985.[4]

From 1980 to 1984, SOMINKI consistently recorded annual profits. Notably, this included some degree of articulation with the Congolese economy. SOMINKI paid its shareholders a total of 46.8 million Zaires during this same period, yet it also paid 267 million Zaires in taxes to the Congolese state, most of which derived from a 50 per cent profit tax.[5] While SOMINKI's gold was refined in Europe, moving from a Belgian to a Swiss refinery in 1981, a large percentage of the final product was sold to the Central Bank of Congo at a fixed price.[6]

Both the profit tax and the sale of gold to the Central Bank represented a continuation of late colonial practice.[7] From 1947 to 1960, MGL paid a total of 106.9 million francs to the state of the Belgian Congo, amounting to 52 per cent of declared profits.[8] Following a legislative ordonnance in April 1946, the state of the Belgian Congo reserved the right to purchase a minimum of 40 per cent of all gold production in the colony, depending upon the needs of the Central Bank (Chirishungu Chiza 2008: 335).[9]

This level of domestic articulation supported expansionary periods of state investment and social service provisioning at the national level, first in the 1950s—when state expenditure rose from 15 per cent to 30 per cent of gross domestic product (GDP), an increasing portion of which was used to finance an expansion of productive activity and invest in public works, health, and education (World Bank 1957, Hesselbein 2009)—and then again during the

---

[2] Personal memoires of Serge Lammens, former SOMINKI director; SOMINKI Annual Reports, 1981 and 1984; Extraordinary General Assembly meeting notes, 30 March 1985.

[3] SOMINKI Annual Report, 1984.

[4] SOMINKI Technical Audit, 1995; personal archives of Serge Lammens, former SOMINKI manager; letter from Marrio Fiocchi, SOMINKI director, to the Congolese Minister of Labour, 21 February 1997.

[5] SOMINKI Annual Reports, 1980–1984.

[6] SOMINKI Annual Reports, 1980 and 1982.

[7] Following a legislative ordonnance in April 1946, the state of the Belgian Congo reserved the right to purchase a minimum of 40 per cent of all gold production in the colony, depending upon the needs of the Central Bank (Chirishungu Chiza 2008: 335).

[8] MGL Annual Reports, 1924–1960.

[9] These policy changes were part of 'a different ideological tendency [...] in the Administration' (Bezy et al. 1981: 36), as laid out in the Ten-Year Plan for the Economic and Social Development of the Belgian Congo, drawn up in the late 1940s to maintain a minimum of social order in the face of growing protest at the injustices and inequalities of colonial rule.

first decade of Mobutu's presidency (as detailed in section 2.1). The sale of gold to the Central Bank provided the state with reserves to help withstand external economic shocks.

It was an external price shock that brought SOMINKI's brief expansionary period to an end. In late 1985, the International Tin Council, formed in 1931, fell apart and the international tin price more than halved, from $5.40 per pound to $2.50 per pound (Mthembu-Salter 2009). Before the price crash, in 1984, tin contributed 74 per cent of SOMINKI's turnover. By 1987, this figure had fallen to 43 per cent. With gold production failing to cover the lost revenue, investment was halted, several mines were shut down, European staff were reduced from around 100 to 40, and 2,400 Congolese workers were laid off.[10]

The measures taken proved insufficient. SOMINKI ran at a loss from 1986 onwards (Kibwe-Kasongo 1994: 33).[11] From 1986 to 1996, SOMINKI's annual tin production decreased from 3,805 tonnes to less than 1,000 tonnes, annual gold production dropped from 530 kilograms to less than 300 kilograms, and the number of SOMINKI staff fell from 10,128 to 5,489.[12] In 1993, SOMINKI's mother company in Brussels, COFIMINES, was liquidated, and the 72 per cent private ownership of the subsidiary passed to Darnay Limited and Cluff Mining. While, at the time, there were 63,000 kilograms of known gold reserves at Twangiza in Luhwindja, it was estimated that more than $100 million of investment was required to bring the deposit to production.[13] Neither the new shareholders nor potential suitors were prepared to make this investment.[14]

The onset of the First Congo War in August 1996 accelerated SOMINKI's final collapse. By this time, gold production represented 80 per cent of the firm's revenue, but the heightened insecurity brought on by the war led to the pillage of gold mines and destruction of machinery by the departing national army and the local population.[15] On 29 March 1997, SOMINKI went into liquidation, ending nearly 100 years of Belgian-owned mineral exploration and exploitation in South Kivu.[16]

---

[10] Personal memoires of Serge Lammens, former SOMINKI director; SOMINKI 1987 Planning Report, 1986; Ministry of Mines SOMINKI meeting minutes, Kinshasa, 1991.

[11] SOMINKI Annual Reports, 1980–1984.

[12] SOMINKI Annual Report, 1987; Ministry of Mines SOMINKI Evaluation Report, 1993; SOMINKI Technical Audit, 1995; 51st Board of Directors meeting notes, Kinshasa, 29 March 1997; personal archives of Serge Lammens, former SOMINKI director.

[13] SOMINKI Annual Report, 1983; annex to SOMINKI correspondence, 16 September 1993.

[14] Interview with former SOMINKI director, Brussels, 10 August 2016; fax from GENMIN to COGEMIN, 26 October 1992; letter from A&M Minerals and Metals president to COFIMINES, 6 May 1993.

[15] Personal memoires of Serge Lammens, former SOMINKI director; 51st Board of Directors meeting notes, Kinshasa, 29 March 1997.

[16] 51st Board of Directors meeting notes, Kinshasa, 29 March 1997.

Not only was SOMINKI foreign owned in the decades leading up to its liquidation, but it was also foreign managed, despite the process of Africanization that had been underway at the corporation's predecessor MGL since at least as early as 1959.[17] The intention of Africanization was to change the management structure of the firm, promoting Congolese workers into senior and managerial positions that had previously been the exclusive reserve of Europeans. In 1961, MGL's European administrative director, Mr Feruzi, was replaced by his Congolese assistant, Martin Musombwa, by order of ministerial decree.[18] That same year, two Congolese were placed in charge of office accounting in Bukavu. In Kamituga, two European accountants, one European store manager, and one European procurement officer were all replaced by Congolese.[19]

Yet, from the outset, European senior management had resolved to manage the process of Africanization within an overall strategy that allowed 'for Europeans to carry out their work in the shadows, while leaving a representative function to Congolese'.[20] This logic was continued as MGL merged into SOMINKI. In 1978, Alexis Thambwe—who went on to hold important ministerial positions under Presidents Mobutu and Joseph Kabila— was promoted to the head of SOMINKI's Kinshasa office, replacing the Belgian Jacques Abel. At a private reception held shortly after his promotion, European colleagues raised concerns about this appointment. Joseph Meuret, soon to become President of SOMINKI, responded by reassuring them that they had nothing to fear, 'Thambwe will be our paid negro.'[21] According to a former member of SOMINKI's Congolese managerial class, 'while SOMINKI succeeded politically in creating the impression of Africanization, the company never Africanized. They had Mr Thambwe who symbolized and was the face of Africanization, but in reality SOMINKI was highly colonial in that all the decisions remained in the hands of Europeans.'[22]

The data supports this view, indicating that while the number of SOMINKI's Congolese managers doubled from 38 to 76 between 1976 and 1984, during the same period the number of European managers remained relatively constant, at 94 in 1976 and 90 in 1984, peaking at 110 in 1978.[23] As observed by Bezy et al. (1981: 89–90) at the state-owned Gécamines

[17] MGL General Assembly meeting notes, 4 October 1961.
[18] Decree Number 40221/123 of 11 December 1961; MGL letter to the president of the Kivu-Maniema Provincial Government, 15 December 1961.
[19] Internal MGL correspondence, Bukavu, 5 September 1961.
[20] Internal MGL correspondence (marked confidential), Goma, 26 January 1961.
[21] Personal memoires of Serge Lammens, former SOMINKI director.
[22] Interview with former SOMINKI director, Kinshasa, 20 August 2016.
[23] Personal archives of Serge Lammens, former SOMINKI director.

in the 1970s, this suggests that Congolese were being promoted into new managerial positions that duplicated, rather than replaced, those of European managers. The size of the European managerial class only began to decline from the late 1980s onwards, as SOMINKI shed staff to stave off bankruptcy. Even under this duress, in its final years, its most senior directors were Europeans. SOMINKI remained, then, firmly under the control of not only Belgian ownership but also European management throughout its two-decade expansion and decline from 1976 to 1997.

In 2002, five years after SOMINKI's liquidation, its major gold deposits were acquired by the Canadian corporation Banro. Fifteen years later, in 2017, Banro would find itself in a very similar situation to that of SOMINKI in 1997, on the verge of financial collapse, having failed to control costs in a context of price volatility.

3.2 Banro (1995–2019)

The liquidation of SOMINKI in 1997 was part of negotiations begun in 1995, during which a group of British-Canadian investors, led by the British mining magnate Algy Cluff, negotiated several agreements with the Congolese government to acquire control of SOMINKI's assets. A protracted acquisition process ensued, as the DRC moved through two wars and three different presidents within the space of four years.[24] A final agreement was reached in April 2002, the same month that the Second Congo War was officially ended by the signing in Pretoria of the Global and All-Inclusive Agreement. The new agreement ceded 100 per cent ownership of SOMINKI's major gold deposits to the Canadian corporation Banro, covering Twangiza, Kamituga, and Lugushwa in South Kivu Province and Namoya in neighbouring Maniema Province. Following this agreement, Banro established the four Congolese subsidiaries of Twangiza Mining, Kamituga Mining, Lugushwa Mining, and Namoya Mining, one to manage each respective concession.

Three years later, in 2005, the Canadian government announced the launch of the Canada Investment Fund for Africa (CIFA), jointly managed by the emerging market private equity investors Actis and Cordiant, to invest in Canadian corporations operating in Africa. In November 2005, CIFA announced a 13 million Canadian dollar investment to support Banro's exploration activities in the DRC, with the head of Actis's mining investments

---

[24] For detailed accounts of this process, see de Failly (2001: 4–8); Mthembu-Salter (2009: 3–5); Geenen (2014: 129–134).

explaining, 'not only do we believe that Banro has extremely attractive commercial prospects, but through this investment we can make a significant contribution to the long term development of the mining industry in the DRC' (CIFA 2005). On closing in 2006, most of CIFA's $212 million corpus had been invested in mining firms (CIFA 2006).

Most of Banro's money in its early years was raised, though, by the issuance and sale of common shares, with the corporation raising 19.5 million Canadian dollars on the Toronto Stock Exchange (TSE) in 1996 to finance the initial acquisition of SOMINKI's gold assets.[25] Raising capital to finance its exploration activities through the sale of shares was the corporation's main strategy over the next decade (a detailed overview of Banro's financing history from 1996 to 2018 can be found in Appendix 1). Between 1996 and 2016, Banro issued shares worth around 300 million Canadian dollars and 100 million US dollars.[26]

By 2012, with the required investment secured, Banro entered commercial production at its flagship Twangiza project. In 2007, Banro had forecast initial production costs at Twangiza of $257 per ounce, yet in 2012 and 2013, the actual production cost was recorded at $879 and $801, respectively.[27] Fortunately for Banro, the annual average gold price had increased across this period from $872 per ounce in 2008 to $1,669 per ounce in 2012 (Figure 3.1). The early profitability of production at Twangiza was, then, entirely the result of a near doubling of the gold price over a short time frame.

Towards the end of 2011, Banro began to construct Namoya, its second mine, in Maniema province. The firm's directors had been encouraged by the rising gold price, which had seen a sixfold increase between 1999 and 2012. According to Twangiza Mining's then general director, this was a major mistake, as 'we went to build Namoya before we started stabilizing at Twangiza', with the decision driven by senior directors who were 'more concerned with the company's share price than the mining fundamentals'.[28] The then general director stated that Namoya was initially budgeted to be built for $100 million using profits generated by Twangiza but on the assumption that gold would, at the least, stay at its current price. Yet, as Figure 3.1 shows, the gold price collapsed by one-third between 2012 and 2015 and had yet to

---

[25] From the 1990s, the TSE in Canada became the major home of the global mining industry, in particular of junior companies focusing on exploration. In 2003, 53 per cent of mineral exploration companies in Africa were Canadian (Deneault et al. 2008). In 2007, 60 per cent of the world's mining companies were listed in Toronto, twice as many as the five major competing stock exchanges combined (ibid.). According to Kennes (2005: 159), they were attracted by a favourable investment climate, minimal government regulation and reporting obligations, and a well-developed industry of financial services.

[26] Banro press releases, 2013–2017.

[27] Banro press release, 30 July 2007; Banro consolidated financial statements, 2012 and 2013.

[28] Interview with Twangiza Mining general director, Twangiza, 6 June 2017.

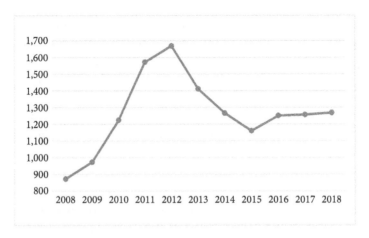

Figure 3.1 Annual average gold price per ounce, 2008–2018 (USD)

Source: World Gold Council, http://www.gold.org/goldhub/data/gold-prices (accessed 17 August 2021).

meaningfully recover by 2018, leading to significant shortfalls in Twangiza's forecasted revenue. In addition, underestimating the industrial machinery required to process gold at Namoya meant 'the [budgeted] $100 million went up in smoke in a month', with construction costs eventually totalling $250 million.[29]

Needing to raise an additional $150 million to finance the Namoya construction overspend, and with a market capitalization on the TSE of $80 million, Banro was pushed 'to take a number of short-term loans that came at a premium'.[30] In 2012, Banro turned to the US debt market to raise $175 million in notes, with a 10 per cent interest rate and maturing (as would later prove critical) in 2017, just five years later. In 2013, Banro secured $30 million in bank loans from the Congolese bank Rawbank and the Nigerian bank Ecobank at high interest rates of 9 per cent and 8.5 per cent, respectively and an additional $53 million from several other unspecified lenders.[31] It was at this juncture that Banro's financial health began to deteriorate. The corporation's long-term debt increased from zero in 2011 to $159 million in 2013, and from 2013 onwards, Banro entered a year-on-year negative working capital

---

[29] Banro consolidated financial statements 2012–2016; interview with Twangiza Mining general director, Twangiza, 6 June 2017.

[30] Interview with Twangiza Mining general director, Twangiza, 6 June 2017.

[31] Banro Annual Information Form 2013; Banro press releases 2013.

position (Table 3.1).[32] This meant it had no available capital to reinvest in the maintenance of infrastructure or other costs related to productive activity.

Requiring further financing to meet its new debt obligations, from 2014 onwards, Banro entered several forward sale and streaming transactions (Table 3.2). Forward sale transactions provide the investor an agreed amount of gold delivered over an agreed time frame, while streaming transactions secure the investor an agreed percentage of the life-of-mine production at an agreed cost. In both cases, the transactions typically result in the mining firm securing investment in exchange for a share of its future production at below market prices, as was the case for Banro.

In 2014 and 2015, Banro completed four forward sale transactions, one with Gold Holding in the United Arab Emirates (UAE), one with the US private equity fund Gramercy, and two with undisclosed investors. Over a four-year period, these agreements committed Banro to deliver 102,985 ounces of Twangiza's gold production—worth around $125 million at the time—in return for $98 million of investment. In 2015 and 2016, Banro completed streaming transactions with Gramercy for the Namoya mine and

Table 3.1 Banro financial overview, 2006–2016 (millions of USD)

Year	Revenue	Net income	Long-term debt	Working capital
2006	0	−3	0	50
2007	0	−4	0	26
2008	0	−8	0	−2
2009	0	−5	0	69
2010	0	−3	0	68
2011	0	−9	0	−27
2012	43	−5	155	4
2013	112	2	159	−73
2014	125	0	201	−68
2015	157	−74	168	−80
2016	228	−51	206	–

Sources: Banro consolidated financial statements, 2007–2016; Morning Star investor website, http://www.morningstar.com (accessed 28 March 2017).

[32] Long-term debt consists of any loans or other financial obligations that require repayment over the course of more than one year. Working capital is calculated by subtracting a firm's current liabilities (debts and other obligations) from its current assets. It is used as an indication of a firm's short and medium-term financial health, with a high level of working capital correlated with strong financial health.

Table 3.2 Banro's forward sale and streaming transactions, 2014–2017 (millions of USD)

Year	Transaction	Investor	Value	Return
2014	Forward sale	Gold Holding (UAE)	41	40,500 ounces from Twangiza (four years)
2015	Streaming	Gramercy (US)	50	8.3 per cent from Namoya at $150/ounce (life of mine)
	Forward sale	Gramercy (US)	40	44,496 ounces from Twangiza (three years)
	Forward sale	Undisclosed	10	9,508 ounces from Twangiza (two years)
	Forward sale	Undisclosed	7	8,481 ounces from Twangiza (thirty-three months)
2016	Streaming	Baiyin (China)	67.5	11 per cent from Twangiza at $150/ounce (life of mine)
2017	Forward sale	Undisclosed	45	51,880 ounces from Namoya (three years)

Sources: Banro annual information forms, 2014–2016; Banro press releases, 2014–2017; Banro Material Change Report, March 2016.

with the Chinese Baiyin Nonferrous Group (hereafter, Baiyin) for the Twangiza mine.[33] Due to these multiple arrangements, in 2016 and 2017, Banro received no revenue for around one-third of Twangiza's production.

Banro's own assessment of its financial structure by the end of this period highlights the extent of the constraints placed on corporate performance by the loans and borrowing agreements it had entered in response to overspend and price fluctuations:

> The Company has a significant amount of indebtedness and other liabilities and obligations (collectively, 'Obligations'), including the notes (the '2012 Notes') issued by the Company in March 2012 under a US$175 million debt financing, gold delivery obligations under forward sale and stream transactions, trade payables, DRC bank debt, and preference shares and preferred shares issued by the Company and certain of its subsidiaries, respectively. This could have important adverse consequences [. . .] Certain financing agreements the Company is a party to, including

[33] At a time when the gold price was around $1,250 per ounce, this second transaction committed Banro to deliver Baiyin 11 per cent of Twangiza's life-of-mine production at $150 per ounce in return for $67.5 million of investment, with the percentage delivered to halve when total production at Twangiza reached 1.14 million ounces, which was approximately eight years away at the time the agreement was made. Until the 1.1-million-ounce target was reached, this transaction secured Baiyin 88,000 ounces of gold—worth around $110 million at the time—at a cost of $80.7 million (the $67.5 million investment plus the $13.2 million paid for the gold at $150 per ounce). After this point, Baiyin would continue to secure 5.5 per cent of production, approximately $10 million per year, for the remainder of the Twangiza's productive lifespan.

the Note Indenture, contain a number of restrictive covenants that impose significant operating and financial restrictions on the Company and may limit the
Company's ability to engage in acts that may be in its long-term best interest.

(Banro 2016a: 20–21)

This warning was to prove prescient. In March 2017, the repayments on the
$175 million of debt financing taken in 2012 became due. Unable to make
the repayments and on the verge of bankruptcy, Banro filed for Canadian
government court protection from its creditors. In December 2017, it was
granted this protection under the Canadian Companies' Creditors Arrange-
ment Act. Banro emerged from creditor protection in March 2018, having
undertaken a major financial restructuring plan that included the deferment
of forward sale and streaming transactions. A few months later, in May 2018,
Banro delisted from the TSE (Banro 2018a, 2018b). In March 2019, the
corporation split its assets and the Chinese investment fund Baiyin International Investment (one of Banro's two principal shareholders at the time)
acquired full control of the Twangiza mine. Six months later, in September 2019, Banro's remaining Congolese subsidiaries suspended all activities,
and its chief executive officer (CEO) wrote to the Congolese Ministry of
Labour requesting the suspension of all worker contracts for reasons of force
majeure.[34]

Internal mismanagement and inefficiencies provide additional contributing factors to Banro's decline, offering a further explanation for the overspend
on the Namoya mine construction. A 2012 third-party audit of Twangiza
Mining highlighted several key issues negatively affecting corporate performance: 'limited effort and results in ensuring process effectiveness; significant inventory and procurement systems inadequacies; [. . .] systems
management, ownership and required structures do not exist or inadequate;
[. . . and] project structure and ownership appears ineffective.'[35] Interviews
with former employees at Twangiza Mining lend support to these findings.
A former auditor and a former procurement officer both observed a preference among non-national procurement managers to use foreign (and often
home-country) suppliers for goods and capital inputs when presented with
domestic suppliers who could procure the same goods at a lower cost.[36] A
former Twangiza Mining procurement manager confirmed this tendency to

---

[34] Letter from Banro CEO Brett Richards to the DRC Government Ministry of Labour, 24 September
2019.
[35] Twangiza Mining External Audit Report, Nubian Africa, 2012.
[36] Interviews with former Twangiza Mining auditor, Bukavu, 15 December 2016 and former Twangiza
Mining procurement officer, Kinshasa, 13 January 2017.

disregard cost efficiency, noting that when he arrived at the mine in 2012, exclusive suppliers were up to 150 per cent more expensive than alternative options.[37]

The financial impact of local-level armed attacks on the corporation's Namoya mine, leading to the temporary suspension of production on three occasions, is a final factor for consideration when assessing Banro's decline to Canadian government protection (the attacks themselves are discussed at greater length in section 7.2).[38] Indeed, popular and corporate accounts of Banro's financial descent have highlighted these incidents as the primary cause behind the corporation's financial difficulties. Quoting one of Banro's shareholders, the Canadian national newspaper *The Globe and Mail* reported, 'The violence has caused significant disruption to Banro's operations in the DRC, which ultimately rendered the company insolvent by late 2017' (McGee 2018).

However, the three temporary production suspensions resulting from the attacks lasted for a total of just 11.5 days,[39] amounting to around $3.6 million in lost revenue.[40] Relative to the scale of Banro's debt repayments, these attacks functioned, at the most, as a short-term trigger for Banro's filing for Canadian government protection in December 2017 (and likely served as a somewhat welcome scapegoat and smokescreen for the corporation when reporting events to its shareholders and the media).

In reality, Banro had been driven to the verge of bankruptcy in 2017 by three longer-term factors: first, poor corporate systems and processes; second, $150 million overspend on the construction of the Namoya mine; third, a gold price collapse starting in 2012, just after Banro had begun construction at Namoya based on the assumption of a stable price. The first two factors can be equated to a general level of corporate mismanagement and inefficiency and the third to exposure to price volatility. Together, these factors pushed Banro into increasing indebtedness, with its long-term debt rising from zero in 2011 to $206 million by 2016. Unable to meet its obligations to lenders and investors as the gold price continued to stagnate, Banro had no choice but to seek Canadian government protection in 2017. The speed of Banro's descent,

---

[37] Interview with former Twangiza Mining procurement manager, Skype call, 23 January 2017.

[38] Banro press statements, 2017.

[39] Banro press statements, 2017; Banro, 'Management's Discussion and Analysis for the Second Quarter of 2017', 2017.

[40] During the first quarter of 2017, just prior to the attacks taking place, Namoya produced 23,100 ounces across a ninety-day period, equivalent to around $28.2 million of value based on the average gold price for that quarter, or $313,333 of revenue per day. Banro, 'Management's Discussion and Analysis for the First Quarter of 2017', 2017; World Gold Council price data from http://www.gold.org/goldhub/data/gold-prices (accessed 17 August 2021).

however, was accelerated by underlying mechanisms of surplus extraction to primarily Northern centres of financial wealth and power.

3.3 Enrich the centre, impoverish the periphery

Despite Banro's poor performance as a viable productive entity, a group of seventeen company directors amassed considerable wealth from the corporation, primarily through share-based compensation. The potential for directors of gold corporations to accumulate wealth through the short-term performance of their firm's shares is a relatively recent phenomenon. From the end of the direct convertibility of US dollars into gold in 1971 through to the 2000s, trade in gold increased to the point where, by 2010, gold had become 'as easy to trade as it is to trade any stock or share' (Shafiee and Topal 2010: 180).

Domiciled between Canada and the United Kingdom, with one in South Africa, Banro's senior directors accrued at least $54.6 million in salaries, share-based compensation, fees, incentives, and bonuses over the twenty-year period from 1997 to 2016 (Table 3.3).[41] This included $36.6 million before the corporation had produced a single ounce of gold, of which around $19 million derived from share-based compensation. Of the $54.6 million, $30.2 million (more than half) accrued to just two directors. The actual earnings are likely a multiple of the $54.6 million identified, given that Banro's stock rose from $0.5 per share in 2001 to around $14 per share in 2007 and

Table 3.3 Banro senior director compensation, 1997–2016 (USD)

Five-year period	Number of directors	Wages	Identified share-based compensation	Fees, incentive, and bonuses	TOTAL
1997–2001	4	967,945	0	497,092	1,465,037
2002–2006	7	2,570,320	10,577,781	894,786	14,042,887
2007–2011	8	6,533,812	8,411,646	6,121,362	21,066,820
Pre-production subtotal	–	10,072,077	18,989,427	7,513,240	36,574,744
2012–2016	9	10,234,251	0	7,820,794	18,055,045
TOTAL	–	20,306,328	18,989,427	15,334,034	54,629,789

Sources: Banro management information circulars, 2004–2016; Enrico Carisch's personal data set.

[41] I am grateful to Enrico Carisch for sharing his own data set on these figures.

that not all share-based compensation is accounted for as the beneficiaries are under no reporting obligation when they exercise them.

The financial difficulties Banro entered from 2012 onwards had little impact on the level of compensation accruing to senior directors. While no share-based compensation was identified during this period (which, to repeat, does not mean that this compensation was not taken), senior director wages actually increased from $6.5 million between 2007 and 2011 to $10.2 million between 2012 and 2016, with this latter period representing the five years leading up to Banro entering Canadian government protection. Fees, incentives, and bonuses also increased from $6.1 million to $7.8 million across the same two periods.

Alongside high and sustained levels of director compensation up until 2017, payments to shareholders provided an additional avenue through which corporate value was rerouted overseas while Banro's indebtedness continued to grow. From the outset, Banro's corporate structure had its DRC-based subsidiaries run through holding subsidiaries in Barbados (Figure 3.2). Under Canada's double taxation treaty with Barbados, signed in 1987, Canadian companies can repatriate profits from Barbados without paying Canadian tax. In December 2013, Banro began making shareholder dividend payments out of Banro Group in Barbados and continued to do so on a regular basis up until the end of 2017, when it entered creditor protection.[42]

To summarize, a few senior directors made tens of millions upfront before production began, and both senior directors and shareholders continued to extract value from 2012 onwards, despite the increasing financial difficulties Banro began to face during this period. To sustain this surplus extraction as long as possible, it was necessary to squeeze the value accruing domestically to the Congolese state and to Congolese firms and labour.

Banro's 2002 mining convention included a ten-year tax moratorium from the start of commercial production and an exemption from royalties. Five years later, in 2007, the Congolese government undertook a review of sixty-three mining contracts signed during the Congo Wars, recommending that twenty-two be cancelled and thirty-nine renegotiated (Lukusa 2016: 45–47). Banro's was among those to be renegotiated, eventually resulting in a 2010 contract amendment which committed Banro to paying a 1 per cent royalty tax and a 4 per cent profit tax.[43]

---

[42] Banro press releases, 2013–2017.
[43] Second Amendment to the Mining Convention of 13 February 1997 between the DRC and Banro, Kinshasa, 13 July 2010.

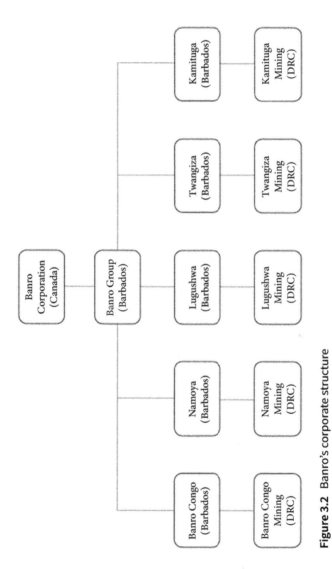

Figure 3.2 Banro's corporate structure

Source: Banro Corporation, Annual Information Form, March 2016.

The negotiated amendment yielded modest results. Data on Banro's post-production tax declarations is only available for the years 2012, 2013, 2016, and 2017.[44] Across these four years, Banro declared a total of $29 million in tax contributions, of which $650,000 went to the Barbadian state and the remaining $28.35 million to the Congolese state (Table 3.4). Due to Canada's double taxation treaty with Barbados discussed earlier in this section, no taxes were paid in Canada. Across 2012, 2013, and 2016, the $20.4 million paid in taxes was equivalent to just 5.3 per cent of Banro's recorded revenue of $665 million for that period (only marginally more than the minimum of $18.1 million accruing to Banro's senior directors in the five-year period from 2012 to 2016).[45] This finding aligns with the work of Bokondu et al. (2015: 10), who calculated that between 2011 and 2014, total Congolese state revenue collected from the mining sector amounted to 6 per cent of total sector revenue during the same period.

Across this same period, Banro appears to have avoided payment of the 4 per cent profit tax in the DRC, agreed to in its 2010 contract amendment. In 2016 and 2017, the tax declarations reported to the Extractive Sector Transparency Measures Act (ESTMA) note that the taxes in the DRC were paid to the *Direction générale des recettes administratives, domaniales, judiciaires*

Table 3.4 Banro's tax payment declarations, selected years (USD)

Year	Country	Taxes	Royalties	Fees	TOTAL
2012	DRC	–	–	–	4,588,473
2013	DRC	–	–	–	4,972,597
2016	DRC	530,000	2,450,000	7,530,000	10,510,000
	Barbados	310,000	0	0	310,000
Subtotal		840,000	2,450,000	7,530,000	20,381,070
2017	DRC	150,000	2,780,000	5,380,000	8,310,000
	Barbados	340,000	0	0	340,000
TOTAL		1,330,000	5,230,000	12,910,000	29,031,070

Sources: EITI DRC Final Reports, 2012 and 2013; Banro Corporation ESTMA reports, 2017 and 2018.

[44] This is due to the DRC's temporary suspension from the EITI in 2014 and Banro's delisting from the TSE in 2018. In the case of the former, this meant mining firms operating in the DRC no longer made fiscal contributions and other data publicly available for a number of years. In the case of the latter, it meant Banro no longer publicly declared its tax contributions to the Canadian government's Extractive Sector Transparency Measures Act, an initiative begun in 2015.

[45] Banro financial statements and press releases, 2013–2017; EITI DRC Final Reports, 2012 and 2013; Banro Corporation ESTMA reports, 2017 and 2018.

et de participation (General Directorate of Administrative, State and Juris-diction Revenue and of Participation, DGRAD), the agency responsible for collecting mining royalties and the annual surface rights tax. The agency at the Ministry of Finance responsible for the collection of profit tax, the *Direction générale des impôts* (General Directorate of Taxation, DGI), was not listed in the declarations. It might be countered that this absence of Congolese profit tax is because it had yet to recuperate its investment. Both corporate and Congolese state data, however, suggest that this was not the case for Twangiza, where, in 2014, total revenue from the mine of $280 mil-lion outstripped total investment for the first time and continued to do so through to 2016.[46]

One way in which Banro might have been avoiding this profit tax is by using an intricate network of intra-company and shareholder loans and trans-fers. In 2010 and 2011, before commercial production at Twangiza began, Banro's Congolese subsidiary Twangiza Mining was credited with a net total of $105.4 million in transfers from its mother company, Banro Corporation in Canada. In 2012 and 2013, the first two years of production, Twangiza generated $154 million of revenue and sent back to Banro Corporation a net total of $62.7 million in transfer and loan repayments (Table 3.5).

Table 3.5 Transfers and loans from Banro to Twangiza Mining, 2010–2013 (millions of USD)

Year	Country	Entity	Movement	Twangiza Mining		Net difference (a −b)
				Credit (a)	Debit (b)	
2010	Canada	Banro Corporation	Transfer	108.0	12.2	95.8
2011	Canada	Banro Corporation	Transfer	9.6	0.0	9.6
PRE-PRODUCTION TOTAL				117.6	12.2	105.4
2012	Canada	Banro Corporation	Transfer	33.9	78.5	−44.6
2013	Canada	Banro Corporation	Transfer	3.6	0.0	3.6
2013	Canada	Shareholders	Loan	65.0	86.7	−21.7
POST-PRODUCTION TOTAL				102.5	165.2	−62.7

Sources: Twangiza Mining annual financial reports, 2010–2013.

---

[46] Banro financial statements and press releases, 2013–2016; *Agence nationale pour la promotion des investissements* (National Agency for the Promotion of Investments) data, 2004–2016.

During these same two years, Twangiza Mining declared retained annual earnings of minus $42 in 2012 and $0 in 2013.[47] When these zero or negative declared earnings were raised in discussion with a former senior financial manager for Banro in the DRC, the former employee explained that Twangiza Mining's retained earnings were counterbalanced against the repayment of loans and transfers.[48] Across the two years of 2012 and 2013, while Banro's Congolese subsidiary retained effectively zero earnings, despite generating $154 million of revenue, Banro's senior directors accrued at least $10 million in compensation and the corporation began paying shareholder dividends.

The purpose of these intra-company financial flows is unclear and might be linked to an effort to maintain the retained earnings of DRC-based subsidiaries at zero so as to avoid profit tax payment to the Congolese state. Similar practices have been documented elsewhere in the DRC during this period. A 2014 study of Swiss-headquartered mining TNC Glencore found that its Congolese subsidiary Kamoto Copper Company had run at losses of hundreds of millions of dollars per year from 2009 to 2013, while its Canadian-registered subsidiary Katanga Mining Limited ran at a net profit of $401 million over the same period (Peyer et al. 2014). Marysse and Tshimanga (2014: 149) found US-headquartered mining TNC Freeport McMoran to artificially reduce its profits made in the DRC through transactions between itself and its subsidiaries. Five TNC subsidiary case studies conducted by Congolese civil society organizations between 2015 and 2017 revealed that 'profit tax payments to the Congolese state are minimized by mining companies, and thus [. . .] this very important flow often remains hypothetical, or even almost zero' (The Carter Center 2017: 4).

In addition, and contrary to MGL and SOMINKI's sale of gold to the Central Bank of the Congo, all Twangiza's gold bars were shipped either to the South African smelter Rand Refinery, just outside of Johannesburg, or the Chinese smelter managed by Baiyin Nonferrous Group, headquartered in Gansu Province.[49] Banro's right to sell all its production on the global market was enshrined by the 2002 Congolese Mining Code and was upheld in the most recently introduced 2018 code.[50]

---

[47] Twangiza Mining financial accounts, 2010–2013.
[48] Conversation with former Banro senior financial manager, Kinshasa, 19 July 2018.
[49] From 2012 to 2016, the North American metals trader Auramet had been the exclusive final buyer of Twangiza's gold until the entry of Baiyin following its 2016 streaming transaction with Banro.
[50] DRC 2002 Mining Code, Article 266; DRC 2018 Mining Code, Article 108.

Banro also did what it could to squeeze the amount of the surplus accruing to Congolese firms and suppliers, as part of its general strategy to stave off bankruptcy while retaining shareholder pay-outs and expected levels of senior director compensation. In June 2017, six months before Banro entered creditor protection, Twangiza Mining's then finance manager revealed that the subsidiary had around $18 million of unpaid debts to firms and individuals subcontracted to procure or provide goods, services, and equipment to the mine. He added that Congolese firms and suppliers had been disproportionately negatively affected as, unlike their foreign counterparts, they didn't have the personal connections to be in daily contact with Banro's CEO, board members, or senior management demanding payment.[51] In a separate interview earlier that year, a former Twangiza Mining procurement officer expressed the same sentiment.[52]

Conversations and interviews with Twangiza Mining's suppliers and subcontractors indicated that initially, in the first few years of the mine's operation, payments were made on time and in full. Delays began in 2013, shortly after the beginning of the gold price collapse and the Namoya construction overspend. In many cases, Twangiza Mining would miss two to three payments, and then begin gradually paying off the first missed repayment, one small percentage at a time. When trying to insist upon the payment of the money owed to them, Congolese suppliers and subcontractors would be told by Banro staff in the DRC that 'we're waiting on Toronto'.[53] A representative from a foreign firm subcontractor was able to meet with one of Banro's senior directors in 2015 and was told that once Banro had undergone debt restructuring it would have more working capital and would be able to pay off its subcontractor and supplier debts.[54]

In 2017, the situation remained unresolved, with the four major Congolese suppliers reporting unpaid debts owed by Twangiza Mining of $500,000, $110,000, $15,000, and $2,000, respectively.[55] Congolese subcontractors reported the same issue, which, in one instance, led to the withdrawal of a domestic firm from this position. Initially, the Congolese firm GINKI Petroleum International (hereafter, GINKI) was Twangiza's main fuel supplier. By 2014, Banro had accumulated a debt of $2.4 million towards GINKI, at which point, GINKI withdrew from the contract as the directors decided

[51] Interview with Twangiza Mining financial manager, Twangiza, 8 June 2017.
[52] Interview with former Twangiza Mining procurement officer, Kinshasa, 13 January 2017.
[53] Interview with Twangiza Mining supplier, Bukavu, 31 January 2017.
[54] Interview with Simba Logistics DRC director, Bukavu, 22 February 2017.
[55] Interviews with Congolese suppliers, Bukavu, January to April 2017.

they couldn't absorb the risk of accumulating more debt. The Malaysian TNC Engen, with far greater liquidity to absorb such debts, won the subcontract in 2015. In 2017, Banro still owed GINKI around $670,000 of unpaid fuel bills.[56] According to one of GINKI's directors, 'Banro has a colossal Congolese debt [...] we were doing better when they weren't here.'[57] At the end of 2017, as Banro entered creditor protection, many of the debts to Congolese subcontracted firms and individual suppliers were still outstanding.

Foreign firms were also affected, with the country manager of the South African catering subcontractor Allterrain Services (ATS) reporting, in 2017, that the firm was owed three to four months of costs amounting to around $900,000–1.2 million.[58] To manage the risk of these debts, the catering firm had postponed payments to its local suppliers at Luhwindja, where the Twangiza mine was located, with the *Cooperative des Eleveurs de Luhwindja* (Livestock Cooperative of Luhwindja)reporting $54,000 of unpaid meat deliveries.[59] Another former local supplier in Luhwindja, supplying foodstuffs such as eggs, bananas, and peanuts sourced from across the region, withdrew from his position in Banro's chain in early 2016 as he could no longer afford to keep pre-financing his orders in the face of late repayments.[60]

Minimizing its fiscal burden in the DRC and overseas, and accumulating debts with subcontracted firms and suppliers, Banro's final strategy to stave off bankruptcy while continuing to secure shareholder and senior director value was to squeeze wages. Between 2012 and 2016, wage levels remained unchanged across all groups, from unskilled workers to senior managers.[61] In addition, between the mine's construction in 2010 and Banro entering creditor protection in 2017, there had been no annual wage increases.[62] From at least 2012 to 2017, then, while Banro paid shareholder dividends and maintained high levels of senior director compensation, the nominal value of Twangiza Mining worker wages stagnated.

To summarize, corporate mismanagement and inefficiencies, combined with the gold price collapse between 2012 and 2014, drove Banro into increasing indebtedness and financial difficulties. By late 2017, and on the verge of bankruptcy, Banro was forced to seek Canadian government

---

[56] GINKI financial archives; interviews with GINKI director, Bukavu, April and May 2017.
[57] Interview with GINKI director, Bukavu, 14 February 2017.
[58] Survey interview with ATS manager, Bukavu, 17 June 2017.
[59] Interview with local farmers' cooperative president, Luhwindja, 7 February 2017.
[60] Conversation with former ATS supplier, Luhwindja, 30 November 2016.
[61] Twangiza Mining worker payroll data, 2012; Twangiza Mining worker payslips, 2012; Twangiza Mining wage classification document, 2016.
[62] Conversations with Twangiza Mining union delegates, June and July 2017; Twangiza Mining worker contract template, 2017.

protection from its creditors. Banro's financial decline was hastened by underlying mechanisms of surplus extraction from the DRC to Northern (and, to a lesser extent, Chinese) financial centres. Banro's trajectory recalls the phenomenon of financialization discussed in section 1.3, whereby processes of surplus extraction from the periphery to financial centres can exert downwards pressure on TNC profits, which is, in turn, alleviated by squeezing the value accruing to actors in the periphery, such as domestic firms and labour (Fine 2008).

The continued redirecting of value to overseas directors and shareholders as the noose of bankruptcy began to tighten (and thus, at the expense of the corporation's long-term productive capacity and viability) is little different to the forms of rent-seeking for which supposedly inefficient and mismanaged African states and state-owned enterprises (SOEs) were so heavily criticized following the failure of state-led developmentalism in the 1960s and 1970s. In this instance, flowing instead to the managers of, and investors in, a foreign corporation which twice required Canadian state intervention and support to sustain its activities (first when starting out in 2005, and again when facing bankruptcy in 2017).

There are clear parallels between the declines of Banro and SOMINKI as the Belgian firm likewise succumbed to a failure to control costs in the face of severe price volatility, having also overinvested as prices rose shortly before a crash. Rather than a story of Congolese mismanagement (as often implied in much of the existing literature on the firm), SOMINKI's demise was one of a Belgian-owned and managed subsidiary subject to the same difficulties and suffering the same fate as its Congolese state-owned mining counterparts of the time, going bankrupt in the 1990s because of a failure to control costs when confronted with the tin price crash of 1985.

Yet, SOMINKI demonstrated a greater degree of articulation with the Congolese economy through the payment of a 50 per cent profit tax and the sale of gold to the Central Bank. By contrast, Banro's Congolese subsidiary, Twangiza Mining, consistently recorded zero profits and all Twangiza's gold bars were shipped overseas. With little fiscal revenue accruing to the Congolese state and none of the gold produced going to the Central Bank of the Congo, at the outset of the twenty-first century, capital-intensive FOM in South Kivu was less financially embedded in the national Congolese economy than had been the case during the twentieth century.

Taken together, the evidence presented in this chapter challenges one of the central assumptions underpinning the African Mining Consensus that capital-intensive FOM will be more efficient and effective at leading mining-based industrialization than the forms of capital-intensive DOM that preceded it. Contrary to these expectations, the evidence indicates that the supposed superiority of capital-intensive FOM has unravelled in South Kivu not once but twice. This suggests that the success or otherwise of mining-led industrialization might not lie in its ownership or management structures but rather in the model itself and its associated constraints, exemplified here in the difficulty of retaining productivity in the face of severe price volatility. In the case of Banro, the deleterious effects of this constraint were compounded by processes of overseas surplus extraction at the expense of domestic capture and reinvestment.

Chapter 4 develops this line of argument by highlighting a second structural impediment to mining-based development in the African periphery in the form of enclavity. As will be shown, in a continuation of trends in South Kivu's capital-intensive FOM sector from around the 1980s, the capital infrastructure driving production at Twangiza in the 2010s was highly specialized, deeply dependent upon diffusion from technological centres (primarily of the global North), and poorly articulated with the Congolese economy.

4

Disarticulation and alienation

Since the 2000s and into the 2010s, a body of global value chain (GVC) schol-arship has been questioning the continued relevance of the enclave thesis to the African mining industry. As noted in section 1.2, the justification for this has been the observation that, since the turn of the twenty-first century, global mining corporations have restructured away from directly managing all their activities (often referred to as vertical integration) towards outsourc-ing the provision of equipment, goods, and services to independent firms (horizontal integration). This has fostered belief that 'the enclave mental-ity to diversification in low-income [African] economies is an anachronism' (Kaplinsky et al. 2011: 29) and that if the opportunities presented by corpo-rate outsourcing are grasped, 'the potential then arises for linkages from the commodities sector to provide a considerable impetus to industrialization' (Morris et al. 2012: 414).

Here, the use of the concept 'linkages' is a reference to the seminal work of the German development economist Albert Hirschman (1977), from which both Kaplinsky et al. (2011) and Morris et al. (2012) draw inspiration, based on the idea that economic development hinges on the incremental unfold-ing of linkages between productive industries and the surrounding economy. This line of thinking has served as a central theoretical justification used by the World Bank, African governments, and development agencies when extolling the potential virtues of capital-intensive foreign-owned mining (FOM).

In this context, the purpose of this chapter is twofold: first, to investigate the degree of articulation between the Congolese economy and the manufac-ture and provision of goods, equipment, and capital infrastructure to FOM in South Kivu during the twentieth century and how the turn to corporate outsourcing since the 2000s has affected this articulation; second, and relat-edly, to analyse the extent to which any articulation is associated with broader processes of domestic capital accumulation and structural transformation.

Based on the findings presented, the chapter questions the strength of the influential policy claim that recent industry restructuring has rendered the African mining enclave an outdated remnant of the past. The core argument of the chapter is, on the contrary, that the technological frontier of mining

Disrupted Development in the Congo. Ben Radley, Oxford University Press. © Ben Radley (2023).
DOI: 10.1093/oso/9780192849052.003.0004

in the twenty-first century has led to a heightened level of disarticulation and technological alienation between Banro's Twangiza mine and the surrounding Congolese economy compared to earlier eras of FOM in South Kivu.

4.1 Assimilation to enclavity

King Leopold II of Belgium's creation and appropriation of the Congo Free State following the Berlin Conference of 1885 led to a profound and violent disruption of, and departure from, the pre-existing social order. Two defining outcomes of Leopold's Congo Free State, which was to last until 1908, were its forced integration of rural regions into production for the international market, on highly exploitative terms, and the disruption and suppression of pre-colonial trading networks (both foreign and indigenous) in favour of Belgian financial capital, solicited primarily to develop the mining and transport sectors (Peemans 1975; Bezy et al. 1981).

Belgian financial capital first entered South Kivu in 1902 when, upon King Leopold II's solicitation, the Belgian industrialist Baron Empain invested an initial capital of 25 million gold francs in founding *Chemins de fer du Congo Supérieur aux Grands Lacs* (Upper Congo Railways of the Great Lakes, CFL) to construct a railway connecting the eastern parts of the Congo Free State. In return, the Baron's company, the Empain Group, was given four million hectares of land and mineral rights stretching from the Congo River eastward to Lake Kivu, a guarantee of capital amortization, and an additional four million hectares for each further investment of 25 million gold francs (Young and Turner 1985: 33). Between 1903 and 1910, CFL conducted ten mineral exploration missions, discovering significant deposits of gold, tin, and other minerals, including in South Kivu (OGP 2010).

In the early decades of the Belgian Congo, from 1908 onwards, and as under the Congo Free State, the emergence of independent African traders and firms continued to be seen by the colonial state as a threat to its authority and by Belgian capital as a threat to profits (by creating upwards pressure on wages). Local, regional, African, and foreign initiatives and trading networks which 'left to their own dynamic, would have obviously led to a larger, more diversified and certainly less concentrated accumulation profile' (Bezy et al. 1981: 35), were disrupted and restricted by state suppression (MacGaffey 1991: 39). Generally, there were few opportunities under Belgian colonial rule for Indigenous capital accumulation outside of state control (Hesselbein 2007; Putzel et al. 2008).

The focus, again as under the Congo Free State, was instead on developing the mining sector through predominantly Belgian mining capital. In 1923, the Empain Group created the *Société manière des Grands Lacs* (MGL) as a CFL subsidiary, responsible for all mineral exploration and exploitation in the eastern region. Production began the following year, as MGL exported 42 kilograms of gold to Belgium.[1] By the end of the 1930s, MGL had 573 mining concessions covering 49,440 square kilometres. Between 1920 and 1932, the Empain Group was one of four financial groups that controlled 75 per cent of all investment in the Congo, three-quarters of which was in mining and related infrastructure, with mineral exports increasing six-fold between 1920 and 1930 (Bezy et al. 1981: 20–21).

In concessions where production was underway, labour-intensive techniques were employed.[2] In Luhwindja, for example, the location of Banro's Twangiza mine, gold was first discovered by MGL in 1927. Prospection work in the early 1930s revealed an estimated 383 kilograms of gold reserves (Empain Group n.d.).[3] In 1938, MGL began alluvial exploitation at Twangiza, establishing a small worker camp of around 100 people at Chiramu (on the same site as one of Banro's worker camps in the 2010s). Here, as at other alluvial gold sites at the time, the ore was manually sieved and ground by workers to remove the shale and mudstone and extract the gold.[4]

The major exception was MGL's Mobale mine in Kamituga, around 150 kilometres south of Luhwindja, where production began in 1932. Over time, Mobale was to become MGL's most mechanized gold mine. Yet, even here, capital infrastructure was used mostly to separate the gold from the ore, while the extraction of the ore itself remained labour-intensive, dependent upon workers entering the shafts to physically excavate the ore and transport it to the surface in small wagons. Many locals considered the work degrading and stayed away (Kyanga 2013: 3–7). Many in Luhwindja, where work took place above ground, likewise saw the work as undesirable. The local *Mwami*,[5] on whom MGL relied for the recruitment of labour, resorted to sending those in conflict with him to work in the mines as punishment (Bisharhwa 1982).

Of the workers who did labour in MGL's mines, some stole gold from the firm (both those working underground at Mobale and those involved

---

[1] MGL General Assembly meeting notes, 17 June 1925.

[2] MGL General Assembly meeting notes, 6 October 1937; MGL Annual Report, 1937.

[3] Internal report on Concession Number 90, SAKIMA, 1995.

[4] Letter from Marrio Fiocchi, SOMINKI director, to the Congolese government, 13 January 1989; interview with former MGL worker, Luhwindja, 18 September 2016.

[5] The *Mwami* (singular) or *Bami* (plural) are traditional customary authorities who, throughout postcolonial Congolese history in South Kivu, have usually fulfilled a dual function serving as both customary and local government authorities.

in surface mining elsewhere on the concession), with those caught beaten, whipped, or imprisoned.[6] From at least as early as the 1950s, with financial investment from foreign traders, a growing number of workers began to engage in an alternative network of gold production, outside of MGL's control and supervision. This development was, no doubt, aided by the relative ease with which the predominantly labour-intensive methods of extraction they had learned at MGL could be assimilated and replicated independently.

Internal MGL correspondence shortly after independence in 1960 details an established network of illegal gold production and trade in South Kivu, from Luhwindja and Kamituga to the provincial capital of Bukavu and onwards to Uganda.[7] By 1963, MGL felt compelled to call upon the provincial state procurer for the Congolese government's support:

> It is of public notoriety that gold theft, clandestine exploitation and illegal exploitation have extended considerably since 1960 [. . .] at MGL, we think the thefts amount to several dozen kilos per month, or 30 to 40 percent of our production. To this must obviously be added important clandestine exploitations [elsewhere in the province], about which we possess no direct information.[8]

The same memorandum notes the arrival of foreigners to set up illegal gold trading houses.

The emergence of an alternative network of mining production and trade occurred alongside the mechanization of labour-intensive FOM, as MGL reinvested profits in the construction of industrial plants and hydroelectric power stations in the late 1940s and early 1950s (Mthembu-Salter 2009). This reflected a similar trend of mining industrialization taking place elsewhere across the country at the time (Bezy et al. 1981: 38–39). At MGL, investment in gold mechanization was heavily concentrated at Kamituga, while many other sites retained the labour-intensity of production well into the second half of the twentieth century. At Luhwindja, for example, while the discovery of a major underground deposit at Twangiza in 1957 led to a transition to shaft mining, production remained labour intensive through to its eventual suspension in the 1970s.[9]

Several smaller mining subsidiaries operated alongside MGL during this period, all under the ownership and control of the same Belgian mother

---

[6] Interviews with several former MGL and SOMINKI workers, South Kivu, September 2017–March 2018.

[7] Internal MGL correspondence, Bukavu, 7 August 1960; MGL letter to state procurer, Bukavu, 30 August 1960.

[8] MGL memorandum to the provincial state procurer, 4 September 1963.

[9] Letter from Marrio Fiocchi, SOMINKI director, to the Congolese government, 13 January 1989.

company, COFIMINES. As mines moved towards more capital-intensive forms of extraction and processing, productive activities and the provision of services were vertically integrated across each of the subsidiaries under COFIMINES' direct control.[10] In addition, procurement to support mining mechanization was channelled exclusively through foreign suppliers. During SOMINKI's period of high reinvestment from 1980 to 1984, discussed in section 3.1, the subsidiary spent a total of one billion Belgian francs on procurement (Figure 4.1). From this, more than two-thirds accrued to Belgian, German, and South African firms, and 99 per cent to firms from North America, Europe, Japan, and South Africa. None accrued to the Democratic Republic of the Congo's (DRC's) national economy, and (outside of South Africa) only 0.1 per cent accrued to African countries, with 0.1 million to Burundi and 8.7 million to Rwanda. Even food produce came to be increasingly sourced overseas by the 1980s, with the neglect and decline of agriculture rendering basic foodstuffs such as rice cheaper to import from Thailand than to source locally.[11]

Twangiza's gold deposit in Luhwindja was not targeted during this period of high investment, partly because the absence of appropriate technology made industrial exploitation of the thinly dispersed gold unfeasible.[12] By the 2000s, the development of a new chemical process known as 'carbon-in-pulp'

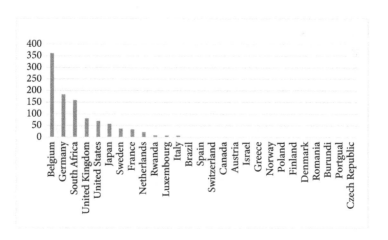

Figure 4.1 SOMINKI procurement by country, 1980–1984 (millions of Belgian francs)

Source: SOMINKI Annual Reports, 1980–1984.

[10] Interview with former SOMINKI director, Brussels, 10 August 2016.
[11] Ibid.
[12] Interview with former SOMINKI director, Kinshasa, 20 August 2016.

or 'carbon-in-leach' had turned the deposit into a commercially viable project, where gold ore with a mineral concentration of around just one to two grams of gold per tonne of rock could be profitably mined.

Constructed by Banro in 2010 as an open pit mine around 2 kilometres long and 0.5 kilometre wide, controlled explosions using dynamite took place every few months to loosen the rock for extraction. Once extracted by bulldozers, the rock was deposited by trucks in a large storage warehouse and then put on a conveyor belt, which carried it a few hundred metres to be crushed in a giant, rotating cylindrical plant, known by workers as 'the scrubber'. The noise from the plant could be heard through the night when lodging in the workers' camp a few hundred metres away, as the large rocks rolled around the revolving cylinder. Upon exit, the crushed rocks travelled another hundred metres or so along a second conveyor belt, where they entered ball mills which ground them down into a muddy liquid.

Here, the carbon-in-pulp process began, as the liquid was mixed with cyanide and carbon in thirteen large tanks to further increase the concentration of the gold. The gold was then released from the carbon solution to enter an electrolysis process on giant steel wood cathodes before being smelted at 1,150 degrees Celsius to around 90 per cent purity. Next, the liquid waste was taken and stored in the tailings' management facility, an artificially constructed reservoir around one kilometre away. The gold bars produced by the smelting weighed 10–15 kilograms and were shipped to refineries in South Africa and China to be smelted to the 99.9999 per cent purity required for sale and trade on the global market.

The use of heavy machinery to extract and process the ore, including the carbon-in-pulp technique, marked the full transition of FOM in South Kivu from a labour-intensive form of production using easily replicable methods and techniques, to a highly specialized, disembedded, and capital-intensive process of gold ore extraction and processing. Simultaneous with this transition has been a shift from the vertical integration practiced by MGL and SOMINKI towards the corporate outsourcing of a range of activities and services to independent firms practiced by Banro.

4.2 Stimulus to Northern economies

Corporate outsourcing can increase a mine's articulation with the domestic economy through two channels. The first is the procurement of goods, capital equipment, and inputs through independent domestic suppliers or manufacturers. The second is by subcontracting the provision of productive activities and services to domestic firms. These two channels can, in turn, provide impetus to broader processes of domestic capital accumulation and structural transformation through the productive reinvestment of profits and by stimulating secondary sectors. This section considers the first of these channels—procurement—and finds most of Banro's procurement in the 2010s to have been managed internally by the corporation. While this stimulated the development of productive capacity and capabilities in the global North, it left only a marginal space for a small group of Congolese suppliers at the low-value and low-tech end of Banro's chain.

From 2010 onwards, as Banro began the construction of its Twangiza mine, the procurement policy of its Congolese subsidiary Twangiza Mining stated, 'Preference will be given to local vendors. Support of local companies in the communities will receive favourable consideration' (Banro 2010b). In reality, Twangiza's industrial structure was wholly dependent upon externally manufactured capital goods, equipment, and inputs, and Congolese firms and suppliers played a negligible role in procuring these for the mine. Banro internally managed the procurement of its high-value and technologically advanced supplies and only outsourced a very low percentage of overall procurement value to a small group of Congolese suppliers for the provision of basic materials and equipment.

The industrial machinery and technology used to drive Twangiza's extraction and carbon-in-pulp processing method heralded almost entirely from North America, Europe, Japan, South Africa, and Australia. The gold-processing plant itself was purchased second-hand from the Australian mining corporation Tamaya Resources.[13] It comprised a ball plant, two ball mills, a carbon-in-pulp chemical treatment facility, a gold storage room, and a smelting laboratory. The plant was transported by sea from Australia and delivered by road through the Kenyan port of Mombasa, via 140 forty-foot containers. It was reassembled by foreign engineers on site (Banro 2009, 2010a).

Both during and in the several years after mine construction, procurement managers at Twangiza Mining reported the subsidiary to have made exclusive use of foreign firms and suppliers.[14] Corporate documentation supports these testimonies and provides insight into the extent of the mine's technological transplantation from predominantly Northern industrial centres. An asset inventory from 2011 lists all machinery and mobile equipment held by Twangiza Mining at the time, including the associated

[13] Twangiza Mining fixed assets listing as of 31 December 2012.
[14] Interviews with former and current Twangiza Mining procurement managers and workers, Twangiza, Bukavu and Kinshasa, January–June 2017.

Table 4.1 Twangiza Mining asset manufacturers by firm and nationality, 2011

Firm	Nationality	Firm	Nationality	Firm	Nationality
Bobcat	United States	La Roche	United Kingdom	Dynapac	France
Bomag	United States	Lister	United Kingdom	Manitou	France
Caterpillar	United States	Logic	United Kingdom	Deutz	Germany
Ditch Witch	United States	Powerscreen	United Kingdom	Mercedes	Germany
Fusion	United States	Thwaites	United Kingdom	Kirloskar	India
Grove	United States	Winget	United Kingdom	Samil	India
Ingersoll Rand	United States	Hitachi	Japan	Sykes	Australia
Miller	United States	Honda	Japan	Kipor	China
Robin	United States	Mitsubishi	Japan	Pramac	Italy
Wilson	United States	Suzuki	Japan	Bell	South Africa
Foden	United Kingdom	Toyota	Japan	Atlas Copco	Sweden
Henry Cooch	United Kingdom	Yamaha	Japan	Liebherr	Switzerland

Source: Twangiza Mining machinery and mobile equipment asset list, 2011.

manufacturer (Table 4.1). Of the thirty-seven manufacturers listed, twenty-five were US, British, or Japanese corporations. The remainder were mostly from European countries, with just four corporations from three countries outside of the global North (China, India, and South Africa).

A depreciation schedule from the end of 2012 lists all the fixed assets held by Twangiza Mining at the time, providing information on the original cost of each asset along with the manufacturer (Table 4.2). The most expensive asset was the second-hand plant procured from Australia, at a cost of $16.4 million. After this, the highest asset value heralded from the South African mining company TNC Bell, which provided $15.3 million of dump trucks, excavators, and other heavy mobile machinery. Of the $20.1 million procured from the remaining firms, just $1.6 million was sourced from countries outside of the global North (the same three countries that featured in the 2011 inventory of China, India, and South Africa). Notably, apart from South Africa, no African firms appear in either of the lists.

It was only at the lower-value, light industrial range of inputs that Congolese and other African firms began to appear. The period 2010–2013 spanned the construction phase of Twangiza through to the beginning of commercial production, in other words, the most capital-intensive period

Table 4.2 Twangiza Mining fixed assets by firm, nationality, and buying value, 2012
(millions of USD)

Firm	Nationality	Value	Firm	Nationality	Value
Tamaya Resources	Australia	16.4	Foden	United Kingdom	0.4
Bell	South Africa	15.3	Thwaites	United Kingdom	0.4
Caterpillar	United States	4.4	Manitou	France	0.3
Hitachi	Japan	4.2	JCB	United Kingdom	0.3
Toyota	Japan	3	Lister	United Kingdom	0.3
Mercedes	Germany	1.7	Motorola	United States	0.2
Mitsubishi	Japan	1	Ditch Witch	United States	0.2
XCYG	China	0.8	Spidersat	United Kingdom	0.1
Winget	United Kingdom	0.6	Xeros	United States	0.1
Liebherr	Switzerland	0.5	Dell	United States	0.1
Powerscreen	United Kingdom	0.5	Miller	United States	0.1
Hydraform	South Africa	0.4	Atlas Copco	Sweden	0.1
Samil	India	0.4	Hewlett-Packard	United States	0.1
TOTAL					51.8

Source: Twangiza Mining fixed assets listing and depreciation schedule, 2012.

of the project in terms of the inputs and equipment required. A review of Twangiza Mining procurement invoices from this four-year period indicates that, during this time, the subsidiary procured inputs from eighty-six suppliers and manufacturers (Table 4.3, with the full list of firms provided in Appendix 2). South African firms were dominant, comprising fifty-three of the eighty-six firms (or 62 per cent), generally supplying industrial parts or high-tech equipment. This included $740,000 of drilling equipment and services provide by Geosearch International,[15] $161,000 of closed-circuit television network supplied and installed by Goldfields Technical Security Management,[16] and $51,000 of steel piping and fittings supplied by Senet.[17]

Other non-African firms mostly supplied similarly high-tech inputs, such as Nowata Limited (a mining chemical manufacturer and supplier headquartered in the low-tax jurisdiction of the Isle of Man), which provided the chemicals used in the treatment process. Nowata invoices show that, in 2012, Twangiza Mining purchased 251 tonnes of sodium cyanide and 132 tonnes of carbon for a total cost of $811,458.[18] Also in 2012, a new chemical

---

[15] Geosearch International invoice numbers 191–332, April–October 2011.
[16] Goldfields' letter to Banro, 'Request for quotation for Twangiza Mine: SECRFQ1/2011', 5 August 2011.
[17] Twangiza Mining purchase order 085 MOD 2, 11 October 2010.
[18] Natawa Limited commercial invoices 5766, 6203, and 6220, March–August 2012.

Table 4.3 Twangiza Mining supplier firms by nationality, 2010–2013

Firm nationality	Number	Firm nationality	Number
South Africa	53	Mauritius	2
Kenya	4	Rwanda	2
United Arab Emirates	4	Tanzania	2
United Kingdom	4	Netherlands	1
Australia	3	India	1
DRC	3	Malaysia	1
Belgium	2	Turkey	1
Canada	2	Uganda	1
TOTAL			86

Source: Twangiza Mining procurement invoices, 2010–2013.

treatment facility was purchased and imported from the Australian mining manufacturer Gekko for $350,000.[19]

Among the eighty-six suppliers, there is, nonetheless, a greater presence of Congolese and African firms than observed in the fixed assets lists or in SOMINKI's procurement data from the 1980s. Three of the eighty-six firms were Congolese and (outside of South Africa) eleven were African: four from Kenya, two from Mauritius, two from Tanzania, two from Uganda, and one from Rwanda. Based on a review of the invoices from across the four-year period, the total revenue earned by the Congolese and other African firms was around $7.2 million (Table 4.4).

Five of the fourteen African firms provided capital and inputs manufactured outside of their registered country of origin (digital equipment, heavy vehicles and parts, and computing equipment), four provided a range of services (customs, transport, and travel), and one firm provided labour. The remaining four firms, none of which were Congolese, provided inputs likely manufactured or extracted in their country of origin: Afriserve in Mauritius (quicklime and steel balls), Neelkanth Lime and Tata Afrique in Tanzania (lime, chemicals, and light industrial goods), and Stone Crushing in Uganda (light industrial goods, such as piping and fencing).

The three Congolese firms were only ephemerally involved, providing services or inputs manufactured outside of the DRC. Ami Congo provided customs support to facilitate imports for several months in 2012, yet was soon replaced by the Belgian corporation Comexas. In November 2011, the Kinshasa-based firm Key Print made a one-off supply of Xerox computing

[19] Gekko commercial invoice 3064, 30 April 2012.

Table 4.4 African supplier firms to Twangiza Mining, 2010–2013

Firm	Nationality	Input/service	Approximate revenue ($)
Freight Forwarders	Kenya	Transport	1,600,000
Logisol	Kenya	Digital equipment	10,000
Neff Auto Spares	Kenya	Vehicle parts	240,000
Union Logistics	Kenya	Transport	500,000
AmiCongo	DRC	Customs	200,000
Forrest Group	DRC	Mobile machinery leasing	16,440
Keyprint	DRC	IT equipment	772,439
Afriserve	Mauritius	Quicklime and steel balls	800,000
Resourcing for Africa	Mauritius	Thai labour	1,200,000
Neelkanth Lime	Tanzania	Lime	106,000
Tata Afrique	Tanzania	Chemicals, light industrial goods	1,500,000
PC World Computers	Uganda	IT equipment	50,000
Stone Crushing	Uganda	Light industrial goods	70,000
Easy Travel	Rwanda	Travel agent	100,000
ESTIMATED TOTAL			7,164,879

Source: Twangiza Mining procurement invoices, 2010–2013.

equipment at a value of $16,440 (requesting payment into a South African bank account).[20] In November 2013, Malta Forrest, a Congolese firm owned by a Belgian entrepreneur, invoiced Twangiza Mining a total of $772,439 for the lease of unspecified mining equipment (likely heavy mobile machinery, given the asset base listed by Malta Forrest on its website).[21]

One barrier faced by domestic firms was the home country market bias of Twangiza Mining's procurement teams. For procurement purchases of more than $5,000, Twangiza Mining's procurement officers presented their line managers with quotes from three different suppliers. From these quotes, the managers made a final decision as to which supplier was chosen. This decision was then authorized by the relevant department manager, finance manager, and the general director of the mine. Reflecting on this process, former employees observed a preference among non-national procurement managers to use foreign (and often home-country) suppliers for goods, such as workers' clothing and computing equipment, even when presented with domestic suppliers who could procure the same goods at a lower cost.[22] Hanlin and Hanlin's (2012: 472) comment on industrial gold mining in East

---

[20] Key Print commercial invoice 533/NMM-KYP/AG/2011, 2 November 2011.

[21] Malta Forrest commercial invoices 21311432–21311443, 11 November 2013, https://forrestgroup. com (accessed 23 August 2021).

[22] Interviews with former Twangiza Mining auditor, Bukavu, 15 December 2016, former Twangiza Mining procurement officer, Kinshasa, 13 January 2017, and former Twangiza Mining procurement manager, Skype call, 23 January 2017.

Africa that 'expatriate procurement officers tended to avoid engaging in local markets, reverting to markets they understood' might hold relevance here. This tendency might also be explained by perceptions that Congolese suppliers would be less efficient than their foreign counterparts or procure goods of lower quality.

It was only at the lowest-value and lowest-tech end of its equipment and supplies that Banro outsourced procurement to a small group of several Congolese suppliers. Around 2009, shortly before mine construction began, Twangiza Mining sent formal correspondence to major commercial traders in Bukavu, listing the items it needed and requesting supplier quotations. The items it sought, in 2009 and into the 2010s, were mostly office equipment and stationery, workers' safety equipment (including boots, jackets, and protective clothing), and basic construction materials (such as steel bars and concrete). The suppliers incorporated into Banro's chain at this level were some of Bukavu's most successful and well-known Congolese entrepreneurs.[23] As documented in section 3.3, Banro accumulated debts to all members of this group as it strove to stave off bankruptcy, with some choosing to withdraw from their integration into Banro's chain as a result.

In 2016, Congolese traders operating in Banro's value chain supplied an estimated $1.5 million of goods and equipment to the mine, while during the same year, Twangiza Mining imported around $41 million of procured goods through foreign suppliers.[24] While Congolese suppliers were incorporated at this low-tech end of Banro's chain, as elsewhere in Banro's procurement network, none of these low-value goods were manufactured domestically. Rather, local suppliers procured predominantly Asian-manufactured goods almost exclusively through Dubai, with the exception of some light industrial materials manufactured in the neighbouring countries of Uganda (steel bars) and Rwanda (concrete).[25]

The documented presence of Congolese suppliers and firms in Banro's procurement network, along with firms from several other African countries, provides some evidence of greater African firm integration into capital-intensive FOM in South Kivu than was the case with SOMINKI during the 1980s. Yet, integration, especially but not just for Congolese, was restricted to the low-value end of the chain with no signs or evidence of moving to higher value-added activities (or 'upgrading'). Instead, and in a continuation

---

[23] One, for example, began as a small trader in hardware goods in Kadutu on the outskirts of Bukavu, going on to construct a five-storey commercial centre on Avenue Lumumba, the main road running through the city centre.

[24] Domestic supplier invoices, 2016; South Kivu list of declared imports, 1 January 2016–31 December 2016, Congolese Central Bank.

[25] Interviews with multiple Congolese suppliers, Bukavu, January–April 2017.

of past practice in South Kivu, Banro managed most of its procurement internally, depending primarily on non-African firms and suppliers (except for South Africa). This, in spite of the capacity of Congolese suppliers at times to procure the same goods at a lower cost than their foreign counterparts. In addition, only a small fraction of procurement was outsourced to Congolese suppliers, and none of the capital procured for Twangiza, whether managed internally or by Congolese suppliers, made use of domestically manufactured inputs, goods, or equipment. Based on this, it can be concluded that the procurement of capital to construct and maintain Banro's Twangiza mine has made little contribution to processes of transformative economic development in the DRC.

4.3 Foreign firm expansion

In the realm of subcontracting, the second channel through which corporate outsourcing can increase a mine's articulation with the domestic economy, Banro's contribution to transformative economic development has been similarly underwhelming. In 2017, Twangiza Mining subcontracted fifteen firms to provide thirteen different activities and services to the mine. Of the fifteen firms, outside of the provision of cheap and mostly unskilled labour (considered more fully in Chapter 5) only two were Congolese (for the provision of sand and drilling services, respectively). The remaining activities and services—customs, electricity, security, road maintenance, fuel, smelting, aviation, catering, gold certification, and transportation—were provided by foreign firm subsidiaries. In South Kivu alone, not considering Congolese firms elsewhere across the country, domestic firms at the time operated in at least five of these areas (security, catering, road maintenance, fuel, and transportation).[26]

An obstacle to domestic firm inclusion has been Banro's requirement, following industry practice, that subcontracted firms cover their own costs for the first sixty or ninety days of the contract before reimbursement.[27] In 2015, Twangiza Mining began contacting domestic suppliers to the catering firm Allterrain Services (ATS)—a subsidiary of the South African corporation Tsebo Outsourcing Group—with a view to having one of them replace ATS as the main catering subcontractor. While some domestic suppliers expressed interest in the opportunity, none had the financial capital required

---

[26] *Fédération des entreprises du Congo* (Congo Business Federation), South Kivu membership list, January 2017.
[27] Interview with Civicon manager, Luhwindja, 29 November 2016.

to front the initial ninety days of costs. In the end, ATS retained its contract.[28] Similarly, a domestic fuel supplier was approached by Twangiza Mining soon after Banro's arrival in the DRC but had to forego the contract due to insufficient financial capital.[29]

Congolese firms have also been hampered by inadequate state policy to support and develop domestic capacity and capabilities, itself a by-product of the earlier mining sector reform led by the World Bank, which restricted the Congolese state to a regulatory role within a liberalized and privatized framework. For the first decade after the 2002 Congolese Mining Code was introduced, the DRC had no local content or subcontracting legislation. This changed in 2014, but the new legislative measures allowed mining transnational corporations (TNCs) operating in the country to continue their practice of procuring through and subcontracting foreign firms, despite rhetoric about prioritizing the promotion of domestic firms and entrepreneurs.

The 2014 inter-ministerial local content decree, for instance, states that mining companies registered in the DRC must procure from domestic suppliers but that imports are permissible 'if the needs expressed by mining companies surpass the capacity of Congolese industries and small and medium enterprises'.[30] Similarly, in 2017, a law was passed which allowed for the continued subcontracting of foreign firms if the required expertise was 'unavailable or inaccessible' domestically.[31] The 2018 Congolese Mining Code is governed by this law.[32] The subcontracting law did, however, address the issue of pre-financing by requiring the transfer of at least 30 per cent of the value of the contract to the subcontracted firm upfront.

Alongside these legislative loopholes, there has been little broader industrial policy to increase the 'capacity', 'availability', or 'accessibility' of Congolese actors to facilitate their inclusion and upgrading in global mining value chains. The Ministry of Industry agency *Fonds de promotion de l'industrie* (Funds for the Promotion of Industry, FPI) provides a notable exception. However, of a total $125.9 million invested by FPI in supporting domestic firms in the three-year period 2013–2015, more than half was invested in Kinshasa and only $2.7 million (or 2 per cent) was invested in South Kivu, in non-mining sector firms.[33] Beyond FPI, there is little evidence of the state's

---

[28] Interviews and conversations with Tsebo Outsourcing Group managers and suppliers, December 2016–April 2017.

[29] Interview with domestic fuel supplier managers, Bukavu, 31 January 2017.

[30] Inter-ministerial decrees 0027/CAB.MIN/MINES/01/2014 and 043/CAB.MIN/IPME/2014 of 11 February 2014.

[31] Law 17/001 of 8 February 2017.

[32] DRC Mining Code 2018, Article 108.

[33] FPI Annual Reports, 2013–2015.

active intervention to support Congolese firms seeking entry into industrial mining value chains.

Assessing the distribution of value accruing to Twangiza Mining's sub-contracted firms confirms the overall picture of domestic marginality in this sphere. In 2013, the most recent year for which data was attained, foreign firms captured $40 million or an estimated 87 per cent of the total revenue accruing to Twangiza Mining's subcontractors (Table 4.5). Of the remaining six million dollars accruing to Congolese firms, nearly half went to firms providing mostly unskilled labour, whose wages have been insufficient for significant reinvestment or to support consumption-led processes of economic transformation (as documented in section 5.2). In addition, two of the five Congolese firms had a strong external orientation. The majority shareholder of Diphil was a well-known and successful Congolese entrepreneur whose primary residence was in South Africa, and Groupe Rubuye was owned by the Rubuye family, a similarly successful group of Congolese entrepreneurs living in Canada.

While foreign firm subsidiaries captured most of the subcontracting revenue, some also expanded their presence in the DRC, having entered the country through Banro. The subcontract awarded to Tsebo Outsourcing Group was its first in the DRC. The firm then went on to secure several new

Table 4.5 Twangiza Mining subcontractor value capture, 2013 (millions of USD)

Nationality	Firm(s)	Service	Value	
			$	%
Congolese	Premium	Sand	3.3	7.2
Congolese	Cinamula, Diphil, Zuki	Labour	2.6	5.6
Congolese	Groupe Rubuye	Drilling	0.2	0.4
Subtotal domestic			6.1	13.2
Malaysian	Engen	Fuel	21.6	46.9
Kenyan	Civicon	Road maintenance	8.4	18.2
South African	Tsebo Outsourcing Group	Catering	3.3	7.2
British	Aggreko	Electricity	2.5	5.4
British	G4S	Security	1.5	3.3
Swiss	Société Générale de Surveillance	Gold certification	1.3	2.8
South African	Savannah	Aviation (helicopters)	0.8	1.7
South African	Rand Refinery	Smelting	0.5	1.1
Tanzanian	Simba Logistics	Transportation	0.1	0.2
Belgian	COMEXAS Group	Customs	Unknown	
Subtotal foreign			40.0	86.8
TOTAL			46.1	100

Source: Twangiza Mining 2013 financial accounts.

contracts in the country, including with mining TNCs Glencore in Lualaba Province and Randgold Resources in Haut-Uélé Province.[34] Since arriving in the DRC through contracts with Banro, the Tanzanian firm Simba Logistics and the Swiss corporation *Société générale de surveillance* (SGS) have gone on to secure additional contracts in the mining regions of Katanga and Haut-Uélé.[35]

From the value accruing to subcontractors (foreign and Congolese), two had significant domestic procurement expenditure that supported, or indicated the possibility of supporting, local processes of capital accumulation. The first was the Congolese firm Premium, which extracted around 200 cubic metres of sand per day from the island of Idjwi on Lake Kivu and Kalehe in South Kivu. Twangiza Mining paid around $7,000 for this daily volume, using the sand to shore up the mine's ever-expanding waste storage reservoir facility. Initially, this was a labour-intensive operation, with around 250 workers extracting the sand and loading it on and off boats and lorries; the firm rented two boats and thirty-two lorries to transport the sand to the mine. In 2016, however, the firm invested in extractive machinery to increase productivity and acquired three lorries.[36]

The second was the South African subsidiary ATS. Under its agreement with Banro (2016b: 23), ATS was 'required under its contract to source basic food commodities, including vegetables and small livestock, from local producers'. This led ATS to form and work closely with two local producer cooperatives in Luhwindja, the *Cooperative des eleveurs de Luhwindja* (Livestock Cooperative of Luhwindja) and the *Cooperative agricole de Lubanda* (Agricultural Cooperative of Lubanda). The former had twenty-eight members and the latter fifteen, and both were comprised mostly of local miners who were displaced from the Twangiza site to allow for the mine's construction (a process discussed at greater length in section 7.1). As the Ghanaian manager of ATS's contract with Twangiza Mining explained:

> In our organization we have a community relations manager whose duty is to go around, sort out from the community what we can buy from them, and train them on what we need to use. Because sometimes, you will go to some of the community, and what you are needing they don't produce it, but they have the land that they can cultivate. So, we train them, and we tell them that what they produce, we can

---

[34] Interview with Tsebo Outsourcing Group administrator, Bukavu, 6 December 2016.
[35] Interviews with Simba Logistics DRC director, Bukavu, 22 February 2017 and SGS manager, Twangiza, 6 June 2017.
[36] Interviews with Premium director, Bukavu, 12 October 2016 and Twangiza Mining Tailing Management Facility manager, Twangiza, 9 June 2017.

buy. So, once the community manager goes down to engage the community and train them, whatever they plant like potatoes, tomatoes, and onions, we buy from them.[37]

The Food and Agricultural Organization (FAO) also worked with the cooperatives to strengthen the insertion of local producers into global value chains, including training the cooperatives to meet the required food control standards.[38] Neither of the cooperatives had a formal contract with ATS, but each month, the livestock cooperative provided Twangiza with around 1 tonne of meat and the agricultural cooperative around 1 tonne of fruit and vegetables.[39]

According to ATS firm data (Figure 4.2), during the first five months of 2017, $287,101 was spent procuring primarily meat and vegetables locally from six suppliers in Luhwindja. Alongside the two cooperatives, the third main supplier (providing fruit and vegetables) was *Cantine Iragi* (Iragi Canteen), owned by a successful local trader. The remaining $418,161 was spent on a combination of domestic and imported produce procured from Bukavu, including fish, meat, coffee, sugar, and rice. From this, it can be extrapolated that the South African subsidiary was spending around $700,000 annually sourcing produce from Luhwindja-based suppliers and procuring around 1 million dollars through domestic suppliers in Bukavu, including some Congolese produce.

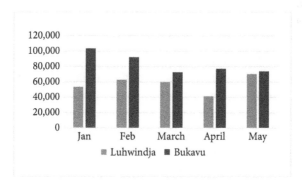

Figure 4.2 ATS local food procurement, January–May 2017 (thousands of USD)

Source: ATS local supplier data, 2017.

---

[37] Interview with ATS manager, Bukavu, 20 June 2017.
[38] Interview with FAO representative, Bukavu, 24 February 2017.
[39] Interviews with cooperative members, Luhwindja, 7 February and 10 February 2017.

In Luhwindja, this represented a sizeable investment in the local economy, and the livestock and agricultural cooperatives reported having used the income to invest in more land to meet the demand as well as sourcing the required produce from other local farmer associations. One of these local associations was the non-governmental organization (NGO) *Action pour la promotion de l'enfant et la femme* (Action for the Promotion of Children and Women, APEF), founded and run by a leading political figure locally, which was providing agricultural employment to around 200 local women.[40] Similarly, according to ATS's corporate data, *Cantine Iragi* was the local supplier earning the most revenue from the catering firm and sourced its chickens and eggs from Ngweshe and Walungu in South Kivu.

South Kivu's FOM economy has undergone a long-run transition from labour-intensive production in the early to mid-twentieth century to highly capital-intensive production in the opening decades of the twenty-first century. The arrival of FOM in South Kivu in the 1920s through the Belgian subsidiary MGL installed a predominantly labour-intensive form of production, and the initial absence of mechanization facilitated the local assimilation of the extractive methods and techniques deployed by Belgian firms. These techniques were soon replicated by Congolese to develop a parallel network of labour-intensive domestic-owned mining (DOM) outside of the control of foreign mining firms. By the 1970s and 1980s, while labour-intensive FOM continued in many areas, mechanization had begun and the capital infrastructure adopted by FOM at its most industrialized sites was highly enclaved from the local and national economy. Procurement data following fresh shareholder investment in the 1980s shows the total dependence of the Belgian subsidiary, at this juncture, upon the foreign supply of goods, capital equipment, and inputs.

By the 2010s, FOM in South Kivu under the tutelage of Banro had become highly capital intensive. Contrary to the expectations of African Mining Consensus proponents, Banro's practice of corporate outsourcing at Twangiza had marginalized Congolese actors in favour of foreign (and predominantly Northern) firms, while doing little to stimulate domestic capital formation and structural transformation. The few domestic firms and suppliers that were incorporated were located at the lowest value-added end of Banro's chain and clustered in areas outside of productive capabilities, primarily in services and the provision of mostly unskilled labour.

Beyond the examples of the Congolese firm Premium and the South African catering subsidiary ATS, there was no evidence that Banro's practice of corporate outsourcing—whether through the channel of procurement

---

[40] Conversation with APEF labourer, Luhwindja, 10 February 2017.

or subcontracting—had contributed to sustained processes of transformative economic development domestically. It had, however, provided significant stimulus to predominantly Northern economies through the demand for manufactured goods and services as well as by providing an opportunity for foreign firm subsidiary expansion into a new domestic market.

Rather than invalidating the enclave position, the findings present an accentuated version of Prebisch's original enclave thesis whereby contemporary resource extraction in the periphery has few domestic linkages and is generally disarticulated from local and national economies due to the periphery's dependence upon external technology and industrial capabilities in the centre. The technological frontier of industrial gold mining in the early twenty-first century, embodied by the carbon-in-leach process at Banro's Twangiza mine, has extended far beyond that of MGL and SOMINKI's earlier eras, leading to a greater degree of technological alienation from the surrounding Congolese economy.

Based on the findings, the wisdom of moving from capital-intensive DOM to FOM, grounded this time in a belief that the global industry shift to corporate outsourcing can provide a stimulus to broader-based processes of industrialization, is once more brought into question. Rather, as with the constraint of price volatility observed in Chapter 3, it suggests that the narrow, specialized, and disembedded industrial composition of the sector undermines its potential to drive broader processes of domestic capital accumulation and structural transformation in the African periphery, regardless of ownership and management structures.

This line of argument is continued in Chapter 5, which draws attention to a final structural constraint restricting the transformative potential of mining-led industrialization in African low-income-country settings, in the form of low labour absorption. The weight of this constraint is accentuated under the model of capital-intensive FOM observed in South Kivu, whereby an ever-decreasing number of workers are employed and a foreign managerial class expends a significant share of total wages outside of the country.

5
Wage polarization and labour fragmentation

Drawing on empirical evidence from a revisionist line of historical scholarship focused on today's industrialized countries (as discussed in section 1.2), African Mining Consensus proponents have argued that capital-intensive foreign-owned mining (FOM) will generate fresh employment and drive higher wages than those available in the surrounding economy, and the expenditure of these increased wages can stimulate broader local processes of economic development and structural transformation. This claim is also frequently promoted by the industry itself. According to the industry-funded World Gold Council (2011: 21), for example:

> on average, mining companies pay significantly more than typical local wages, and this differential increases in less developed economies. For example, in lower-middle income gold producing countries such as Côte d'Ivoire or Mongolia, the lowest paid mine worker will on average earn 3.5 times more than the typical local wage and may earn almost seven times more.

The main purpose of this chapter is to problematize this line of thinking. It does so, in part, by incorporating wage data from labour-intensive domestic-owned mining (DOM) so often left out of industry assessments such as the World Gold Council's above under the justification that 'reliable and comparable data [...] is not currently available' (World Gold Council 2011: 6). One of Rio Tinto's (2018: 7) sustainability reports, for example, notes that 'our business is often the major source of jobs and livelihoods, and sometimes, one of few avenues to opportunity'. In the 100-page report, labour-intensive DOM is not discussed. Similarly, a report by the industry-funded International Council on Mining and Metals (2016: 39) found industrial mining jobs to be better paid then available alternatives but noted that labour-intensive DOM 'is not included in the analysis as reliable estimates for employment [...] do not exist'.

The main argument is that most worker wages associated with FOM in South Kivu since its inception in the first half of the twentieth century have

Disrupted Development in the Congo. Ben Radley, Oxford University Press. © Ben Radley (2023).
DOI: 10.1093/oso/9780192849052.003.0005

been comparable to, or below, those found in labour-intensive DOM and generally stagnant, declining significantly in real terms during the 1940s (under the *Société manière des Grands Lacs*, MGL), the 1960s to the 1990s (under SOMINKI), and the 2010s (under Banro). Meanwhile, by expanding labour informality and entrenching spatial separation between workers, the global industry shift to corporate outsourcing in the twenty-first century has weakened the collective strength of workers at Twangiza to resist and transform their conditions. Together with a far lower level of labour absorption than was the case historically and the external orientation of most of the managerial stratum, who consume and invest their wages outside of the Democratic Republic of the Congo (DRC), the ability of wages derived from capital-intensive FOM to stimulate economic development in South Kivu has been limited.

5.1 Low worker wages, high foreign capture

Throughout the 1930s and early 1940s, in the beginnings of what was then predominantly labour-intensive FOM in South Kivu, and in a context of labour scarcity compared to the early twenty-first century, MGL wages to workers were low and stagnant, declining in real terms. The average monthly worker wage was relatively constant from 1930 to 1937, at around 70 francs.[1] Between 1937 and 1944, two MGL workers based in Mwenga territory of South Kivu—one in Kamituga and one in Luhwindja—earned between 40 and 50 francs per month, with no meaningful or consistent wage increase across this period.[2] Yet, between 1944 and 1946 alone, the cost of basic foodstuffs and clothes in Mwenga territory more than doubled (Witangila bin-Mubya 1982: 26), indicating the stagnant wages received by MGL workers to have declined in real terms during this period. MGL wage dynamics in South Kivu reflected trends at the national level, where real wages to local labour in the Belgian Congo in 1945 were less than those earned in 1914 (Bezy 1957: 166).

In the late 1940s, declining wages sparked a series of worker revolts across the country (Bezy et al. 1981: 36). In the Kivu region, local wages in 1946 ranged between 26 and 216 francs per month, while European wages were as high as 3,000 francs per month, or 115 times greater than the lowest paid workers, giving rise to mass protests and the slogan 'Equal work, equal pay' (Witangila bin-Mubya 1982: 37). The following year, 1947, the *Association*

---

[1] MGL Annual Reports, 1930 and 1937.
[2] MGL worker payment books, 1937–1944.

du personnel indigène de la Colonie (Association of the Colony's Indigenous Workers) was founded, the first workers' union formed by and for the
Congolese (Ntampaka 1978: 30). In 1948, the colonial state introduced a
regionally adjusted minimum wage (Bezy 1957: 65), which rose in the Kivu
region from 1 franc per day in 1948 to 5.5 francs per day in 1955 (Ntampaka
1978: 44).

In response to the introduction of a rising minimum wage, wages for the
lowest category MGL worker at Kamituga increased more than five-fold from
1949 to 1959 (from 1.5 to 8.1 francs per day), and wages for the highest
categories of African employment at MGL more than doubled (Witangila
bin-Mubya 1982: 98). Towards the end of the colonial period, in 1957, the
colonial state granted workers the right to association (Ntampaka 1978: 39).
In 1959, MGL began the process of 'Africanization', promoting Congolese
workers into senior and managerial positions from which they had previously
been excluded.

For these reasons, the 1950s have often been considered 'the "golden age"
of the Congolese working class' (Peemans 1975: 152). This, in turn, initiated
a new process of social stratification in South Kivu (and elsewhere). Many
of MGL's workers during this period owned bicycles, sewing machines, and
even vehicles, differentiating them from the surrounding peasantry (Ntampaka 1978: 44). A former MGL worker in Luhwindja, still alive in 2017,
recalled using his wages in the 1940s to pay his dowry and buy several cows.[3]
However, as mineworker wages improved during the 1950s, the total units
of labour employed declined dramatically as MGL began to slowly mechanize production. The number of African workers employed by MGL fell from
16,692 in 1948 to 5,845 in 1960, narrowing the size of the region's emerging
groups of FOM labour.[4]

Congolese independence in 1960 appeared to do little for worker wages.
The period 1960–1975 saw a general decrease in real wages at the national
level (Bezy et al. 1981: 76). At MGL in the late 1960s, both workers and the
government derided what they perceived as unacceptably low wages and criticized the disproportionate remuneration of European managers.[5] In 1968,
the average European MGL wage was eight times higher than that of Congolese administrative middle management and forty-two times higher than
worker wages.[6]

---

[3] Interviews with former MGL workers, Luhwindja, 18 September 2016 and 9 April 2017.
[4] MGL Annual Reports, 1948–1960.
[5] Internal MGL correspondence, Kamituga, 6 February 1968; MGL workers' letter to management,
Kamituga, 12 July 1968.
[6] MGL workers' letter to management, Kamituga, 12 July 1968.

Table 5.1 SOMINKI annual wage distribution, 1984 (in Zaires)

Labour category	Units of labour	Monthly wage per unit	Annual wage per unit	Total annual wages	Share (%)
Workers	11,793	1,042	12,502	147,441,758	56.2
Supervisors	199	5,349	64,192	12,774,283	4.9
Directors	76	22,247	266,960	20,288,979	7.7
Foreigners	89	76,773	921,277	81,993,636	31.2
TOTAL	12,157	–	–	262,498,656	100

Source: SOMINKI Annual Report, 1984.

By the 1980s, following MGL's 1976 merger with several other subsidiaries into SOMINKI, the process of Africanization begun in the late 1950s had nonetheless begun to bear fruit. Members of the emerging Congolese managerial stratum earned significantly greater wages than workers and had access to credit, with which they bought cars, land, and property in Bukavu and Kinshasa, where many of their families were from or had moved to.[7] In addition, in an extension of colonial practice, this stratum was spatially segregated from the rest of the workers. At SOMINKI's gold mining town in Kamituga, Congolese managers lived in superior housing in a different neighbourhood, ate imported European food in a separate canteen, and had exclusive access to a social club.[8] They received the best medical care, including overseas treatment if required, and the subsidiary established schools for their children to attend.[9]

Nonetheless, foreign labour remained in a dominant position. In 1984, foreign labour captured 31 per cent of wages at SOMINKI, despite representing less than 1 per cent of the total workforce (Table 5.1). Congolese supervisors and directors meanwhile, despite outnumbering foreign staff by two to one, captured just 13 per cent of total wages that same year.

Meanwhile, real wages to workers appeared to have fallen below the revenue earned in labour-intensive DOM. Reflecting on the 1980s, a former SOMINKI geologist recalled that 'we were looking for workers, but we couldn't find them because they were all going to dig for gold'.[10] Noting increasing worker desertion, SOMINKI's 1980 annual report argued that the problem 'finds its origin in the growing attraction of artisanal gold exploitation, which procures for those interested revenue and savings and the means

---

[7] Interviews with former SOMINKI workers, Bukavu, 12 September 2016.
[8] Interviews with former SOMINKI workers, Luhwindja and Bukavu, 12 and 16 September 2016.
[9] Interviews with former SOMINKI workers, Bukavu, 12 September 2016.
[10] Interview with former SOMINKI geologist, 6 September 2016.

to acquire [. . .] consumer goods available on the market'.[11] The implication, supported by testimonies from former SOMINKI workers, is that worker wages at SOMINKI were too low to save or purchase consumer goods.[12]

SOMINKI's 1979 annual report notes, 'the purchasing power of manual labour has reduced catastrophically over the course of the preceding years. This situation led to violent strikes in April'.[13] Real wages continued to decline into the 1980s, falling far behind inflation, despite their negotiation every two years with the unions.[14] Frequent strikes throughout the 1980s failed to redress the situation.[15] With inflation spiralling during the 1990s, by the time SOMINKI went into liquidation in 1997, the value of real wages to Congolese workers had almost completely collapsed.

Banro's entry into South Kivu's mining economy in the 2010s, through its flagship Twangiza project, generated an eight-fold increase in labour productivity compared to SOMINKI in the 1980s, and a twenty-five-fold increase in labour productivity compared to labour-intensive DOM at Kadumwa, the largest labour-intensive DOM site in Luhwindja, situated just a few kilometres downhill from the Twangiza mine (Table 5.2). It is notable from this data that SOMINKI was only an estimated three times more productive than Kadumwa, underlining the relatively low level of capital intensity underpinning FOM production in the twentieth century, even as late as the 1980s. The data also highlights the far lower level of labour absorption associated with production at Twangiza, with approximately five units of labour employed per kilogram of gold produced by SOMINKI in 1984 compared to just half a unit of labour at Twangiza in 2013.

To determine whether, and to what extent, the increased productivity generated by Banro's arrival drove higher wages to workers, worker wages in the surrounding labour-intensive DOM economy must first be presented. Table 5.3 shows the wage levels in 2017 across different worker categories at Kadumwa.[16] The data shows that shaft workers, who descend underground to extract the ore and who accounted for nearly three-quarters of workers at Kadumwa, earned an average monthly wage of $163. Meanwhile, water carriers, ore carriers, and ore washers—site workers, who all work above ground—earned average monthly wages of $27, $54, and $68, respectively.

---

[11] SOMINKI Annual Report, 1980 (author translation).
[12] Interviews with former SOMINKI workers, 18 February 2017, Bukavu and 22 April 2017, Kamituga.
[13] SOMINKI Annual Report, 1979 (author translation).
[14] SOMINKI Technical Audit, 1995; personal memoires of Serge Lammens, former SOMINKI director.
[15] Interviews with former SOMINKI workers, Kamituga, 22 April 2017.
[16] As discussed at more length in Chapter 6, the managerial group overseeing labour at Kadumwa earns profits and not wages and so has not been included here.

Table 5.2 Labour productivity of mining in South Kivu (based on 2017 average gold price)

Company/ site	Year	Gold production (kg) (a)	Value created ($) (b)	Units of labour (c)	Productivity ($) (b/c)	Units of labour per kg of production (c/a)	Ratio to Kadumwa
Kadumwa	2017	59.7	2,341,772	762	3,073	12.8	1:1
SOMINKI	1984	435.5	17,602,039	2,100	8,382	4.8	3:1
Twangiza	2013	2,564.9	103,668,128	1,366	75,892	0.5	25:1

Sources: See Appendix 3.

Table 5.3 Kadumwa annual wage distribution, 2017

Group		Units of labour	Monthly wage per unit ($)	Annual wage per unit ($)	Total annual wages ($)	Share (%)
Site workers	Water carriers	30	27	324	9,720	0.8
	Ore carriers	80	54	648	51,840	4.5
	Ore washers	80	67.5	810	64,800	5.6
Shaft workers		528	163	1,956	1,032,768	89.1
TOTAL		718	–	–	1,159,128	100

Sources: See Appendix 4.

To determine wage levels set at Banro's Twangiza mine, workers were divided into three main categories: first, hired labour, composed of informal day labourers working at and around the mine for local Congolese firms; second, subcontractor workers, who work for firms subcontracted by Banro's subsidiary, Twangiza Mining, to provide goods, services, and activities to the mine (as with hired labour, many subcontractor workers were also informal); finally, Twangiza Mining workers directly contracted by the Canadian subsidiary. Congolese managers and directors worked across labour hire firms, subcontracted firms, and Twangiza Mining, while foreign managers and directors worked at subcontracted firms or Twangiza Mining only.

The data indicates that during the same year of 2017 as the data presented for Kadumwa, the average hired labour monthly wage of $187 is broadly comparable to the average shaft worker monthly wage at Kadumwa of $163 (Table 5.4). The lowest paid category of hired labour—composed of 169 workers, or 15 per cent of all workers at Twangiza—earned $110 per month,

Table 5.4 Twangiza wage distribution, 2017

Group				Units of labour	Monthly wage per unit ($)	Annual wage per unit ($)	Total annual wages ($)	Share (%)
Workers	Hired labour			323	187	2,244	724,812	4.4
	Subcontractor workers			285	274	3,288	937,080	5.7
		Unskilled	I	214	319	3,824	818,293	5.0
			II	24	446	5,350	128,405	0.8
	Twangiza Mining		III	128	634	7,608	973,824	5.9
		Skilled	IV	42	796	9,555	401,310	2.4
			V	133	1,281	15,369	2,044,077	12.4
Subtotal workers				1,149	–	–	6,027,801	36.6
Congolese managers				140	2,311	27,735	3,882,919	23.6
Congolese directors				6	6,847	82,159	492,955	3.0
Subtotal Congolese				146	–	–	4,375,874	26.6
Foreign managers				63	6,817	81,804	5,153,655	31.3
Foreign directors				8	9,270	111,239	889,910	5.4
Subtotal foreign				71	–	–	6,043,565	36.7
TOTAL				1,366	–	–	16,447,240	100

Notes: The employment data in Twangiza Mining's financial accounts divides unskilled workers across categories I and II and skilled workers across categories III, IV, and V; wage data includes overtime and allowances. On top of their base wage, workers and managers at Twangiza Mining receive lodging, transport, and child and spouse allowances, with managers also receiving a responsibility allowance. Overtime makes a significant difference to worker wages, often as much as doubling the base wage in the case of subcontractor workers.
Sources: See Appendix 5.

below average shaft worker wages. While wages begin to significantly increase at the level of labour directly employed by Twangiza Mining, most workers at the mine were employed by labour hire or subcontractor firms.

In addition, and in a continuation of trends for most of the twentieth century, wage levels to all worker and manager categories at Twangiza Mining were stagnant from (at least) 2010 to 2016.[17] In 2010, Twangiza Mining annulled its 3 per cent annual wage increase agreed to in the DRC's inter-professional collective agreement to which the *Fédération des entreprises du Congo* (Congo Business Federation, FEC) and its partners (which included Banro) were signatories. At the time this decision was taken, there was no formally recognized union at the company to resist the change.

A union was eventually formed following a 2013 decree from the Congolese labour minister requiring all companies to hold union elections by June 2014.[18] The newly formed union worked to reinstate the annual raise in Twangiza Mining's inaugural collective agreement that was being drafted in 2014 but was ultimately unsuccessful.[19] The final agreement stated only that 'the parties agree to an annual evaluation of the salary scale taking account of the cost of living'.[20] According to union delegates, this was not respected and no increases were accorded since they were last annulled in 2010. This was supported by a 2017 worker contract template, provided by Twangiza Mining's senior human resources officer, which made no reference to annual wage increases. Since at least 2010, then, wage scales at Twangiza Mining don't appear to have been adjusted, neither were wage increases given. As the annual inflation rate from 2010 to 2017 was 7.5 per cent, while the nominal value of Twangiza Mining worker wages over this period stagnated, the real value decreased substantially.[21]

Similarly, both hired labour and subcontractor workers consistently reported the absence of wage increases, with some reporting having worked at a firm for five years or more on the same wage. In 2015, workers at the Congolese labour hire firm Rubye wrote to management requesting a wage increase but never received a response.[22] When workers at the Swiss corporation *Société générale de surveillance* (SGS) raised the same issue, management refused to permit increases, pointing to the benefits workers enjoy such as

[17] Twangiza Mining worker payroll data and worker payslips, 2012; Twangiza Mining 2016 wage classification.

[18] Circular note No. 39/CAB/MIN/ETPS/MBL/NMC/pkg/2013 of 24 July 2013.

[19] Conversations with Twangiza Mining union delegates, June and July 2017.

[20] Twangiza Mining Collective Agreement, Article 67.

[21] Central Bank of the Congo inflation data set, 1991–2017.

[22] Interview with Rubuye worker, Luhwindja, 7 October 2016.

on-site lodging and food.[23] Security workers at G4S reported that when the British firm arrived in around 2015 to replace Erinys International, they experienced a wage decrease from $250 per month to $185 per month.

Two factors help explain low and stagnant wages at Twangiza. First, as discussed in section 3.3, was Banro's incentive to suppress wages, as a significant cost component the corporation could control when it was confronted with financial difficulties from 2012 onwards. The second factor was the downwards pressure on wages exerted by the shift in Luhwindja's labour supply from scarce to abundant.

At the beginning of the twentieth century, the *Mwami* customary authorities of Luhwindja mobilized labour for the Belgian mining subsidiary MGL during a period of labour scarcity, often forcibly recruiting members of families with whom he was in conflict. Similarly, in the mid-twentieth century up to as late as the 1980s, MGL and SOMINKI often noted the difficulty of mobilizing local labour. Yet, by the 2010s, the situation had reversed. As one manager at the Luhwindja office of a labour hire firm reflected:

> There are days when ten people come to ask for work when we don't have any. We reply clearly that there's no work and it's of no use to insist. Unfortunately, they still insist. In any case there are a lot of people who come to ask. We even receive text messages. It's enough just to have heard there's a job available and you'll find even 100 people for the one job.[24]

While demographic pressures do not alone account for this shift (the crisis of Congolese and African agriculture and the weight of structural adjustment are other important considerations), they are, nonetheless, a significant factor. The population of Luhwindja increased from 8,200 at the beginning of the twentieth century to 97,080 in 2017. This represented a population density increase from around 44 people per square kilometre to around 530 people per square kilometre in 2017.[25]

Meanwhile, with workers receiving low and declining wages, the foreign managerial group at Twangiza, representing just 5 per cent of employment and one-third of the managerial stratum, captured 37 per cent of total wages and 58 per cent of the wages accruing to managers. This represents a continuation of dynamics at SOMINKI, where, to recall from Table 5.1, the foreign cohort in 1984 represented less than 1 per cent of the total workforce and

[23] Interview with SGS manager, 13 December 2016.
[24] Interview with Diphil manager, Luhwindja, 2017 (exact date mislaid).
[25] Luhwindja civil registry office data.

captured 31 per cent of total wages. This high level of wage capture by non-nationals, alongside the low level of labour absorption at Twangiza and low wages to most workers, explains the limited impact of wage expenditure on stimulating broader, local-level processes of economic development.

5.2 Externally oriented wage expenditure

The vast majority of hired labour, subcontractor workers, and unskilled Twangiza Mining workers—comprising more than half of all labour at the mine—was from local herder–farmer families, who consumed or invested most of their wages locally. Hired labour workers, the lowest-paid category at the Twangiza mine, reported using their wages on rent, food, school fees, and medical expenses, with little left over to save or invest. As one noted,

> I earned something [when cultivating my land] and was able to make some small savings, as I didn't need to buy many things, such as manioc flour, sweet potatoes and so on. Today, I must buy all that because I no longer have time to farm. The money I earn allows me just to survive. When I get paid, it goes straight to clearing debts accumulated to buy flour and other things.[26]

Similar testimonies were given by subcontractor workers, who earned equivalent wages to hired labour workers, such as guards at the security corporation G4S, who, as already mentioned, earned $185 per month. One G4S guard decided to leave his job in 2017 after two years of service, having failed to make any savings.[27]

Yet, the investment patterns of some local subcontractor workers, earning higher wages than most, showed more diversified and significant local investments across construction, land, and livestock, as the following two summaries of worker testimonies demonstrate:

> He works as a laboratory assistant for SGS. He is using his wages to build a brick house in Luhwindja. Last year he bought 1.2 hectares of land for $1,800, but he doesn't yet have a state title. He grows manioc, beans, and sweet potatoes for sale to the local market, and hires four or five agricultural day labourers. He has also bought seven cows, fifteen goats and around thirty sheep, and is supporting his uncle through university in Bukavu.[28]

---

[26] Life history with Utralu worker, Luhwindja, 12 April 2017.
[27] Interview with G4S worker, Luhwindja, 14 April 2017.
[28] Interview with SGS worker, Luhwindja, 9 October 2016.

He works as a waiter for ATS and spent $1,500 buying land in Luhwindja under a customary agreement. He is currently building a brick house and hopes to have it finished soon. He thinks he will spend around $1,800 on the construction. He also bought half a hectare of land on which he grows beans and vegetables for his family. He has two people that come and work the land from time to time.[29]

Among Twangiza Mining's skilled workers, there was a greater representation of people from the local area whose parents were wage earners (in mines or plantations), state agents, teachers, clerks, military officers, and traders, as well as of urban families based in Bukavu. This was a result, in part, of the requirement of a university degree to access this level of employment. In contrast to the lower strata of workers who lodged locally outside the Twangiza camp, most skilled Twangiza Mining workers lived in Bukavu, were transported to and from the site by Banro, and were lodged and fed on-site during their four-to-six-day shifts.[30] As a result, they rarely set foot outside of the mine. This meant that the consumption and investment patterns of skilled Twangiza Mining workers, who captured 57 per cent of the value accruing to workers and 21 per cent of the total value accruing to all labour at the mine, were generally directed away from the local economy and towards Bukavu.

Many skilled workers reported having invested in housing in Panzi, a suburb on the outskirts of Bukavu where many of Luhwindja's rural–urban migrants reside. The following account is typical of this group:

I supported my father with a small trading business that he started in 2014, with an extra $200 on top of what he already had. I also helped him finish building his house, by buying some tiles for the roofing. I helped my younger brother by giving him $250 to relaunch his small trading activity which had collapsed a few years ago. I supported my younger sister in secondary school, which she finished last year. This year she said she wants to take some professional training before beginning university [. . .] The most important investment is perhaps the land I bought in Bukavu in 2015 for $2,200, on which I'm currently building a house. I also bought some land near my father's village for $450 where I planted some trees [. . .] I have

---

[29] Interview with ATS worker, Luhwindja, 9 October 2016.

[30] This included formerly rural-based skilled workers who had relocated to Bukavu. The outward migration of rural skilled workers to Bukavu was facilitated by two factors. First, while hired labour was paid locally in cash, all Twangiza Mining workers were paid directly into bank accounts in Bukavu. With no formal bank branches locally, this forced them to travel to the city at least once a month to access their wages. Second, and probably of more importance, Twangiza Mining provided free transportation for all its workers to and from Bukavu in between rotations. The most common rotation cycle for these workers was to work four days and four nights followed by four days off, which they generally spent at their homes in Bukavu, making use of the free transport to make the three-to-four-hour journey to and from the city. Many subcontractor workers, by contrast, worked six-day weeks or a shift cycle of two days and two nights followed by two days off, rendering regular travel to and from Bukavu less feasible.

five children. Three are at school, and I support others. My sister-in-law, my cousin, my nephew [. . .] I earn around $700 a month from which I can easily save $100 each month. It's just the rent and school fees that are expensive.[31]

Around 30 per cent of surveyed skilled workers reported having invested in commerce alongside construction, land, and livestock. This was generally an investment in petty trade or opening a store, although there was some investment in productive activity, such as one worker from Luhwindja who opened a welding workshop locally, investing several thousand dollars in the required capital.

At the level of Twangiza's managerial group, most wage expenditure was directed outside of the country. Managers and directors at subcontractor firms and Twangiza Mining worked mostly on a rotation of seven weeks on site followed by three weeks holiday. When on site, they worked eight to twelve hour days, six days a week. Both foreign and Congolese managers from outside of South Kivu formed a 'fly-in, fly-out' stratum of labour at the mine, with Banro and subcontracted firms covering the transport costs to and from their home residence in between rotations.

Once on site, as with Bukavu-based skilled workers, Twangiza Mining's managerial cohort ate and drank at company restaurants and bars and rarely left the compound. As one subcontractor manager said, 'I'm not familiar with the locals. I come for one month then after one month I fly back.'[32] As a result, the local wage consumption of this group was generally limited to the food and alcohol consumed on site (some of which, as noted in section 4.3, was sourced locally). This aside, managerial consumption and investment took place outside of Luhwindja.

Some Congolese managers directed their investments domestically into construction, agriculture, and business, as the following three accounts from Congolese Twangiza Mining managers testify:

I can say that I supported at least twenty family members at university in Goma, Bukavu and Kinshasa. Honestly, around twenty people. The children of uncles, aunts, and so on. Amongst us Africans, when you have revenue, all the medical expenses, that's on you [. . .] I bought land here in Goma on which I built a house. I also bought land in Bukavu [and] in Kinshasa, where there's a house under construction. I also thought of my childhood passions and bought a 100-hectare concession.[33]

---

[31] Interview with Twangiza Mining worker, Twangiza, 9 June 2017.
[32] Interview with SGS manager, Twangiza, 6 June 2017.
[33] Interview with former Twangiza Mining manager, Goma, 28 January 2017.

First, I've invested in land [. . .] I buy for construction here in Bukavu and for agriculture in the Ruzizi Plain [in South Kivu . . .] I acquired a tractor, I had to get a driver for the tractor [. . .] I know I'm supporting other families. The driver has a family, then there's the three other guys working on my land [. . . We grow] maize and cassava.[34]

My work here at Banro doesn't only benefit me but a lot of people, because there are people whose studies I support and there are other people [who work at my home]. I also opened a butchery and three people work there, just nearby at Mulamba [in Bukavu]. It's called Mikado. We also sell a lot of alcohol there [. . .] We built a house in Goma and we've already bought land there but it's still empty [. . .] We've also bought some cars that we didn't have when we were students [. . .] I can plan holidays with the children. Last year we went to Dubai and after Dubai to Belgium.[35]

The patterns described in these testimonies demonstrate some signs of increasing productivity and capital accumulation domestically, such as the acquisition by one manager of a tractor.

The wage expenditure of foreign managers, by contrast, was oriented almost entirely outside of the DRC. As two foreign subcontractor managers explained:

When we stay on site, we spend very little. The largest expenditure is phone communication with family, that is what we spend mostly [. . .] I'm investing back home [in Kenya] because first thing accommodation is paramount for the family, alongside education for the children. And I've done some investment with the family through a business venture. We opened a business that my wife is running back home, a hardware shop because that's my field. An electrical shop. Most of it though goes on education for the children and protection for my parents.[36]

I'm investing in cocoa farming [in Ghana]. That's where my salary goes, to build up a farm. Currently, I have two farms and I'm building another one. That's what I'm doing with my salary, and I'm also setting up a company to do catering. A small catering company if one day I want to retire and do my own things. I have that ambition also, that can maybe join with the farms. I also have animals, like I have goats, so those are the investments that I do [. . .] Locally no, as the duration is unpredictable. You can't predict, tomorrow you might be leaving.[37]

---

[34] Interview with Twangiza Mining manager, Bukavu, 29 September 2016.
[35] Interview with Twangiza Mining manager, Bukavu, 30 September 2016.
[36] Interview with Aggreko manager, Twangiza, 6 June 2017.
[37] Interview with ATS manager, Bukavu, 17 June 2017.

Some Congolese managers had similarly oriented external investment patterns, as their families were based outside of the country, predominantly in South Africa but also overseas in the United States, Canada, and Europe. Others aspired to join this group, such as one manager whose goal was to buy a house in South Africa and have his children live and study there.[38]

Fifty-eight per cent of the total wages accruing to Twangiza's managerial group was captured by foreign managers. Including the additional external orientation of some Congolese managers with families living outside of the DRC, the general flow of managerial wages at Twangiza was outside of the country, at a ratio of around two-thirds external to one-third internal. Given that the managerial group captured 63 per cent of all wages accruing to labour at Twangiza, this meant that around 40 per cent of total wages left the country, significantly hampering the ability of wage consumption and investment patterns to stimulate economic development domestically.

The high level of foreign managerial wage capture is perhaps surprising when recalling that non-nationals accounted for only 5 per cent of labour at the mine, and that the 146 Congolese managers and directors outnumbered the 71 foreign managers and directors by around two to one. Two factors help to explain this finding. First, nearly half of the Congolese managers at Twangiza Mining were at the lowest managerial level of supervisor, with many of these employed at labour hire and subcontractor firms.[39] Most foreign managers, by contrast, were employed by Twangiza Mining. Second, foreign managers at Twangiza Mining earned a 'double salary'. As a former financial manager at the subsidiary explained:

> take a Congolese and an expatriate director. The difference is the expatriate has two salaries. They have one in Congo and one overseas. When I left Banro I was earning around $4,000 net per month. An expatriate at the same level also had $4,000, but the difference if he is South African or Ghanaian is that he'll have another $4,000 in his overseas account, so he has $8,000 [. . .] It was only us in accounting who knew that the expatriates had two salaries.[40]

This account was confirmed by company payrolls from 2012. The foreign salary payment, representing a loss to the Congolese economy, marks a continuation of past practice, when, following Congolese independence, half of

---

[38] Interview with Twangiza Mining manager, 8 June 2017.

[39] For example, the head of personnel at the labour hire firm Cinamula was from the Idudwe grouping in Luhwindja. The director of labour hire firm Zuki was an entrepreneur from the neighbouring collectivity of Burinhyi and an elected deputy in the National Assembly.

[40] Former Twangiza Mining financial manager, Bukavu, 28 January 2017.

MGL's wages to European staff began to be paid in Belgium.[41] Accounting for the fact that foreign labour only paid a 10 per cent tax rate on their wages, compared to the 30–50 per cent rate paid by most of the Congolese managerial group on a 'single salary', non-nationals effectively earned more than double their Congolese counterparts. Cumulatively, then, distributional dynamics resulted in most of the wages accruing to labour at Twangiza being drained outside of Luhwindja, a significant proportion of which went on to leave the country.

5.3 Weakening of worker power

From the 1970s to the 1990s, labour militancy at SOMINKI was high. To recall from section 5.1, low and declining wages led to frequent and, on occasion, violent strikes during this period. In 1992, the severity of the situation culminated in a fifty-eight-day strike at the Kamituga and Lugushwa gold mines. The strike was eventually put down by the national army, following which union leaders were imprisoned and tortured and 255 workers were fired (Kyanga 2013: 16).[42] Worker mobilization during this period was facilitated by the fact that all workers were contracted by SOMINKI (as had been the case dating back to MGL in the 1940s) and mostly lived together in mining towns. The largest of these was at Kamituga, where two or three thousand workers lived with their families in the same neighbourhoods and near the mine (Kyanga 2013).

By the 2010s, with the onset of corporate outsourcing, subcontracting at Twangiza had led to the fragmentation of the mine's workforce across fifteen different organizations. This high level of organizational fragmentation has weakened the position of Congolese workers and erected new barriers to labour organization and collective action, hampering workers' ability to mobilize for increased wages or to resist and transform their conditions.[43]

First, the outsourcing of labour has expanded worker informality. Of Twangiza's 1,149 workers in 2013, 323 (or 28 per cent) worked across hired labour firms.[44] In 2017, these workers continued to be engaged as informal day labourers with no form of contract, no paid holiday, and limited medical

---

[41] Cobelmin and MGL director meeting minutes, Bukavu, 7 April 1961.

[42] Interviews with former SOMINKI workers and union leaders, Kamituga, 22 April 2017; SOMINKI correspondence to Ministry of Labour, 30 October 1992.

[43] Similar dynamics have been observed in South Africa (Bezuidenhout and Buhlungu 2011; Bolt and Rajak 2016) and Peru (Manky 2018).

[44] During the mine construction phase around 2010, this number was much greater. Hired labour management reported having around 2,100 workers at this time, around 1,800 more than in 2013.

insurance. This was even though many had spent several years working for the same firm or for several different firms and were legally entitled to a contract according to Congolese labour law, having repeatedly worked more than twenty-two days over a two-month period (Mushagalusa 2018).[45] The situation was the same for an additional 127 workers at the subcontractor firms Groupe Rubuye, Premium, Simba Logistics, and Tsebo Outsourcing Group. In total, around 40 per cent of the mine's workforce was employed informally.

By rendering workers more easily disposable, informal status discourages collective action. Most of the approximately 2,100 labour hire workers involved in mine construction were made redundant overnight once construction was complete and the mine moved to production (Geenen and Radley 2014: 62). During the production phase, day labourers were let go due to the seasonal nature of their work or simply because their labour was no longer required. Workers in this position, unsurprisingly, had a sharp appreciation of their precarity: 'When you work for several years without having a contract, it worries you. Everyone wants to have a work contract but unfortunately, it's not the case for all of us. We pray to God though that perhaps one day we will also have a contract.'[46] Many informal day labourers bemoaned their conditions but were fearful of engaging in any form of labour militancy, given their informal status. According to the president of the trade union confederation in Bukavu, informal day labourers at Twangiza Mining who had attempted to claim their contractual rights had been dismissed (Mushagalusa 2018).

Second, by entrenching a spatial separation between workers, corporate outsourcing has further weakened the collective power of FOM labour. This has functioned along three dimensions. First, and as noted earlier, most hired labour, subcontractor, and unskilled Twangiza Mining workers heralded from local herder–farmer families, and their subsistence wages maintained them in this social class position. Skilled Twangiza Mining workers, by contrast, heralded mostly from wealthier and often urban families, and their higher wages allowed them and their families to live a commensurate urban lifestyle in the nearby city of Bukavu.

This rural–urban divide fed into union dynamics. As already mentioned, the Twangiza Mining union was established following a 2013 decree from the Congolese labour minister requiring all companies to hold union elections by June 2014.[47] As of 2018, the urban-based union leaders—all skilled Twangiza Mining workers—had shown no signs of engagement with, or interest

---

[45] DRC Labour Code, Article 40.
[46] Life history with Zuki worker, Luhwindja, 12 April 2017.
[47] Circulate note No. 39/CAB/MIN/ETPS/MBL/NMC/pkg/2013 of 24 July 2013.

in, the experiences and struggles of the predominantly rural-based workers. When asked about the issues of low wages and informality confronting sub-contractor workers, the vice-president of the Twangiza Mining union simply replied, 'They don't concern us.'[48]

In the second instance, the demarcation was present between different groups of rural workers themselves. As the manager of a labour hire firm explained, when Twangiza Mining mobilized informal day labourers, 'all the local collectivities send [candidate] lists, and Banro's human resources department selects from these lists according to their needs [. . .] afterwards, they send us the names of those retained.'[49] To be included on a list, labourers had to come from the corresponding *collectivité-chefferie* (a rural government locality, hereafter collectivity), with each collectivity representing historically distinct Bushi kingdoms (of the ethnic Bashi people).[50] Assodec and Utralu mobilized labour from the collectivity of Luhwindja, while Zuki mobilized labour from the neighbouring Burinhyi.[51] Cinamula mobilized most of its labour from Luhwindja, with some workers originating from neighbouring collectivities. All workers at Diphil were from Luhwindja or the neighbouring Bashi collectivities of Burinhyi and Kaziba.[52]

An anecdote told by a senior human resources manager at the subsidiary Banro Congo highlights the effect of these spatial labour mobilization logics on worker organization. In 2016, he noted the imbalance in the number of workers between the different labour hire companies Cinamula, Diphil, and Zuki. He decided to impose an approximately equal number of workers across the three companies, and to do so, he requested that a certain percentage of Cinamula workers (generally from Luhwindja) be affected to Zuki (generally from the neighbouring collectivity of Burinhyi). When he spoke to the Cinamula director to request this change, he was told 'my people will never cross that river [from Luhwindja into Burinhyi] to collect their money'. It was with much difficulty, he recalled, that the adjustments were made.[53]

These local-level labour mobilization logics fed into a third and final demarcation between 'locals' (perceived as Bashi from Luhwindja or neighbouring collectivities) and 'non-locals' (those outside of this definition). One G4S worker noted the difficulties he encountered as an ethnic Warega,

---

[48] Interview with Twangiza Mining union vice-president, Twangiza, 7 June 2017.
[49] Survey interview with Diphil manager, Luhwindja, 23 March 2017.
[50] Although some migrants negotiated their inclusion as local workers, often through payment to local political elites submitting the lists.
[51] Letter from employment subcommittee moderator to CODELU president, 25 February 2016; interview with Assodec director, Cinjira, 10 October 2016; interview with Zuki site manager, Burinhyi, 12 October 2016.
[52] Interview with Diphil head of personnel, Bukavu, 3 October 2016.
[53] Conversation with Banro Congo senior human resources officer, Bukavu, 22 February 2017.

commenting, 'there's always conflict, as someone who's not from here [...] it's like a cold war between the locals and people who aren't from here.'[54] A Zuki worker from Rutshuru in North Kivu province, who negotiated his recruitment as a local worker, had moved to Luhwindja with his wife, who was from the Kasai region further west in the country. The couple reported feeling a tension between their family and local people and that they had been the victim of numerous burglaries and aggressions since arriving in Luhwindja.[55]

By facilitating worker informality and spatial separation, the organizational fragmentation of labour induced by corporate outsourcing has undermined the collective strength of workers to counteract their marginality. This helps explain the near total absence of labour militancy at the mine, despite the fact that a large segment of the mine's workers experience subsistence-level and declining wages and poor access to benefits. Only two strikes had taken place at Twangiza since mine construction began in 2010. The first was a sit-in staged by security workers in 2011 during the visit of Banro's board of directors from Canada, resulting in a small wage increase.[56] The second was an impromptu six-hour strike in 2014 of around two dozen machine operators in the mining department over proposed changes to overtime remuneration.[57] The general acquiescence of labour at Twangiza contrasts strongly to the militancy of SOMINKI workers in the 1980s and early 1990s, at a time when workers were contracted directly by the Belgian subsidiary and often lived together with their families in mining towns.

The findings presented in this chapter question Consensus proponents' belief that capital-intensive FOM can raise wages and, through the investment and consumption patterns arising from these raised wages, stimulate broader processes of economic development. FOM in South Kivu has demonstrated an enduring tendency to deliver low and stagnant wages to most workers while delivering high wages to a narrow and predominantly externally oriented managerial group. That worker wages have appeared consistently comparable to, or below, those earned in labour-intensive DOM contradicts the World Gold Council's (2011: 21) claim that in low- and middle-income countries the lowest-paid mine workers earn 'on average 3.5 times more than the typical local wage, and may earn almost seven times more'.

---

[54] Conversation with G4S worker, Luhwindja, 30 November 2016.
[55] Conversation with Zuki worker, Luhwindja, 11 April 2017.
[56] Conversation with Twangiza Mining senior human resources officer, Twangiza, 6 June 2017.
[57] Conversation with Twangiza Mining union president, Twangiza, 10 June 2017.

While wage expenditure among the Congolese managerial group demonstrated some signs of increasing productivity and capital accumulation in other sectors, the small size of the group commanding sufficient wages for these kinds of investments, numbering around 100 or so members, greatly constrains the potentially transformative impact of these patterns. The main labour beneficiary of FOM's deeply polarized wage structure in South Kivu has been the foreign managerial stratum. While comprising less than 1 per cent and 5 per cent of labour under SOMINKI and Banro, respectively, this stratum captured around one-third of all wages, nearly all of which was expended outside of the country.

While more fully domesticating the managerial stratum might help alleviate the external orientation of wage expenditure, this would run up against the structural constraint of the low level of labour absorption required for capital-intensive mining operating at the technological frontier. While approximately five units of labour were employed per kilogram of gold produced by SOMINKI in the 1980s, by the 2010s under Banro, this had fallen to around half a unit of labour at Twangiza. The development of increasingly automated industrial gold mines, including in the DRC, where the foreign corporate-owned Kibali project opened a fully automated underground mine in 2018, will only serve to further lower the labour absorption capacity of capital-intensive mining in the future (Randgold Resources 2018).

The evidence presented in Chapters 3–5, centred around the three structural constraints of price volatility, enclavity, and low labour absorption, bears out many of the concerns raised by the critiques of peripheral development reviewed in section 1.3. Consensus proponents envisaged, to draw from the United Nations Economic Commission for Africa report (UNECA 2011: 101–102) *Minerals and Africa's Development*, that capital-intensive FOM sites would become 'centres of growth not enclaves, an agglomeration of not only increased workforce productivity, but also raised incomes among the local population and economic growth more widely'. While increased workforce productivity was certainly achieved, findings concerning the distribution of this greater productivity challenge assumptions about its anticipated transformative effects.

From around the 1980s onwards, and certainly by the 2010s, the dependence of FOM in South Kivu upon capital and technology emanating from and developed in global technological centres had created an externally oriented production structure, disarticulated from the domestic economy. Meanwhile, the industry shift towards corporate outsourcing had, à la Sunkel

(1973) and Vaitsos (1973), facilitated the penetration and expansion of foreign firm subsidiaries into the Congolese economy, marginalizing domestic firms.

In addition, and in accordance with Arthur Lewis's (1954) theorization that wages in the periphery will be set according to the productivity of 'subsistence sectors' rather than in capitalist export sectors, FOM worker wages in South Kivu appear to have been consistently comparable to, or below, those earned in labour-intensive DOM. This, even though Banro's Twangiza mine was around twenty-five times more productive than the nearby Kadumwa mine.

Finally, the supposed superiority of capital-intensive FOM ran aground twice in South Kivu, first in the 1980s and 1990s under SOMINKI and again in the 2010s under Banro, due to the difficulty of retaining productivity in the face of severe price volatility. The damaging effects of price volatility were exacerbated, at least in the case of Banro, by corporate mismanagement, inefficiencies, and underlying mechanisms of surplus extraction which prioritized director and shareholder compensation over the productive viability and long-term future of the corporation. Based on these findings, which align more closely with Prebisch's (1950) earlier characterization of peripheral enclave economies that Consensus proponents have either dismissed as anachronistic or ignored, the Consensus position that capital-intensive FOM will be more efficient and effective at leading structurally transformative processes of mining-based development than the state-owned enterprises (SOEs) that preceded them is brought into question.

Chapters 6 and 7 now turn to a consideration of labour-intensive DOM and how Banro's arrival has interacted with this alternative model of mining-based development. Drawing on evidence from South Kivu, it is argued that this form of mining better meets the needs of peripheral African economies for rising productivity, labour absorption, and the domestic retention of the value generated by productive activity than the currently favoured but disarticulated model of capital-intensive FOM.

6
Dynamic domestic accumulation

The title for this chapter is taken from the work of the late Tanzanian academic and novelist Seithy Loth Chachage. In his extended essay, *The Meek Shall Inherit the Earth But Not the Mining Rights: The Mining Industry and Accumulation in Tanzania*, Chachage (1995: 104–105) argued that while the accumulation associated with capital-intensive foreign-owned mining (FOM) in Tanzania largely disappeared overseas, 'genuinely dynamic domestic accumulation' was taking place in labour-intensive domestic-owned mining (DOM) through technological adaptation and innovation as well as through the stimulation of local-level capitalist growth in other sectors of the economy.

The evidence presented in this chapter aligns with these earlier findings of Chachage. The main argument is that labour-intensive DOM in South Kivu has been a site of dynamic domestic accumulation through techno-logical innovation, capital formation, and productive investments outside of mining. Moreover, the capital–labour social relation underpinning labour-intensive DOM in South Kivu has delivered higher wages to workers than those available in the surrounding economy, while facilitating the emergence of a capitalist class of dynamic and prosperous rural Congolese, all within a form of production that retains a high share of value domestically. These findings question the African Mining Consensus dismissal of labour-intensive DOM due to its low productivity and supposed inefficiency.

For the study of class formation in this context, guidance was taken from the prior work of Schatzberg (1980: 13–31), who warned against adopting an overly rigid prior conception of class in the Democratic Republic of the Congo (DRC). For Schatzberg, the great diversity of localized ways in which class identities intersected with other social markers of identity, such as ethnicity, meant that class positions and processes of class formation in the DRC could only usefully be determined through inductive reasoning made in a specific location, based on sustained and in-depth fieldwork. The analysis in this chapter is informed by such an approach.

The chapter is structured in three sections. The first charts the growth of labour-intensive DOM in South Kivu from the 1950s through to the present day. Attention is drawn to state–corporate efforts to suppress this growth

Disrupted Development in the Congo. Ben Radley, Oxford University Press. © Ben Radley (2023).
DOI: 10.1093/oso/9780192849052.003.0006

and the predominantly informal nature of production, most of which has been smuggled out of the country, facilitated by foreign traders, at times in alliances with armed groups. The second focuses on the DOM economy of Luhwindja, the government collectivity home to Banro's Twangiza mine. Emphasis is placed upon the rural background of the workers, managers, and traders involved in this economy and the social relations underpinning production. The section closes by presenting a schematic overview of the distribution of the end value created by labour-intensive DOM in Luhwindja between and within different groups. This overview demonstrates how, contrary to the distributional dynamics observed at Banro in Chapter 3–5, labour-intensive DOM in South Kivu has the distinct advantage of creating value that is mostly captured by, and distributed among, different groups of Congolese labour and traders. The third and final section builds on this distributional assessment to document the differentiated consumption and investment patterns associated with the wages and profits derived from labour-intensive DOM in South Kivu. The analysis reveals processes of class formation, increasing sectoral productivity, and capital accumulation arising from these patterns.

Before beginning, it is important to note that, as was the case during the twentieth century, not all forms of labour-intensive mining in South Kivu during the 2010s were under domestic ownership and management. At the height of a gold boom in the territory of Shabunda in the early 2010s, the Chinese-owned company Kun Hou Mining ran four river-dredging machines along the Ulindi River (Global Witness 2016). By 2019, several Chinese companies had established semi-industrial mining operations across the province (Verweijen et al. 2022). In late 2021, tensions between Chinese and Congolese heightened when the Chinese embassy in the DRC advised its citizens to leave the country's eastern provinces following the kidnapping of eight Chinese nationals involved in gold mining in Ituri province to the north of South Kivu. The Congolese Ministry of Mines responded by prohibiting the involvement of foreign nationals in all forms of labour-intensive mining.[1] While the ownership and management of labour-intensive mining in South Kivu is not homogeneous, DOM remains, nevertheless, by far the most dominant form of labour-intensive production across the province's several hundred gold sites.

Finally, a brief note on terminology is required. Historically in Luhwindja, shaft managers—those who mobilized and organized labour in production and made the required investments to finance the endeavour—sold their gold

---

[1] Provincial decree No. 21/081/GP/SK, 20 August 2021; Kavanagh (2022).

to local traders, who would sell it on in Bukavu. This was no longer the case by the 2010s, as many of Luhwindja's shaft managers bought some or all the gold from their workers and nearly all of them sold it directly to the traders in Bukavu. In so doing, they bypassed and replicated the role of local traders, who buy gold on site or locally in Luhwindja to sell in Bukavu, assuming a dual position as both traders and managers. Similarly, many of the Bukavu-based gold traders made part of their profits from shafts that they owned and managed in Luhwindja. For this reason, throughout the chapter and the remainder of the book, the two groups are, at times, referred to collectively as trader-managers.

6.1 A locally led alternative

As mentioned in section 4.1, from at least as early as the 1950s, a growing number of Congolese and foreign nationals were beginning to engage in a form of mining in South Kivu that sat outside of the control and supervision of MGL. The nascent network of gold production in South Kivu proved extremely lucrative to traders, who used their profits to buy property, stores, and even yachts from departing Belgians in Bukavu.[2] At this early juncture, the Indian Bhimji family were likely the final buyers in Uganda, exporting the gold to international markets, having established the first regional gold trading business in Kampala in the 1950s (Carisch 2014: 36).

Across South Kivu, this new network was causing significant disturbance to MGL's operations and profits. In Luhwindja, MGL correspondence to the Congolese government in 1974 noted the infiltration of local miners at the subsidiary's Mwana site, forcing the guards to flee, and denounced the lack of local government response to the problem.[3] The following year, MGL suspended production at Twangiza following thirty-seven years of continuous exploitation in Luhwindja, citing insecurity as the determining factor.[4] MGL's withdrawal, conjoined with a rising gold price at the time, facilitated the continued expansion of labour-intensive DOM in the area.

Providing further impetus to the growth of labour-intensive DOM in Luhwindja and across South Kivu was the liberalization of the sector in November 1982. Prior to this, the 1967 Mining Code had required Congolese to own an official exploitation permit (Owenga Odinga 2014: 200). Due to the costliness of this permit and the bureaucratic procedures involved,

---

[2] Internal MGL correspondence, Bukavu, 7 August 1960.
[3] MGL letter to local government authorities, 2 July 1974.
[4] Internal report on Concession Number 90, SAKIMA, 1995.

this excluded many Congolese from legally engaging in productive activity. Following liberalization, all Congolese were allowed to engage in production, with or without a permit, and the sale of gold was legalized at authorized locations in major towns (MacGaffey 1986: 147).

SOMINKI, which, by this time, had taken over the Belgian mining mantle from MGL, responded to the continued growth of labour-intensive DOM in two ways. First, mining brigades from the Congolese national army were deployed to secure the corporation's mines from the illegal encroachment of local miners on its concessions (Kyanga 2013: 13). Second, SOMINKI established seven gold trading houses from which it bought gold produced outside of its control for sale at a fixed price to the *Société Zairoise de commercialisation des minerais* (Zairian Mineral Commercialization Company), a subsidiary of the state-owned Gécamines.

This system didn't last long. While official gold exports initially increased, by 1986, they had fallen below the 1982 level as gold traders preferred smuggling to the lower prices offered by official trading houses (MacGaffey 1992: 251). By 1995, around 200 Congolese were trading an estimated 4 tonnes of annual gold production from Bukavu, of which an estimated 98 per cent was being smuggled out of the country (Bishakabalya 1995: 18–38; OGP 2010: 116). Burundi and Uganda were the primary destinations, with both countries having lower gold export taxes than the DRC (Carisch 2014: 40–47). The foreign exchange earnt from this activity was used to import vehicles, fuel, consumer goods, medical products, and construction materials into eastern DRC. In Butembo in North Kivu, for example, four to five truckloads of consumer goods, paid for entirely in gold, were being imported monthly (MacGaffey 1992: 252). The trade also gave rise to a gold jewellery industry, both in Bukavu and neighbouring Burundi (Geenen 2015).

The 200 or so Congolese gold traders in Bukavu were dependent upon foreign financiers who controlled export out of Africa, at times in alliance with armed groups. In 1996, the rebel militia *Alliance des forces démocratiques pour la libération du Congo-Zaire*—Alliance of Democratic Forces for the Liberation of Congo-Zaire—led by the soon-to-be President Laurent Kabila, gave the established Belgian gold trader Alan Goetz a gold export licence in return for a 1.5 per cent export tax. Goetz was the largest gold trader in the region at the time, with the rest of the trade primarily controlled by the Indian Bhimji, Pattni, and Lodhia families.

By the end of the two Congo Wars, lasting from 1996 to 2002, the mutually beneficial alliance between labour-intensive DOM and non-state armed groups had become entrenched, the latter providing security in return for a share in profits. In Kamituga, for example, the Rwandan-backed militia

Rassemblement Congolais pour la démocratie (Congolese Rally for Democracy) levied taxes on local miners (Vlassenroot and Raeymaekers 2004). The wars had also further hardened ethnic ties. What was left of rural markets, trading networks, and mineral extraction 'was all shaped by patterns of ethnic power brokerage and transactions between Congolese actors and interests from the belligerent external powers involved in the war' (Putzel et al. 2008: viii). Ethnicity had become the fundamental organizing principle of politics, production, and trade.

In addition, by this juncture, 'almost 100 percent of [economic] activity had become informal' (Hesselbein 2009: 2018). Official gold production in the DRC collapsed following SOMINKI's liquidation in 1997 and was not to recover until Banro began commercial production at Twangiza in 2012. During the fifteen-year interim, labour-intensive DOM continued to grow, stimulated by a rising gold price—from $279 per troy ounce in 2000 to $1,669 per troy ounce in 2012—and a peasantry for whom the cumulative result of institutional change in land tenure, continually rising population density, and the Congo Wars had been the exhaustion of the soil and the demise of agriculture as a viable livelihood (Van Acker 2005). By the 2000s, there were an estimated 200,000–350,000 local miners working in the neighbouring provinces of South Kivu and North Kivu (Geenen and Radley 2014).

During this period of growth, independent Congolese traders with direct connections to the international market began to emerge. The most important in South Kivu were Evariste Nshamamba and Mutoka Sefu Ruganyira (the latter based out of Bujumbura), both former employees of, and suppliers to, Goetz (Carisch 2014: 36). As the gold price continued to soar, these traders were able to make significant profits, including by using part of the foreign exchange acquired through the sale of gold to bring consumer goods, construction material, and food produce into the DRC (Geenen 2014: 255–260). Nshamamba also reinvested in founding Congolese air and bus companies, although ostensibly to support and provide cover for his gold trade (Carisch 2014: 63).

In 2016, the major trading houses in Bukavu were *Mines Propres* (Clean Mines), Namukaya, and Kasereka, of which *Mines Propres* accounted for two-thirds of all officially recorded exports.[5] All official exports went to Dubai in the United Arab Emirates (UAE), the destination for around 70 per cent of the DRC's labour-intensive gold production and home to a largely unregulated gold industry worth around $75 billion, where Congolese gold traders have been doing business since the 1960s (Carisch 2014: 56). From

[5] South Kivu Ministry of Mines export data, 2016.

here, the gold was exported primarily to Indian- and Swiss-based refineries, which comprise the majority of the world's refineries selling to transnational corporations (Sharife 2016).

Most production by this point, however, remained informal and continued to be smuggled to intermediary trading houses and refineries before reaching Dubai. Between 2007 and 2016, officially recorded annual gold exports from labour-intensive mining in South Kivu hovered between 25 and 100 kilograms.[6] This equated to between 0.5 and 2.2 per cent of the estimated 4,800 kilograms of annual gold production in South Kivu at the time (Kamundala et al. 2015). In addition, the presence of the *Forces armées de la République Démocratique du Congo* (Armed Forces of the DRC, FARDC) or non-state armed groups had been documented at around 80 per cent of the several hundred labour-intensive gold mines across South Kivu, levying illegal taxes at most of them (Weyns et al. 2016).

Efforts to address these issues by more tightly regulating and formalizing labour-intensive DOM in South Kivu have made little progress. The 2002 Mining Code accorded this form of production a legal status but, in a departure from the 1982 liberalization measures under the Mobutu administration, required local miners to work in officially recognized *zones d'exploitation artisanale* (artisanal exploitation zones, ZEA). Within these zones, they must self-organize into cooperatives, apply for individual exploitation cards, and comply with security and environmental regulations. Progress has been slow, with only seven ZEAs covering an area of 250 square kilometres established in South Kivu as of late 2018, none of which were for gold. This contrasts with the 16,000 square kilometres covered by foreign-owned mineral research and exploitation permits that same year.[7] Such an imbalance might warrant redressing when considering that, contrary to the bleeding out of value associated with capital-intensive FOM documented in Chapters 3–5, an extremely high share of the value generated by labour-intensive gold mining in South Kivu is captured domestically by differentiated groups of Congolese workers, managers, and traders.

6.2 Internally oriented value capture

As mentioned in section 5.1, DOM labour at gold mines in Luhwindja can be grouped along the three categories of site workers, shaft workers, and shaft managers. Most workers were from herder–farmer families, some of whom

---

[6] *Centre d'expertise, d'évaluation et de certification*, Congolese Ministry of Mines, gold export data 2007–2016.
[7] South Kivu Provincial Ministry of Mines mining permit data set, 2018.

had parents who had worked in mining locally. They were generally asset poor, owning few livestock and often owning no land, with only some having completed secondary education.[8] The median reported land ownership across surveyed workers was 0.1 hectares per person, with a highest reported ownership of 5 hectares (Table 6.1). This in a local context where soil fertility and land productivity were low and some families owned from dozens up to several hundred hectares of land.

Shaft workers laboured underground and usually fulfilled specific roles, such as timber specialists, drillers, or supervisors but also worked as generalists. Each shaft had two team leaders, a *sous-PDG* (vice-president) and a *secretaire* (secretary), who held additional responsibilities including recording production and managing the workers. Site workers were composed of *mamans bidons* (female water carriers), *motards* (ore carriers), and *loutriers* (ore washers). At Kadumwa, the largest labour-intensive mine in Luhwindja following the construction of Twangiza, site and shaft workers comprised around 95 per cent of all employment.

Site and shaft workers participated in a six-day working week. There was some activity on a Sunday, but noticeably less than on other days. Workers tended to start shortly after sunrise and finish around mid-afternoon, but there were no fixed hours and the site was operational, albeit to a far lesser extent, throughout the night. Shaft work involved long shifts of eight to ten hours, equipped with iron hammers, chisels, and headlamps. The shafts were narrow with little room to manoeuvre, and once they surpassed 20–30 metres in depth, the air thinned and the labour became demanding and dangerous. In April 2017, a nineteen-year-old worker in Luhwindja died from asphyxiation after the machine used to circulate oxygen through the shaft broke down.[9]

Table 6.1 Mineworker land ownership (in hectares), Luhwindja

Group	Number surveyed	Landless (%)	Mean	Median	Max
Site workers	58	69	0.2	0.0	3.3
Shaft workers	233	46	0.3	0.1	5.0
All workers	291	51	0.3	0.1	5.0

Source: Author labour survey.

[8] While most land in Luhwindja was still owned under customary arrangements, through the colonial practice of *bugule* it had become commodified in the sense that customary land could be assigned a monetary value and bought and sold under private ownership.
[9] Shaft collapses are also commonly reported across the province, resulting in miner deaths, although none occurred in Luhwindja during the course of the research.

Once the gold ore had been extracted from the shafts by workers, it was given to carriers, who balanced 25-kilogram bags of ore on their shoulders and transported them to the treatment sites, either on site or at nearby riverways. Once at the treatment sites, the ore was sieved, ground, and sluiced by ore washers using mercury and other gravitational techniques to extract the gold from the ore.

Water carriers transported water from riverways to the treatment sites. Their work was arduous, involving a steep climb of around 2 kilometres, carrying 20-litre water cans tied to cloth laced around their foreheads to bear the weight. All water carriers were female, and most were widowers or divorcees.[10] As one of the women recounted:

> My parents were farmers. My father had three fields. During my childhood, I didn't go to school. I worked on our land. When I was twenty years old, I got married and I continued the same work. I had three children with my husband, who died shortly after. My husband's family tried to force me to marry the son of one of his other wives. I refused and was imprisoned for a while. After that I left his family and came here to carry water for people, as I have sole responsibility for looking after my children now.[11]

Women reported that they were not allowed to perform any other work at the site, and as a result, they held little hope of moving off the bottom of the labour hierarchy.

The labour of site and shaft workers was overseen by shaft managers. Known locally across the eastern DRC as *présidents-directeurs généraux* (chief executive officers, PDGs), shaft managers occupied a critical role in the production process at Luhwindja. They invested the finances required to construct and maintain the shafts, mobilized and organized labour in production, and managed the distribution of payment to workers through a combination of piece rates for each quantity of ore produced alongside (in most instances) a share of total production. Some also operated as local traders, compelling their workers to sell any gold from their in-kind payment directly to them while also buying from other mineworkers. In this sense, while they were not conducting formal bookkeeping, they were, nonetheless,

---

[10] All other workers and managers were male, predominantly young adults, although some ore washers were teenagers or younger boys. Most often, the boys' fathers or uncles worked at the mine, and they came to the site during school holidays, yet sometimes they had come following the death of one or both of their parents and lived in one of the few dozen on-site houses. It was rare, though, to see children enter the shafts.

[11] Life history with water carrier, Luhwindja, 31 May 2017.

accruing profits from their role as financiers, owners of capital and land, employers of disguised wage labour, and traders.

Most shaft managers in Luhwindja heralded from farming or herder families, around half of which combined agriculture and livestock raising with mining. The parents of shaft managers had on average five times more livestock and nearly three times more land than the parents of site workers and twice as much livestock and around one-third more land than the parents of shaft workers (Table 6.2).

Shaft managers came, in other words, from a wealthier rural background than workers. The following summary is illustrative:

> My father raised and sold cattle and my mother worked on the farm at home. It was a good childhood. I didn't lack anything as my parents were rich. They had a lot of cows. At that time, there was a lot of free pasturelands. You could take your herd anywhere. We produced a lot of milk and sweet potatoes. I studied without any problem but failed the fourth year of secondary school. The long walk to and from school made me too tired to concentrate in class. At this point I was around eighteen years old and started working in mining, as a shaft worker. I did this for one year, then my elder brother sent me on a six-month mechanics apprenticeship in Bukavu. After this, I returned to Luhwindja and carried on working in mining.[12]

For most shaft managers, their wealthier origins played a decisive role in assuming their position within the production process. Many sold family assets to raise the required financing for shaft construction. One sold three cows inherited from his father to raise $1,000, which he used to buy land

Table 6.2 Assets held by the parents of labour-intensive DOM groups, Luhwindja

Group	Livestock		Land (Ha)	
	Mean	Median	Mean	Median
Site worker parents	2	2	1.0	0.6
Shaft worker parents	5	3	1.9	1.0
Shaft manager parents	10	9	2.9	2.5
Small trader parents	6	6	4.8	5.0
Big trader parents	24	15	4.8	4.5

Source: Author labour survey.

---

[12] Life history with shaft manager, Luhwindja, 9 April 2017.

in 2005 to begin shaft construction.[13] Another was the son of the collectivity secretary (the third most senior position in local government), whose father provided the $3,600 he used to buy land ($600) and construct a shaft ($3,000).[14] Some used money saved from their time as shaft workers or as gold traders. One saved $3,000, using $500 to buy land and $2,500 in the shaft construction phase.[15] Another began as a site worker around 1980, saved enough money to become a trader in the 1990s, and eventually saved enough to buy land for shaft construction in 2012.[16]

Others had been financed by Bukavu-based traders, to whom they were obliged to sell their production in return and were often indebted. As one shaft manager said:

> the manager of a pit here always has some debts picked up here and there. I owe $125 to one trader and 110,000 Congolese francs [around $90], 80,000 Congolese francs [around $65] and 60,000 Congolese francs [around $50] to three others [. . .] My debts, though, are not so bad. There are others who have debts of $1,000 or more.[17]

These debts could often lead to financial difficulties, particularly if shaft construction failed to enter the production phase or a manager experienced a serious family illness.

Once the gold had been extracted, it was sold on to *petits négociants* (small traders), most of whom operated on site. Local traders would heat the gold over a coal stove using a blower, raising the temperature to around 500 degrees Celsius to evaporate the mercury and other impurities. Local traders would then sell their gold to *grands négociants* (big traders) in Bukavu, who would heat it with nitric acid over a hot stove to rid it of most remaining impurities. As with shaft managers, some local traders were independent, while others had a financier relationship with a *grand négociant* in Bukavu, to whom they had to sell their gold in return.

Next, all the Bukavu-based traders buying from Luhwindja either sold their gold to *Mines Propres* in Bukavu, one of the gold refineries operating in the city, or smuggled it out of the country, usually to Bujumbura. At *Mines Propres*, the gold was heated to 1,500 degrees Celsius in a cylindrical furnace, and once melted, the molten gold was poured into a graphite ingot mould for casting. While some of this production was officially declared, most of

---

[13] Interview with shaft manager, Kadumwa, 21 September 2016.
[14] Interview with shaft manager, Kadumwa, 23 September 2016.
[15] Interview with shaft manager, Kadumwa, 17 September 2016.
[16] Interview with shaft manager, Kadumwa, 6 October 2016.
[17] Shaft manager life history, Luhwindja, 9 April 2017.

the ingots produced by *Mines Propres* in Bukavu were smuggled to Dubai refineries in the UAE, which refine the gold to the purity required for sale on the international market.[18]

Most small and big traders operating in the Luhwindja gold market were born locally to parents who worked as farmers, pastoralists, or miners (or some combination of the three). As with shaft managers, they were from a wealthier background than workers, with their parents owning considerably more livestock and land (see Table 6.2). Also, and, again, as with shaft managers, this relative family wealth was critical in enabling the financial investments required to get started in the trade. Some had worked as shaft managers, having inherited the shafts from their fathers and used the profits they made to begin trading. Two brothers who worked as local traders said their father worked in mining and had bought thirty cows from the money he made, and then sold some of these to raise the financial capital required to help them start up as traders.[19] The father of another local trader was close to the *Mwami* customary authorities and owned several hectares of land and a few dozen cows. He sold some of his herd for a few thousand dollars, which his son then used to begin trading.[20]

The social composition of labour and traders at Luhwindja, then, is almost exclusively local, and production is underpinned by a profit–wage relation within the capital–labour social relation between workers and managers. Workers received wages from trader-managers, who in turn made profits by virtue of their position in the production process. As well as representing a 'class in itself' through their shared position in relation to the production process, there was some indication that trader-managers represented a 'class for itself' with a degree of consciousness, 'aware of their collective strength, pursuing joint interests in an organized manner to achieve common goals' (Melber 2016: 7), at least at the local level. Trader-managers comprised most of the board members presiding over the *Comité des creuseurs artisanaux de Luhwindja* (Artisanal Miners' Committee of Luhwindja, CCALU), an elected committee representing the interests of Luhwindja's labour-intensive miners through advocacy and organizing with political elites at the local and provincial levels. Through this committee, as discussed in section 7.1, the trader-manager class played a central role in successfully mobilizing local resistance to the closure of Kadumwa.

---

[18] Conversations with Bukavu traders and Ministry of Mines civil servant based at *Mines Propres*, Bukavu, January–March 2017.

[19] Conversation with two local traders, Luhwindja, 22 September 2016.

[20] Interview with local trader, Luhwindja, 31 May 2017.

The CCALU also functioned to discipline and control workers. In the first instance, in the case of serious infractions, such as the stealing of gold, workers were sent to the local state police, who often imprisoned them for a few days and released them upon the payment of a fine. As a last resort, as was the case in March 2017 with several shaft workers who were repeatedly stealing gold at night-time from unguarded wash basins, workers were forcibly excluded from the site. A group of informal *police minière* (mining police) was employed by the committee to enforce such decisions, all of whom were former militia members. The CCALU also used its authority and exclusionary power to suppress labour militancy, such as when it refused the creation of a site workers' committee following a three-day strike led by ore carriers in February 2017 to protest a reduction in their piece-rate pay for each bag they transported.

Data taken from Kadumwa gives an indication of the distribution of wages and profits between and within the different groups of workers, managers, and traders involved in Luhwindja's labour-intensive DOM economy (Table 6.3). Average monthly shaft worker wage estimates of $163 correspond with other studies of labour-intensive gold mining in South Kivu, which have placed them in the range of $25–150 per month (Perks 2011; Geenen et al. 2013; Spittaels et al. 2014; Stoop et al. 2016). Site worker wages all compared favourably to agriculture, which was remunerated locally at a daily rate of around one dollar per worker. They also compared favourably with more skilled forms of local labour, such as teaching, with local primary and secondary school teachers earning similar monthly wages to those earned by ore carriers and washers. Strikingly, shaft worker wages were significantly higher than both site worker wages, as well as those in the surrounding economy, by around a factor of six. The profits made by traders and shaft managers—around $5,000, $20,000, and $60,000 per year for local traders, shaft managers, and Bukavu-based traders, respectively—propelled these groups into the local economic elite.

In addition, and considering the foreign ownership of *Mines Propres*, around 95 per cent of the end value created by production at Kadumwa was captured domestically by Congolese workers, managers, and traders (Table 6.4).[21] Scaling this finding up to the provincial level of South Kivu,

---

[21] The data was collected through interviews with local and Bukavu-based traders buying gold from Kadumwa and with management at *Mines Propres*, the Bukavu-based smelter to whom these traders sold a portion of their gold. *Mines Propres* employees also discussed how they calculated their selling price to the Dubai-based Golden and Jewellery Refinery. These interviews were then complemented by data collected either directly from traders' financial records or, for those who didn't keep comprehensive records of their transactions, from monthly financial logbooks developed in consultation with them and which recorded their buying and selling price.

Table 6.3 Kadumwa wage and profit distribution, 2017

Group		Units of labour	Monthly wage/profits per unit ($)	Annual wage/profits per unit ($)	Total annual wage/profits ($)	Share (%)
Site workers	Water carriers	30	27	324	9,720	0.4
	Ore carriers	80	54	648	51,840	2.0
	Ore washers	80	67.5	810	64,800	2.5
Shaft workers		528	163	1,956	1,032,768	39.6
Subtotal workers (wages)					1,159,128	44.5
Shaft managers		44	1,674	20,088	883,872	33.9
Small traders (Luhwindja)		30	395	4,740	142,200	5.5
Big traders (Bukavu)		7	5,000	60,000	420,000	16.1
Subtotal managers and traders (profits)					1,446,072	55.5
TOTAL					2,605,200	100.0

Sources: See Appendix 4.

Table 6.4 Kadumwa value capture and distribution, 2017

Group	Per gram ($)			Nationality/ownership	Share (%)
	Buying price	Selling price	Value capture		
Workers and managers	–	31.21	31.21	Congolese	77
Subtotal labour			31.21	–	77
Small traders (Luhwindja)	31.21	36.55	5.34	Congolese	13
Big traders (Bukavu)	36.55	38.47	1.92	Congolese	5
Subtotal traders			7.26	–	18
Mines propres	38.47	39.01	0.54	Foreign	1
International	39.01	40.42	1.41	Foreign	4
Subtotal refineries			1.95	–	5
TOTAL			40.42	–	100

Note: This model is based on the value of a gram of gold on the London Gold Fixing of $40.42 (the average price for 2017).
Sources: Author calculations based on trader and refinery interviews, trader financial records, and trader financial logbooks. See Appendix 6 for further detail on how the small trader buying price of $31.21 was estimated.

where it can be approximated that around $200 million of value is created each year by labour-intensive DOM, this data suggests that around $190 million of this total is retained domestically by Congolese groups.[22] Of this, around $150 million would accrue to labour and around $40 million to traders.

From this, however, consideration must be given to how much accrues to the FARDC or non-state armed groups. This is particularly important since the Consensus dismissal of labour-intensive DOM in Africa has been due, in part, to its association with conflict financing. In the case of Luhwindja, the appropriation of value by armed groups was negligible. Every Friday, a battalion of the FARDC stationed in Luhwindja came to collect 3,000FC ($2.5) from each shaft manager as a form of informal taxation. Over the course of 2017, this amounted to around $6,000 or 0.2 per cent of the total value captured by Congolese labour and traders from productive activity in Luhwindja.

This finding corresponds to other studies, which have found the equivalent share of the value generated by labour-intensive DOM accruing to the FARDC or non-state armed groups to range between 0.4 per cent and 1 percent (Kamundala et al. 2015: 172; UNEP 2015: 24). At the provincial level, based on the above approximation of $200 million of annual value generated by the labour-intensive gold sector in South Kivu, this would equate to around $2 million. Most of the value, as has been shown, goes directly to Congolese workers, managers, and traders in the form of wages and profits, a sizeable part of which—as section 6.3 demonstrates—has been productively reinvested both in and beyond mining, driving broader-based processes of locally led technological innovation and capital accumulation.

6.3 Productive reinvestment and industrialization

As with the lowest categories of workers at Banro's Twangiza mine, most labour-intensive DOM workers in Luhwindja reported little left over from their wages to save or invest once subsistence needs had been met. The minority that had made investments reported doing so primarily in small livestock (mostly chickens and goats), constructing wooden or clay housing locally, or (far less frequently) buying small parcels of land. There were, nonetheless, dozens of stalls and shops across Kadumwa selling clothes and goods to miners, such as DVD players, radios, mobile phones, and solar-powered

---

[22] This approximation was reached using the best available estimate for the total annual volume of labour-intensive gold production in South Kivu of 4,800 kilograms (Kamundala et al. 2015) and the same 2017 average gold price of $40.42 per gram.

lamps. There were also a few cinemas, showing mostly American action or Asian martial arts films, and just off site there was a bar screening European football matches through a satellite dish, charging a small fee to miners for attendance. In this sense, through their increased consumption habits, workers at Kadumwa gained access to modern consumer goods and film and satellite television that remained beyond the reach of many rural families in Luhwindja. With just a few exceptions, however, workers remained in the rural class position from which they came; *les villageois* (the villagers), as they are labelled by many urban Congolese.

The trader-manager class in Luhwindja, on the other hand, had made significant investments from their profits. Nearly all shaft managers had purchased land and constructed houses in the Bukavu suburb of Panzi at a cost of up to $15,000. Many had also built several houses locally in Luhwindja, renting them out to tenants, commenting that real estate was the most secure investment, given the climate of insecurity that had characterized the surrounding area in the 1990s and early 2000s. Most had bought land locally, with some using it as a long-term investment for commercial tree planting and others as agricultural land on which they often employed daily wage labourers. Most had also accumulated several cows along with smaller livestock. Those reporting having reinvested in commerce had done so primarily in petty trade and local stores, including one manager who had opened a clothes store at a cost of $1,800 in the neighbouring collectivity of Kaziba. One reported engaging in productive activity outside of mining and agriculture, moving into brick production locally in Luhwindja.

Most shaft managers had their children in school or university in Bukavu, having migrated their families to the city and having supported the education of other children or siblings either locally or in Bukavu. A typical story from the older generation of shaft managers was of one manager who, having obtained his shaft in 1985, put all five of his children through university in Bukavu. In 2017, one of his children was a university professor, one an engineer, and one a senior provincial government official. In two generations, his family had moved from rural farming to the urban professional and bureaucratic classes.

The following investment summaries from two shaft managers provide some more detailed insight into these patterns:

I bought land and built a home in nearby Kaziba, and recently bought land at Panzi in Bukavu, where I have started to build a second home for my family. I've also bought land locally, to grow cypress and other trees. I support my two younger brothers in secondary school at Bukavu, and other children who study here. I've loaned a lot of money to various people who are always asking for some, around $2,000 in total. Last month, I spent $1,100 on construction of my home in Bukavu, around $70 on school fees, and $150 to buy a storage room for my work items at Kadumwa.[23]

I've built four houses with the money I've made, three in Luhwindja and one in Bukavu. Once I completed the house in Bukavu, my family left Luhwindja to live there. My children are also in school in Bukavu, and I hope one day they will go to university. I rent the houses in Luhwindja to tenants, which earns me an extra hundred dollars or so each month. I also used my money from mining to invest in flour and beer. My wife manages the flour depot in Bukavu, and I distribute beer locally here in Luhwindja.[24]

Similarly to shaft managers, and recalling the findings of Raeymaekers (2014: 20) on the investment patterns of Nande traders in North Kivu, most local gold traders in Luhwindja reported using their profits to buy land and construct houses for their families in Panzi, the same predominantly Bashi suburb of Bukavu to which many of Twangiza's skilled workers reported migrating. They also reported constructing homes and investing in land and large livestock locally in or around Luhwindja and employing wage labourers to work the land.

The big traders living in Bukavu were generally situated closer to the city centre, owning more expensive land on which they had built multi-storey houses. Their homes were equipped with flat-screen televisions, satellite dishes, solar panels, fridge-freezers, and other high-end consumer goods, and most of the traders owned at least one vehicle. All of them had children or family in university in Bukavu, elsewhere in the DRC, or in neighbouring Burundi and Uganda.

Most gold traders used their access to US dollars to import modern consumer and other goods through Bukavu. The largest local trader at Luhwindja, who ran a small gold trading house, invested his mining profits in rice, beer, and clothing, which he distributed locally to buyers.[25] Similarly, one of the Bukavu-based traders regularly brought clothes, cosmetics, and other consumer goods back from Dubai.[26] Another two of the Bukavu traders owned small supermarkets, one in the suburb of Essence (where most gold

---

[23] Conversation with shaft manager, Kadumwa, 6 March 2017.
[24] Conversation with shaft manager, Luhwindja, 8 October 2016.
[25] Interview with Luhwindja trader, Luhwindja, 13 April 2017.
[26] Interview with Bukavu trader, Bukavu, 21 February 2017.

trade in Bukavu takes place) and another closer to the city centre. Their supermarkets were full of imported goods, from chocolates and liquor to electronics and household appliances.

The following summary of the trajectory of Luhwindja's most successful Bukavu-based trader captures the generational process of class formation they move through:

> His father worked for MGL during the colonial period, after which his father began to work locally as a miner in Luhwindja. All seventeen of his siblings were educated through the wages his father earned from this work, and he graduated from university in Bukavu with a degree in business management. After he left university, he worked for eleven years as a language teacher at Ifendula in Luhwindja, but the pay was bad; he would receive one bar of soap and seven chickens per month. In 1998, he was nominated as the *Chef de Poste* in Luhwindja [the most senior local government post beneath the *Mwami*]. He left this role in 2003 and used the money he had made to begin working as a gold trader. Today, he lives in a four-storey home he built in Bukavu, and his eldest child just graduated with a degree in psychology from a university in Bujumbura, Burundi.[27]

The investment patterns of Luhwindja's trader-manager class echo those observed for labour-intensive DOM elsewhere in South Kivu, where investment of wages and profits has been documented in agriculture, livestock, education, dowry, property, vehicles, motorcycles, commerce, and transport (Geenen et al. 2013; Geenen 2015; Rothenberg 2014).

Alongside these investments, a significant share of shaft manager profits was reinvested in production. In 2017, an estimated total of around $200,000 was reinvested in capital inputs at Kadumwa, or 9 per cent of the total value created by the site that year.[28] The main inputs were timber to construct, maintain, and extend the shafts, sourced locally, and the use, when needed, of generator-powered machines (manufactured in China and Japan and imported by Bukavu-based traders through Dubai) to circulate oxygen through the shafts and evacuate water. Elsewhere in South Kivu, there was evidence that productive reinvestment was stimulating increasing sectoral productivity through a locally led process of mechanization. Kamituga lies just south of Luhwindja in the same territory of Mwenga and was one of Banro's four main concessions. As foregrounded in section 4.1, Kamituga was the main colonial mining town during the era of MGL, home to Mobale, the most industrialized gold mine in the region during the twentieth century.

---

[27] Interview with Bukavu trader, Bukavu, 14 October 2016.
[28] Shaft manager monthly logbooks.

Following SOMINKI's departure from Kamituga and subsequent liquidation in the late 1990s, local miners, previously operating on the margins of SOMINKI's sites, gained full access to the town's most productive deposits. During this period, dynamite was used in some areas to blast through rock. This led to the emergence of a group of female workers, known as *mamans twangaises*, to crush the extracted rock manually using mortars and a wooden pounder. Around a decade later, miners in Kamituga noticed a decrease in the quality of the extracted ore. Many sites, no longer profitable to exploit, emptied out.

In 2007, a German gold trader, who owned the trading house Aurex in Bukavu, wanted to access the Kamituga gold market. To do so, he entered a partnership with *Société minière du Congo* (Congo Mining Company, SOMICO), a state-owned mining enterprise established by President Laurent Kabila in 1998, and sent six ball mills to Kamituga. Initially, shaft managers were distrustful of the mills, suspecting that they would lose some of their gold in the machines. Around four years later, in November 2011, a Congolese entrepreneur brought three ball mills to Kamituga from Misisi, a large labour-intensive site in South Kivu, where the mills had been in use since around 2009. He had imported the mills from Tanzania at a cost of around $7,000 each.[29]

Following their arrival, another Congolese entrepreneur set up a ball mill repair workshop in Kamituga. Shortly after, the mills began to be manufactured locally. The locally manufactured mills were first tried out in Lugushwa, another of Banro's concessions.[30] About the size of a cement mixer, the mills were powered by generators to grind large rocks into a fine powder at a faster rate than manual labour. They could also grind what was previously considered *déchets* (waste). While a *maman twangaise* could break down around 15–25 kilograms of rock per day, a single ball mill could process 300 kilograms in around half an hour.

Mill owners used locally available vehicle parts and other machinery to repair and maintain the engines, which would wear down quickly. This included sourcing gearboxes from vehicles and joining the gearbox to a connecting rod by a belt. In the connecting rod, about 400 lead or steel balls were used to crush the stones and finely grind the ore.

By the end of 2012, there were around seventy ball mills active across the three main labour-intensive DOM sites in Kamituga.[31] Around ten of the mills were owned by shaft managers, with the remaining sixty owned by local

---

[29] Interview with shaft worker, Kamituga, 23 April 2017.
[30] Interview with shaft manager, Kamituga, 22 April 2017.
[31] Interview with Kamituga civil society representative by telephone, 9 February 2018.

gold traders or businessmen. Those wanting to use the mills paid the owners 10,000 Congolese francs (around six dollars) for every 100 kilograms of treated ore.

Around the same time as the ball mills were being introduced at Kamituga, shaft managers were also attempting to connect sites to the local electricity grid (run by a hydroelectric power station). The aim was to facilitate the use of water and oxygen machines in the shafts which, by circulating oxygen and extracting water, would allow for production to continue at deeper levels underground. In many cases, explosives were used alongside these machines to blast through the hard rock encountered at these deeper levels of shaft construction. Pneumatic drills were also increasingly present in the mining town, used by shaft workers underground in place of hammers and chisels. Through the increased use of machinery, explosives, and ball mills, then, a locally led form of industrialized production was beginning to organically emerge in the area, with origins in extractive techniques previously adopted at other sites in South Kivu. As a result, sites that had been exhausted by manual techniques once again became productive.

The upper stratum of labour involved in South Kivu's DOM economy consists of its trader-manager class who, in Luhwindja, make the initial investment to finance shaft construction, mobilize and organize labour in production, own the means of production, and reinvest profits in production, including in mechanization. In this sense, these trader-managers might be considered an emerging capitalist class, seen also through their commercial and productive investments in other sectors that, in agriculture at least, include the use of wage labour.

These findings question the assumptions that have contributed to the marginalization of labour-intensive DOM within the African Mining Consensus. Around 95 per cent of the end value generated by labour-intensive DOM in Luhwindja accrues to Congolese groups, of which an extremely low share contributes to conflict financing. In addition, Luhwindja's labour-intensive DOM economy has raised wages for workers compared to surrounding conditions, driving structural transformation through sectoral shifts in the labour market.

These shifts are linked with increasing productivity through a locally owned and managed process of technological innovation and capital formation towards an industrialized form of production, as well as commercial investments in other sectors (which might themselves be linked to a more diversified process of capital accumulation and increasing productivity). In other words, the productivity of labour-intensive DOM in South Kivu might be low—the criticism often labelled against it by Consensus proponents—but it appears to be increasing, and the sector has contributed to broader processes of structural transformation and capital accumulation, led and managed by an emergent capitalist class of dynamic and prosperous Congolese. The developmental trajectory of this sector, however, has been disrupted by Banro's arrival.

7
Marginalization and conflict

As discussed in Chapter 1, efforts to sever the link between labour-intensive domestic-owned mining (DOM) and conflict financing in the eastern Democratic Republic of the Congo (DRC) resulted, from 2010 onwards, in a raft of Northern and domestic legislative and policy measures designed to pressurize the world's largest electronics corporations, such as Apple and Intel, to conduct due diligence in their global supply chains to ensure that the minerals used in their products were not funding conflict in the DRC. Under these measures, throughout the 2010s, Banro was the only entity in South Kivu that could legally export its gold production to effected international markets. The 'closed' supply chains managed by foreign mining corporations were more readily assumed to prevent armed group profiteering from productive activity, in contrast to the 'open' supply chains managed by local traders.

The falsehood of this assumption is demonstrated in this chapter, where the major argument put forward is that, contrary to the hopes of African Mining Consensus proponents, the return of capital-intensive foreign-owned mining (FOM) to South Kivu has led to an intensification of local conflict rather than its alleviation. As a result of Banro's arrival, the dynamic domestic accumulation associated with labour-intensive DOM in South Kivu has been subjected to processes of displacement, subversion, and suppression. This, in turn, has given rise to new forms of protest, violence, and killings as different groups of local actors have sought to resist their newfound marginality.

Section 7.1 documents these multiple processes of marginalization. It opens by showing how the displacement of labour-intensive DOM following Banro's arrival in Luhwindja decreased the volume of locally available mining employment. It then documents how Banro's arrival subverted the pre-existing social relations underpinning the mobilization and organization of mining labour as local groups moved from occupying the upper strata of the DOM hierarchy to the lower strata of the FOM economy that was replacing it. Together, these two processes induced a general deterioration in local conditions following Banro's arrival. The section closes by highlighting Banro's suppression of locally led industrialization in Kamituga and, indirectly, Luhwindja.

Disrupted Development in the Congo. Ben Radley, Oxford University Press. © Ben Radley (2023).
DOI: 10.1093/oso/9780192849052.003.0007

Section 7.2 considers how local groups have responded. While peaceful strategies to resist met with some early success, Banro's alliance with local and national political elites, backed with the security apparatus of the Congolese state, has limited their effectiveness. From 2015 onwards, resistance strategies increasingly began to reproduce historical processes of violence and conflict, including Banro's financing of state and non-state armed groups operating in the region.

7.1 Displacement, subversion, and suppression

In 2010, Mbwega, the largest labour-intensive DOM site in Luhwindja at the time, was appropriated from local miners to make way for the construction of Banro's Twangiza mine. Several thousand miners were forced off the land by state policy and military, and a further 2,500 residents were forcibly relocated to the nearby hilltop of Cinjira. Shortly after, displaced miners opened the three additional labour-intensive mine sites of Cinjira, Lumpumpu, and Ntagare, yet they soon proved unproductive. As a result, many who had been relatively prosperous through their employment in labour-intensive DOM fell into difficulty, as the following testimony summaries detail:

> He was a shaft manager at Mbwega and owned two shafts. His family owned maize and manioc fields near to the mine, along with five cows. When they were displaced to Cinjira they received $500 in compensation for their land. He used the money to construct two shafts at the new mine at Cinjira, but both are now closed as they only led to a very small amount of gold. They sold all their cows to generate some income, and today his two wives work as agricultural day labourers. He is looking for work.[1]

> Life was very good at Mbwega. They owned three fields totalling around 1 hectare of land. She grew maize, beans, and manioc and sold it at the local market. Her husband was a shaft worker at the site. They received $500 in compensation when they were displaced. Her husband worked for a while at the new site in Cinjira but stopped shortly after as production was too low. Life in Cinjira is difficult. They are hungry, and struggle to keep their children in school. They sold all their livestock—four cows and some goats and chickens—to survive. Today, they are growing potatoes on the land of a friend to get by.[2]

[1] Interview with former Mbwega shaft manager, Cinjira, 7 April 2017.
[2] Interview with former Mbwega farmer, Cinjira, 7 April 2017.

He was a shaft worker at Mbwega. His family had around three hectares of land where they grew maize and potatoes. They didn't want to leave but they were forced by armed police who came to their home. They were compensated with $2,500 for their land. They had five cows, four goats, and five chickens, but today they have nothing left as they sold them all to keep the family going. He tried working in mining at Cinjira for a while but didn't find anything. He managed to borrow some money from a friend. He used this money to start his business and today he bakes bread to sell to others at Cinjira.[3]

Despite the continued operation of Kadumwa and other smaller DOM sites across Luhwindja, the volume of mining labour available locally in Luhwindja has declined significantly since the construction of the Twangiza mine in 2010. A labour census conducted at Mbwega prior to its appropriation estimated the presence of 500 shaft managers and 5,000 workers (OGP 2008). Discussions with *Comité des creuseurs artisanaux de Luhwindja* (CCALU), the elected committee representing labour-intensive miners in Luhwindja, suggested that there were a further 500 miners working at other sites across the collectivity at the time. This leads to an estimated total of 6,000 people directly employed in labour-intensive DOM in Luhwindja prior to 2010.

Site visits and data provided by the CCALU suggest that, by 2017, there were an estimated 2,000 units of labour across seven labour-intensive DOM gold sites in Luhwindja. This represented a considerable decrease from the estimated 6,000 prior to 2010 (Table 7.1). Conversations with trader-managers supported this impression, such as the remark of a Bukavu-based trader buying gold from Luhwindja: 'It's become very difficult. I have very little work since Banro arrived and closed Mbwega. Even if I spend my days here at my office, it's become very complicated.'[4]

In addition to displacement, the labour regime associated with Banro's Twangiza mine subverted pre-existing logics of labour mobilization and organization in Luhwindja. Hoffman (2021: 254) has traced how Belgian colonial rule in South Kivu ushered in 'the construction of a new ethno-territorial order, and the privileges, rights and benefits that would accrue to it' and how, in the present, this ethno-territorial order is 'appropriated, reactualised and deployed by "ethnic subjects" themselves'. This can be seen in Luhwindja, where the capital-labour social relation underpinning labour-intensive DOM functioned through precisely such reactualized ethno-territorial and kinship identities.

---

[3] Interview with former Mbwega shaft worker, Cinjira, 7 April 2017.
[4] Interview with gold trader, Bukavu, 18 April 2017.

Table 7.1 Units of DOM labour in
Luhwindja, pre-2010 and 2017

Site	Units of labour	
	Pre-2010	2017
Mbwega	5,500	0
Kadumwa	200	800
Lulimbowe	100	100
Lugunkuri	100	400
Mwana	100	275
Cinjira	0	225
Lumpumpu	0	100
Ntagare	0	100
TOTAL	6,000	2,000

Sources: Site visits, CCALU data, local
government data.

Up until the 1970s, proximity to the *Mwami* customary authorities was
required to receive mineral-bearing land and become a shaft manager.
This practice continued through to the 2000s, with mineral-bearing land sold
to shaft managers by *baganda*—members of the *Mwami*'s inner circle. In
return, a share of production went to the *Mwami*, outside of official local
state revenue. As a result, nearly all trader-managers at the time were Bashi
from Luhwindja with either close ties to the local political elite or part of this
elite themselves.

By the 2010s, mineral-bearing land no longer belonged directly to the
Mwami, and *baganda* were no longer involved in its distribution. Former
Bami had distributed it via *kalinzi*—an indefinite loan in return for tribute
and loyalty—and the *Mwami* at the time had not exercised the right to claim
it back.[5] Indicative of the decreased influence of the *Mwami* in this sphere,
while Babofa was the clan of Luhwindja's royal family and most local political elites during this period, shaft managers represented a broad range of
local clans with no single clan dominant. While proximity to local political
elites was no longer as important in Luhwindja as it once had been, ethno-
territorial identity nonetheless remained a critical determinant in assuming
one's place within the local trader-manager class.

In a continuation of past practice, only Bashi from Luhwindja were permitted to become shaft managers. This criterion was applied by landlords
(themselves all Bashi from Luhwindja) when selling use rights to their land,

---

[5] Conversations with local government tax collectors (who were also *baganda*), Luhwindja, February
and March 2017.

often in favour of family or clan members. As one manager recalled, 'My father and [one of the landlords] are cousins. That's why I got a shaft there easily, because they're cousins. For example, Constantin, who you know, he married into the same family. That's why he got a pit at Kadumwa, because they're now in the same clan.'[6] The ethno-territorial and kinship logics associated with the place of shaft managers in production were commonly acknowledged, and generally uncontested, by both locals and non-locals alike.

The ethno-territorial and kinship structures shaping the social composition of shaft managers in Luhwindja flowed down to the mobilization and organization of labour. Many of the shafts were known as *puits familiaux* (family pits), composed exclusively of family or clan members, whereas others (but not all) were strongly oriented along similar kinship logics. Those with a family or clan connection to a shaft manager could more easily gain access to shaft work. Those without were asked by shaft managers to pay up to $100 or an equivalent livestock contribution to join the team, which many could not afford. Reflecting these logics, almost all workers were Bashi from Luhwindja or one of the neighbouring collectivities.[7]

Local traders were also Bashi from Luhwindja or (to a lesser extent) the neighbouring collectivity of Burinhyi. All the Bukavu-based traders who bought gold from Luhwindja were Bashi from the local area. The three most important Bukavu-based traders, in terms of their share of the Luhwindja gold trade, had a common history, and many noted that it would be difficult to enter the Luhwindja market without their approval. Two of the three were from the same local area of Luhwindja, and while the third was from Burinhyi, they all went to the same primary school in Luhwindja. There were also some familial connections between the Luhwindja network of traders and the Bukavu-based refinery, *Mines Propres*, to whom they sold most of their gold. The main laboratory technician at *Mines Propres* was the nephew of one of the three major traders controlling the Luhwindja gold market.

The mobilization logics underpinning Banro's managerial class at Twangiza, however, were altogether different. The families of Congolese managers generally came from the urban educated and professional classes, often the mining sector. One operations director, for example, was the son of a former SOMINKI manager. His father used his earnings at SOMINKI to put him through university in Kinshasa.[8] Two other directors were brothers

---

[6] Interview with shaft manager, Luhwindja, 10 February 2017.

[7] A group of six ethnic Warega from nearby Kamituga worked at Kadumwa in 2017. They had been granted access due to their technical proficiency in shaft construction and ore extraction (one was a former SOMINKI worker).

[8] Interview with operations director, Luhwindja, 9 October 2016.

whose father, also a former SOMINKI manager, had paid for their university education in Canada, where they trained as engineers and remained for twenty years after completing their studies.[9] Foreign managers were predominantly from South Africa, Ghana, Kenya, and Tanzania. With their families based outside of the country, they constituted Twangiza's 'fly in, fly out' managerial stratum. In 2017, the community relations manager was the only managerial employee heralding from Luhwindja.

Thus, while the local DOM trader-manager class was composed entirely of Bashi from Luhwindja or neighbouring collectivities, these same groups were almost entirely absent from the managerial class at the Twangiza mine. Instead, as documented in section 5.1, local groups were restricted to the lowest strata of Twangiza's labour hierarchy. This transformation of the established social order inflicted a significant degree of cultural shame and resentment against Banro's presence, which would often surface in conversations. During a discussion over drinks between a local shopkeeper and his friends, for example, much time was spent lamenting the fact that the brother of the former *Mwami* of Luhwindja had been reduced to working as a guard for the British security corporation G4S.[10]

As a result of displacement and subversion, alongside the low level of industrial employment and low wages to most industrial workers, Banro's arrival induced a shrinking of the pre-existing mining economy in Luhwindja, rerouting mining income away from, rather than into, the local area. Extrapolating backwards from the wage data presented in sections 5.1 and 6.2, and drawing on the DOM labour data presented in Table 7.1, it is possible to make an approximate comparison between the mining wages and profits earned, consumed, and invested locally prior to and seven years after the construction of the Twangiza mine (Table 7.2). From this comparison it can be seen, first, that the total number of people locally employed in Luhwindja's mining economy (considering DOM and FOM together) has decreased from around 6,000 to fewer than 3,000 across this time frame. Second, the total annual income accruing to groups of mining labour who consumed and invested their income locally has also decreased from around $11.4 million to $6.4 million, around 45 per cent.[11]

While not too much should be read into the exact figures presented due to the level of approximation, the scale and directionality of these findings are nonetheless congruent with the many testimonies from local farmers,

[9] Interviews with Simba Logistics director and senior manager, Bukavu, 17 and 22 February 2017.
[10] Conversation with local shopkeeper, Luhwindja, 27 November 2016.
[11] Only one-third of shaft manager profits has been included in this estimation due to the predominantly Bukavu-based orientation of much of this group's expenditure and investment.

Table 7.2 Locally expended mining wages in Luhwindja, pre-2010 and 2017

Time period	Group	Units of labour	Total annual wages/profits ($)
Pre-2010	Artisanal site workers	1,496	994,961
	Artisanal shaft workers	4,157	8,132,031
	Artisanal shaft managers	346	2,319,874
TOTAL PRE-BANRO		6,000	11,446,866
2017	Artisanal site workers	499	331,654
	Artisanal shaft workers	1,386	2,710,677
	Artisanal shaft managers	115	773,291
	Industrial workers (unskilled)	846	2,608,590
TOTAL POST-BANRO		2,846	6,424,212

Notes: Unskilled denotes hired labour, subcontractor workers, and unskilled Twangiza Mining workers. To determine the units of labour across each category in labour-intensive DOM, the same weighting was used as observed between the three categories at Kadumwa. To determine the total annual wages of site workers, the wages earned by water carriers, ore carriers, and ore washers were likewise weighted as observed at Kadumwa.
Sources: Author calculations based on site visits, CCALU data, local government data.

herders, teachers, hospital workers, priests, civil servants, and youth, who, in conversation, consistently foregrounded the relative strength of Luhwindja's local economy prior to Banro's arrival. The following three statements are illustrative:

I think that local mining is very important for us. All of us grew up in this system and made progress in this way. Our parents had a market thanks to the work of local miners. When a miner comes from work, he buys something, and this something allows me to study. Since Banro has arrived, you see parents saying 'I don't have money to pay school fees' and children staying at home [...] We hadn't experienced that before.[12]

Someone who digs, once he's found some gold, the money he earns at least circulates locally. Even those who sell flour, or something else, are going to benefit. Even those who sell *fretins* [local fish]. If we compare now with Banro, you will see that the company pays its workers in Bukavu. Even a native from here is paid in

[12] Luhwindja parish youth focus group discussant, Luhwindja, 27 November 2016.

Bukavu. All the money goes there, while we have our commerce here, but who can now buy from us?[13]

When local miners come home from Kadumwa, they contribute a lot to local development here. They buy flour for example, far more than the workers at Banro. I've seen that all the contracted workers at Banro, the majority, live in Bukavu with their families. So, what do they have to do with Luhwindja now? They have nothing to do with the people of Luhwindja. They won't even buy their cooking oil here. Banro gives them food and soap. What can they buy here? That's the difficulty we have.[14]

Banro's arrival, then, has led to an overall decrease in the total level of mining employment and mining income consumed and invested locally. Rather than strengthening the economy through the provision of additional and well-remunerated labour, the process of transnational corporation (TNC)-led mining (re)industrialization in South Kivu has, on the contrary, led to a generalized deterioration in local conditions.

Alongside displacement and subversion, and recalling SOMINKI's efforts in the 1980s to protect its concessions from local miners, Banro has enlisted the support of the Congolese state to undermine and hold back the locally led process of mining industrialization documented in section 6.3. In the early 2010s, Banro initially tolerated the presence of labour-intensive DOM on its Kamituga concession. The corporation had not yet moved to the construction phase, and its presence in the area was relatively lightly felt, run out of a small office in the town.

Yet, due to the increased productivity of labour-intensive DOM, generated in particular by the use of ball mills from 2012 onwards, Banro's strategic deposits were being exploited and exhausted at a much faster rate than had been the case previously. In 2017, Banro's chief executive officer (CEO) at the time explained that the corporation's strategy was to have the Kamituga and Lugushwa mines in the production phase in the next ten years.[15] The mechanization of labour-intensive DOM in Kamituga posed a direct threat to this longer-term vision by more rapidly depleting the value of the corporation's deposits in the area. The public relations manager of Banro's subsidiary Kamituga Mining succinctly articulated the crux of the problem for the corporation: 'For us, it is about the mechanization of mining exploitation [. . .]

---

[13] Luhwindja parish youth focus group discussant, Luhwindja, 27 November 2016.
[14] Interview with Zuki worker, Luhwindja, 12 December 2016.
[15] Interview with former Banro CEO, John Clarke, United Kingdom, 26 October 2017.

we continue to tolerate the presence of miners up to now, but under the condition that they remain in artisanal mining only' (cited in Buraye et al. 2017: 361–362).

Banro made its first move in January 2012, as the mining administration at the level of Mwenga territory attempted to formally ban the use of ball mills due to their illegal encroachment onto Banro's Kamituga concession. This proved ineffective, so in early 2013, Banro opened legal proceedings against the mill owners, informing them that the mills would be appropriated by the Congolese state if they were not moved off the Mobale deposit. In September 2013, after owners failed to heed this warning, around thirty of the seventy mills in the area were appropriated by state agents with the support of local military and police, and transferred to state custody in Bukavu. According to one of the local policemen involved in the operation, 'police officers and soldiers were instructed to clear all the ball mills at Mobale. This was difficult for us, but we had to follow orders.'[16] In 2015, Banro enlisted the support of the local Mining Police and the *Forces armées de la République Démocratique du Congo* (FARDC) to cut off access to electricity in five labour-intensive DOM sites, close ten new mineshafts, and restrict access to its most valuable deposits in the area (Stoop et al. 2016).

The cumulative effect of Banro's open hostility to locally led mechanization was to create a climate of doubt and insecurity among both workers and the trader-manager class. As the president of a local miners' association reflected in 2017, 'Since 2012, local miners have been leading a life of uncertainty. They continue in their work, not knowing what day their enemy will surprise them, inciting local authorities, police, and military to appropriate their machinery.'[17]

The news of Banro's suppression of mechanization efforts in Kamituga travelled to nearby Luhwindja, where it had a similarly inhibitive effect. By 2017, Luhwindja's trader-manager class was facing similar issues to those of Kamituga prior to the introduction of ball mills. According to shaft managers at Kadumwa, while, around 2011, the gold was nearer to the surface, plentiful, and relatively easy to access, by 2017, the site was nearing the extractive limits of predominantly manual production methods.

An ore washer captured this shift when asked what he was treating: 'That's just gravel. Before we would throw it away, it wasn't sold. When there was a

---

[16] Interview with local policeman, Kamituga, 22 April 2017. The 2013 Annual Report of the South Kivu Provincial Mining Division understatedly noted that 'the arrival of ball mills [...] has made cohabitation between the artisanal and industrial miners even more delicate'.

[17] Interview with Miners' Association president, Kamituga, 24 April 2017.

lot of gold, we didn't sell that. But given there's no longer much gold around, it's now being sold.'[18] A conversation with Bukavu-based gold traders buying from Luhwindja further illustrated the site's decline:

> Trader 1: Before, there was a lot of gold [at Kadumwa]. There was really a lot.
>
> Trader 2: It's true that at the beginning, production levels were high when Kadumwa started.
>
> Trader 1: [Today] they no longer have the means to reach the veins.[19]

Shaft managers explained that the problem was that, in many places, they had reached the level of hard rock and could only descend deeper by making use of the same explosives and ball mills used in Kamituga. Yet, they were doubtful Banro would tolerate mechanization at the site, considering its suppression of similar efforts in Kamituga, and were reluctant to invest in the required capital as a result. Part of this reluctance also stemmed from their fear that Banro would soon force them off the site in the same way that it had enclosed Mbwega back in 2010 and its most valuable deposits in Kamituga.

7.2 From peaceful protest to violence

In the face of their subjection to processes of displacement, subversion, and suppression following Banro's arrival in South Kivu, local Congolese have responded with acts of protest, evasion, and resistance. In 2010, eighty families resisted the appropriation of Mbwega, resulting in the local imprisonment of each household head. This led to most relenting, but the six who continued to protest were eventually sent to the central prison in Bukavu. While in prison, their fields were taken and their homes destroyed.[20] Some local miners attempted to continue working at Mbwega but were similarly arrested and sent to Bukavu's central prison.[21] Local government authorities closed any shafts that Banro deemed to have been constructed too close to its Twangiza mine.[22]

In June 2010, just prior to Mbwega's enclosure, Banro signed a memorandum of understanding with local government authorities in Luhwindja to prohibit labour-intensive DOM at nearby Kadumwa and Lukunguri,

[18] Interview with ore grinder, Kadumwa, 13 July 2017.
[19] Conversation with gold traders, Bukavu, 14 December 2017.
[20] Conversations with residents, Luhwindja, July 2017.
[21] Conversation with former Mbwega shaft worker, Bukavu, 16 May 2017.
[22] Letter from the Luhwindja head of collectivity to the Twangiza Mining director general and the Mwenga territorial administrator, 'The Closure of Underground Shafts Used by Illegal Miners in Twangiza Mining's site', 24 March 2015.

alongside Mbwega.[23] Immediately after Mbwega's closure, hundreds of local miners barricaded the road to Banro's Twangiza construction site for three days and demanded that Kadumwa and Lukunguri remain open.[24] As one of Kadumwa's shaft managers described, 'Kadumwa was threatened with closure so many people stood up. Kadumwa was the only site that allowed a lot of people to find some revenue, small as it might be, to survive. You can't close it without providing other employment.'[25] Their protest was successful, and both Kadumwa and Lukunguri were left open for local miners to continue their work.

The two sites were again threatened with closure in 2013 when, once more recalling SOMINKI's earlier attempts to call on the Congolese state to protect its concessions, Banro's vice-president of government relations wrote to the Congolese minister of mines requesting that action be taken against 'the proliferation of illegal artisanal mining in the concessions belonging to Twangiza Mining, which is facing difficulties in its exploration activities considered a priority for extending the life of the mine.'[26] In response, the *Comité de développement de Luhwindja* (Luhwindja Development Committee, CODELU), a political group of Luhwindja elites based in Bukavu, and CCALU, the elected committee representing local miner interests in Luhwindja, wrote a letter which was signed by 679 miners.

Addressed to the minister, with several Banro representatives in copy, the letter stated 'we resist any attempt to displace us for the second time from this site which supports our families today [...] We denounce this latest attempt at displacement. Our peaceful and pacifist attitude should not be mistaken for naivety.'[27] Despite this warning, in early 2014, military and police descended upon Kadumwa and attempted to close the site, reportedly using tear gas.[28] CODELU and local government authorities contacted the Ministry of Mines in Kinshasa to urge that Kadumwa be left open and were eventually successful. Police and military withdrew, and work continued at Kadumwa as before.[29]

Around the same time, in Kamituga, state efforts to appropriate ball mills were resisted and evaded by the local trader-manager class. While around thirty mills were seized by state security forces in 2013, the remaining forty or so were hidden from sight by owners, who had some forewarning of their

[23] Twangiza Mining and Luhwindja Collectivity memorandum of understanding, 5 June 2010.
[24] Interview with community leader, Luhwindja, 16 September 2016.
[25] Interview with Kadumwa shaft manager, Luhwindja, 9 April 2017.
[26] Letter from Banro's vice-president of government relations to the minister of mines, 28 May 2013.
[27] Letter from CODELU and CCALU to the minister of mines, 21 June 2013.
[28] Interview with CODELU member, Bukavu, 15 June 2017.
[29] Interview with Luhwindja head of collectivity, Luhwindja, 9 February 2017.

impending seizure. In 2017, mill owners formed and registered the cooperative *Développement de Kamituga* (Kamituga Development) to represent and defend their interests.[30] While mills were no longer present at the main site of Mobale, they continued to operate elsewhere across the town.

The subversion of the social relations underpinning labour mobilization and organization was also resisted by local inhabitants. In 2014, a workshop was held in Luhwindja between Banro, local government authorities, and civil society representatives, the latter of whom asked 'why the marginalization of community members? Why do we not respect the Memorandum of Understanding which stipulates that employment priority is accorded to community members?' The workshop concluded by requesting that the memorandum be respected and that ten managerial positions be given to appropriately qualified candidates from Luhwindja.[31]

The request was not followed, so, in 2015, locals founded the *Union des habitants de Luchiga* (Union of Luchiga Inhabitants, UHLU). UHLU brought together people from the *groupement* (grouping) of Luchiga,[32] the largest grouping in Luhwindja by size and population, and in which both the Twangiza mine and nearly all Luhwindja's labour-intensive mines were located. UHLU immediately established sub-committees in each of Luchiga's six villages with the ultimate goal of holding Banro accountable for the commitments it had made in the 2010 memorandum of understanding.

As one of its first acts, UHLU wrote a letter to the general director of Twangiza Mining, copying the provincial minister of mines. In the letter, UHLU requested appropriate compensation for those who had been displaced, more and better job opportunities for local people at the mine, and for Twangiza Mining employees to be paid locally in Luhwindja, 'to allow for the circulation of money here and not elsewhere.'[33] On the issue of job opportunities, the letter demanded the removal of all the subsidiary's senior human resource managers on the grounds that they 'promote the exclusion of people from Luhwindja from access to managerial positions to the benefit of agents coming from elsewhere.'[34] The letter stated that if UHLU's demands were not met by June, protests would be organized.

No response was received to the letter so, as promised, UHLU organized a three-day protest and blockade of Twangiza's supply routes, beginning on

[30] Interview with Kamituga Development founder and president, Kamituga, 24 April 2017.
[31] Final Workshop Report, Luhwindja, 3 February 2014.
[32] The collectivity of Luhwindja is composed of twenty-six villages organized in nine local government authority groupings, known as *groupements*.
[33] Letter from UHLU to Twangiza Mining director general, 'Reclamations of the Luchiga Population', 12 May 2015.
[34] Ibid.

Friday 12 June. Hundreds of people set up and occupied three roadblocks to disrupt the movement of workers and goods to and from the Twangiza mine. A total of around $250 was raised locally to provide food and drink to support the protestors. The following day, the *Mwami* and *Mwamikazi* travelled to Luhwindja from Bukavu[35] but failed to convince demonstrators to remove the roadblocks, despite negotiations long into the night with protest leaders at the local government office.

On Sunday morning, the *Mwamikazi* called one of the protest leaders to communicate that Banro was missing cyanide and other materials to continue production and warned that if the protest continued, she would be compelled to resort to force. At midday, three police vehicles arrived from Bukavu firing live bullets in the air, using teargas, and throwing stones into people's homes and stores to disperse protestors.[36] Protestors, fearing for their safety, returned to their homes.

To respond to local discontent following the protest, the *Mwami* established a new labour hire firm, Utralu, subcontracted by Twangiza Mining to provide road maintenance support and build a local football stadium. The firm provided around 150 local workers with monthly wages of $110, at the very bottom of Twangiza's labour hierarchy.[37] In a letter written by UHLU to Twangiza Mining in August 2015, these new jobs were dismissed as having not 'responded to our preoccupation [of securing] decent work'.[38] The same demands laid down prior to the protest were repeated.

In 2016, frustrated by the lack of any visible progress on any of its demands, UHLU withdrew its support for the Community Forum, which had been founded to facilitate dialogue between the local community and Banro.[39] A conversation with a local subcontractor worker in 2017 captured the general mood in Luhwindja at the time:

You know that the company operates in Luhwindja, but in terms of managers, I don't think that we even have one senior manager at the company. At the most we have one. At a certain point, that frustrates our leaders. I just told you I'm a university lecturer, but it's been nearly seven years that I'm in this situation with a

---

[35] The *Mwamikazi* of Luhwindja, Espérance Barahanyi, assumed the throne and her position as the senior government representative of the collectivity of Luhwindja on the death of her husband, while her son was a still a minor. Upon her son, *Mwami* Naluhwindja Chibwire V Tony, reaching adulthood, he assumed the throne, yet they continued to share their duties.

[36] Interviews with UHLU members and protestors, Luhwindja, November–December 2016.

[37] Ibid.

[38] Letter from UHLU to Twangiza Mining director general, 'Contestation', 15 August 2015.

[39] Conversation with UHLU president, Luhwindja, 1 December 2016.

subcontractor. It's the same treatment up until today. And at a certain point I can also ask myself, what's going on?[40]

Local level mobilization had met with some early success, especially in keeping Kadumwa and Lukunguri open for Luhwindja's miners. Yet, as the examples of imprisoned protestors and UHLU's failed blockade demonstrate, the alliance between Banro, political elites, and the state's security apparatus severely constrained the effectiveness of local efforts to secure more favourable terms for the continued existence of labour-intensive DOM in the area or more attractive employment opportunities at Twangiza.

This alliance was forged from the outset. Banro's arrival was facilitated by then President Joseph Kabila, the *Mwamikazi* of Luhwindja, and the FARDC, the latter launching a successful operation in 2005 to clear the non-state armed group *Forces démocratiques pour la libération du Rwanda* (Democratic Forces for the Liberation of Rwanda) from the area and protect Banro's infrastructure and personnel. According to Geenen (2014: 134):

> In his search for a new legitimate intermediary between the company and the local population, [President Joseph] Kabila contacted [the former *Mwami*] Philemon's widow, Espérance Barahanyi, who bore the title of '*Mwamikazi*'. At that moment, she was residing in Belgium with her children. The President reasoned that if she were able to win legitimacy in the eyes of the population, she could facilitate Banro's instalment.

In return for their support, the *Mwamikazi* and those close to her were well rewarded. Co-opted as a provincial deputy for South Kivu at the Assembly in Bukavu, the *Mwamikazi* was heavily involved in many of the domestic firms subcontracted by Banro. She was the largest of Cinamula's six shareholders, with a 30 per cent stake,[41] and held a 20 per cent stake in Premium, alongside the son of the national senator for Mwenga, among others.[42] She also founded and ran *Action pour la promotion de l'enfant et la femme* (APEF), one of the local associations providing agricultural produce to Banro.

The *Mwamikazi* and senior state authorities in Luhwindja and neighbouring collectivities also received direct monetary payments from Banro. In 2011, according to corporate documentation, these included $4,000 per month to the *Mwamikazi* (logged either as a community relations payment or for consulting fees) as well as a $6,000 scholarship contribution

---

[40] Interview with subcontractor worker, Twangiza, 7 June 2017.
[41] Cinamula statute, 26 August 2014. She was joined here by her sisters-in-law, close friends, Luhwindja's chief administrator, and the son of the former Luhwindja Secretary.
[42] Premium statute, 18 August 2014.

logged as a donation. This amounted to more than $50,000 of payments across the year. That same year, numerous other payments to local *Bami* in neighbouring collectivities across Banro's South Kivu concessions were made, including $2,000 as a marriage donation, $3,100 for room hire and cocktails, $3,000 for medical assistance, and regular $200 per diems alongside fuel, transport, and accommodation payments.[43]

People in Luhwindja were well aware of the nature of the relationship between Banro and local political elites. As a shaft manager recounted:

> The people of Luchiga, and across Luhwindja, haven't had their interests protected since the *Mwamikazi* came back here. She is the one who brought Banro here and defends it to the detriment of the interests of the local community. It's the *Mwamikazi* who should defend the local population, but she only sees her personal interest. The population is no longer defended. That's the heart of the problem.[44]

With the limits of peaceful protest in the face of the alliance between Banro, political elites, and the state's security apparatus becoming increasingly evident following the failed 2015 demonstration, local-level resistance strategies turned increasingly violent. The increased violence was linked to shifting alliances between local miners, local militia, and national army leaders, all of whom stood to lose out from the continued marginalization of labour-intensive DOM (Geenen and Verweijen 2017; Verweijen 2017). It also had historical precedent, as *Société minière des Grands Lacs'* (MGL's) artisanal operations at Twangiza experienced armed attacks in 1961, and between 1963 and 1965, most of MGL's southern mines were occupied by Simba rebels (eastern adherents to a nationalist, anti-imperialist insurgency, launched by Pierre Mulele in western Congo).[45] This led to the killing of MGL's secretary general, Mr Malengreaux, damage to machinery in Maniema, and mineral and vehicle theft totalling 23.4 million Congolese francs in 1964 alone.[46]

On the night of 9 July 2015, just one month after the state-led repression of local protest, there was an armed attack on the Royal Palace in Luhwindja. Made by members of the Ruvura clan with a claim to the throne, seven of the attackers were sentenced to life in prison.[47] Next, at around one o'clock in the morning of 7 February 2017, a few dozen armed attackers broke into the Twangiza mine through the main entrance to the camp where Twangiza Mining's workers and managers were lodged. Three state police guarding

[43] Banro Congo Ledger Report, 2011.
[44] Life history with Kadumwa manager, Luhwindja, 9 April 2017.
[45] Internal MGL memo, April 1961; personal memoires of Serge Lammens, former SOMINKI director.
[46] MGL letter to the Congolese Business Federation, 12 December 1964.
[47] Interview with CODELU member, Bukavu, 21 February 2017.

the mine and one attacker were killed by gunfire, and one of G4S's security guards was shot (but survived). Some attributed the attackers to a local militia group from Luvungi, around 60 kilometres away across the mountain range of the Ruzizi plain, although this remains unconfirmed.[48] Following the attack, Banro increased the military and police protection at the mine, securing the perimeter with extra weaponry and with the addition of a military battalion from the tenth division. This brought military personnel at the site up to around 100 alongside around 40 police.

Violent resistance also emerged around the same time at Banro's Namoya mine in neighbouring Maniema province, where similar processes of marginalization had been underway since the mine's construction in 2013. According to a local association from the area, 'since 2013, the central government's decision to force local miners to leave Banro's concession led to a wave of protest and discontent at the heart of the surrounding community'.[49] Discontent at Namoya was further amplified in January 2016, following the killing by a senior police officer of a local activist during a peaceful march against, among other issues, the displacement of local miners.[50]

Resistance turned violent in September 2016, when six convoy trucks delivering goods through South Kivu to the Namoya mine were burned and thirteen drivers of Kenyan or Tanzanian nationality were taken hostage. All were later released following the intervention of the FARDC (Wilson 2016). Next, in March 2017, an armed attack was launched against Namoya. Two Congolese, one Tanzanian, and one French national were kidnapped. Attacks continued from May to September, resulting in the deaths of Congolese military and police.[51]

In August 2018, another attack on trucks belonging to Banro carried out by the militia Maï-Maï Malaika led to two passengers being killed and four people being kidnapped (Reuters 2018). Through these incidents, beginning with the attack on the Royal Palace in Luhwindja in 2015, processes of marginalization unleashed by Banro's arrival in the provinces of South Kivu and Maniema eventually began to reproduce historical patterns of local conflict along new and increasingly violent trajectories.

As well as inciting violent conflict, Banro has also contributed to conflict financing via three channels, first, through the likely payment of ransoms. In 2016, a Tanzanian hostage was allegedly released in exchange for a

---

[48] Conversations with Twangiza Mining employees and local and state authorities in Luhwindja and Bukavu, February and March 2017.

[49] Memo from Maniema Libertés to non-governmental organizations, 16 February 2016.

[50] Ibid.

[51] Banro press statements, 2017. https://sedar.com (accessed 10 August 2018).

ransom payment (Congo Research Group 2019). In 2017, a senior manager at Banro Congo divulged that an initial ransom of $1 million was requested in exchange for the kidnapped French national and that the corporation brought in a South African negotiation team to secure the French national's release, which eventually took place a few months later.[52] All kidnapped staff were eventually released unharmed. Considering the documented ransom payment in 2016 and the testimony of a senior manager at the corporation in 2017, it seems plausible that, in at least some instances, their release was negotiated in exchange for a ransom. In this way, Banro might have financed the activities of non-state armed groups linked to the kidnappings, such as Maï-Maï Malaika.

Second, a subcontracting firm providing transport and logistics services to Banro's Namoya mine appears to have made regular payments to another non-state armed group, Maï-Maï Yakutumba, over an extended period. Maï-Maï Yakutumba was operating at the southernmost point of South Kivu province bordering with, and crossing over into, Maniema province. Its territory included part of the transport route running from the city of Uvira in South Kivu down to Namoya, through which convoys carrying goods and inputs to the mine regularly travelled.

The claim that a subcontractor had been financing this armed group first came to light in 2011, when a report by the UN Group of Experts on the DRC (2011: 97) noted that 'a Banro representative informed the Group [. . .] that some transporters contracted by Banro had made small payments to armed groups on the route between Bukavu and Namoya'. This claim was repeated in an article published by the Wall Street Journal in 2015 (Scheck and Patterson 2015). One respondent claimed that the subcontractor paid $20 per truck to Maï-Maï Yakutumba when using the Uvira–Namoya transport route. Two other sources regularly travelling the route for the subcontractor independently claimed that they had seen money change hands between the convoys and militia members waiting on the side of the road.[53]

Third, and as already mentioned, by 2017, Banro was dependent upon around 100 FARDC soldiers and 40 police to secure its Twangiza mine, to whom it paid individual stipends in return for their services. This is little different to the payments made by the trader-manager class at Kadumwa and elsewhere across South Kivu to armed groups in return for protection, for which labour-intensive DOM has been so heavily criticized in the past.

---

[52] Conversation with Banro Congo senior manager, Bukavu, May 2017 (exact date mislaid).
[53] Interviews with respondents who requested full anonymity, July 2016.

Through forced displacement, subverting labour relations, and suppressing locally led processes of mining industrialization, Banro has marginalized and come into conflict with various groups. Affected groups initially adopted non-violent strategies of protest, evasion, and resistance against both the corporation and the local political elites who helped sustain its presence. From 2015, resistance took on increasingly violent dimensions, including an armed attack on the Twangiza mine in 2017, which led to several deaths. In addition, Banro appears to have contributed to conflict financing through payments to both state and non-state armed groups.

A re-examination of the Consensus literatures on 'blood diamonds' and 'conflict minerals' is therefore required. By highlighting the link between labour-intensive DOM and conflict financing in Africa, the literatures implicitly or explicitly extoll the comparative virtues of capital-intensive FOM, assumed to operate in isolation from conflict dynamics. The evidence presented in the chapter problematizes this belief as the view that Banro's mines are 'conflict-free' (Bafilemba and Lezhnev 2015: 3) fails to hold up to scrutiny. On the contrary, the corporation has been directly involved in generating and perpetuating local conflict and violence.

Moreover, in a repeat of SOMINKI's efforts detailed in section 6.1 to stifle the emergence of labour-intensive DOM, Banro has disrupted the developmental trajectory of South Kivu's trader-manager class, working to restrict the capital intensity of DOM by all available means, including the appropriation of machinery, this in addition to inducing a generalized deterioration in local conditions, both materially and culturally, through the displacement of DOM labour and the subversion of the social relations underpinning labour mobilization and organization. Taken together, the evidence presented in Chapters 6 and 7 challenges the Consensus dismissal of labour-intensive DOM as a desirable form of mining-based development in the African periphery.

8

The fragile foundations of the African Mining Consensus

To recall, the African Mining Consensus holds that African countries should leverage their comparative advantage in metals and minerals to drive productivity growth and that the resultant distribution of value from these productivity gains will stimulate the structural transformation of local and national economies. For this, both capital-intensive and labour-intensive forms of domestic-owned mining (DOM) are deemed unsuitable. The Consensus holds, instead, that mining (re)industrialization should be led by the superior expertise and efficiency of transnational companies (TNCs).

Based on the findings presented, three critiques of the Consensus position can be made. First, the wisdom of overlooking the developmental potential of labour-intensive DOM based on its perceived low productivity, inefficiency, and links to conflict financing is questioned. While productivity might be low, this does not mean it is static. In South Kivu, labour-intensive DOM was shown to be embedded in a capital–labour social relation that was associated with increasing sectoral productivity via technological innovation and capital formation.

This process was led by a trader-manager class of dynamic and prosperous rural Congolese that was also making commercial and productive investments in other, non-mining sectors. This class raised finance to make the required investments, mobilized and organized labour, owned the means of production, and reinvested profits, including in mechanization. As such, this class might be considered as advancing a domestically embedded form of peripheral capitalism.

By analytically centring the profit–wage relation within the capital–labour social relation underpinning labour-intensive DOM in South Kivu, relations so often concealed in the existing literature,[1] the findings challenge one of the recurring arguments and policy recommendations from African mining scholarship, namely, that labour-intensive DOM can, or should, 'coexist'

---

[1] This occurs either by avoiding mention of profits and referring only to the 'revenues' or 'income' earned by miners or, when profits are acknowledged, by collapsing the distinction between workers and managers and referring to all miners as making profits.

Disrupted Development in the Congo. Ben Radley, Oxford University Press. © Ben Radley (2023).
DOI: 10.1093/oso/9780192849052.003.0008

with capital-intensive foreign-owned mining (FOM). This line of thinking can be seen in both the Democratic Republic of the Congo (DRC) scholarship (Geenen 2011; Kamundala, 2012) and the broader African literature (Hilson 2002; Hilson and Yakovleva 2007; Nyame and Blocher 2010). It has also been promoted by the World Bank, for whom 'mining together' is a key solution for conflicts between labour-intensive and capital-intensive mining (Verbrugge and Thiers 2021). This perspective is based on the perception that labour-intensive and capital-intensive miners are usually not in competition for the same deposits as capital-intensive mining targets deeper veins while labour-intensive mining targets more easily accessible surface deposits.

Yet, if labour-intensive DOM is conceptualized not as a low-productivity, pre-capitalist, or non-capitalist subsistence activity but as a capitalist and mechanizing form of production, it can be understood that it is in more direct competition with capital-intensive FOM for the same deposits than is commonly assumed. What a mining TNC exploits industrially today is nothing but the riches that, over a longer time frame, a mechanizing form of labour-intensive DOM could exploit tomorrow (or, more prosaically, many decades from now).

This invites a reconsideration of the merits and consequences of the 'coexistence' argument. While intended to support labour-intensive DOM, this line of thinking might serve to further reinforce its marginalization by cementing its existence on the same terms as Banro in South Kivu (to recall from earlier): that TNCs tolerate the presence of labour-intensive miners but under the condition that productive activity remains labour intensive.

In addition, Banro has created and reproduced local conflict in and around its mines, including through direct payments to armed groups. This suggests that conflict financing is less related to ownership structures, or the form of production, and more a consequence, as Laudati (2013) has argued, of operating in a conflict setting where armed groups attempt to claim a share in the value generated by productive activity, both in mining and other economic activities. Moreover, the data from Luhwindja, supported by previous studies in the DRC, demonstrated the low share of value accruing to armed groups from labour-intensive DOM.

The second critique is that the high level of disarticulation between capital-intensive FOM in South Kivu and the Congolese economy provides little support to the Consensus argument, advanced by the global value chain (GVC) literature, that global mining industry restructuring away from vertical integration and towards corporate outsourcing means 'the enclave mentality to diversification in low-income [African] economies is an anachronism' (Kaplinsky et al. 2011: 29). The general picture seems to confirm rather than invalidate Prebisch's original enclave thesis whereby resource extraction in the periphery has few domestic linkages and is generally disarticulated from local and national economies due to the periphery's dependence upon external technology and industrial capabilities in the centre.

Moreover, far from supporting the emergence of a Congolese private sector, Banro's arrival, while helping accelerate gross domestic product (GDP) growth in the DRC, has facilitated the entry of foreign firm subsidiaries, some of whom have since expanded and consolidated their presence in the Congolese economy. This is reminiscent of the process described by Sunkel (1972: 518) for 1960s Latin America, whereby:

> industry was taken over to a large extent by foreign subsidiaries, with the result that much of the benefit expected from industrialization has gone abroad in payment for capital equipment and in a transfer of profits, royalties, and other financial payments. This has effectively denationalized and eroded the local entrepreneurial class. Although the massive penetration of foreign firms has accelerated growth rates, especially industrial, it has also accentuated the uneven nature of development.

While bearing similarity to Sunkel's analysis, the twenty-first-century capital-intensive FOM enclave in South Kivu signifies a heightened version of its twentieth-century counterpart. From the 1940s onwards, the Congolese Central Bank bought a percentage of the gold produced in the country at a fixed price, providing the state with a source of foreign exchange for development financing. The Belgian-owned subsidiaries *Société minière des Grands Lacs* (MGL) and SOMINKI also paid profit tax rates of up to 50 per cent to the Congolese state, which, in turn, supported expansionary periods of state investment and social service provisioning at the national level, first in the 1950s and then again during the first decade of Mobutu's presidency (1965–1974). In the 2010s, by contrast, Banro was selling all its gold outside of the country and had failed to pay even the already low 4 per cent Congolese profit tax.

In addition, the labour-intensive production techniques underpinning Belgian-led gold mining in its infancy, which continued to be used in many areas, including Luhwindja, up until the latter part of the twentieth century, offered scope for these techniques to be assimilated and adapted through innovation. Yet, gold mining in the twenty-first century has become a highly capital-intensive, technologically advanced, and specialized activity. This restricts the potential for local technological innovation, as occurred in the previous century, particularly within a regulatory framework where state industrial policy to guide such a process is almost entirely absent. At the onset of the 2020s, the technological frontier of gold mining lies far further away from low-income economies like the DRC than it did in the previous century, heightening the enclaved nature of its underlying productive structure.

Further intensifying twenty-first century enclavity and a theoretical counterpoint to the general enthusiasm for corporate outsourcing found in the GVC literature, the organizational fragmentation induced by outsourcing weakened the collective power and strength of the predominantly local industrial workers at Twangiza to negotiate higher wages or improved terms of incorporation. Through the marginalization of labour-intensive DOM locally, low wages to industrial workers, and a low level of employment, Banro's arrival led to an overall decrease in the total amount of mining income consumed and invested locally. This led, in turn, to a generalized deterioration in local conditions. This casts serious doubt over the Consensus position that capital-intensive FOM can raise local wages and improve living standards in the African periphery. The development of increasingly automated industrial gold mines will only continue to accentuate these detrimental effects in the future.

The third and final critique is a questioning of the Consensus assumption that capital-intensive FOM will be more efficient and effective at leading mining industrialization than DOM alternatives. In South Kivu, the corporate-led model has twice proved ineffective in delivering sustained economic development, principally for the same reason. The Belgian subsidiary SOMINKI went into liquidation in 1997 and exactly twenty years later, in 2017, the Canadian corporation Banro went into Canadian government creditor protection to save it from bankruptcy.

In both cases, the foreign corporations had failed to control costs in the face of price volatility. For SOMINKI, the tin price halved in 1985 and failed to recover. For Banro, the gold price dropped by one-third between 2012 and 2014 and then stagnated. In the case of Banro, inefficiencies, mismanagement, and processes of surplus extraction contributed to this failure, including continued corporate rent-seeking as it descended ever closer to the verge of bankruptcy. These trajectories highlight that far from bastions of efficiency and effectiveness, foreign corporations are equally beholden to the vagaries of volatile prices, undermining the ability of capital-intensive FOM to drive broader processes of capital accumulation and structural transformation in the African periphery, just as such volatility had damaged capital-intensive DOM in the mid-1970s.

The African Mining Consensus rests, then, on fragile theoretical foundations. Together, these three lines of critique suggest that, while helping to drive high GDP growth rates, TNC-led mining (re)industrialization in African LICs might be reproducing similar processes of peripheral polarization, marginalization, and exclusion to those identified by earlier structuralist and dependency thinkers.

Pro-labour and regulatory industrial policy certainly have a role to play in alleviating some of these effects. In 2017, the Congolese state intervened to address the twin issue of labour informality and low worker wages by passing a law forbidding subcontractors from engaging in 'the illegal lending of labour [. . .] a fraudulent operation that removes the status of the employee [. . .] to profit from the price that should have been paid for the same work'.[2] This same law moved to make it easier for domestic firms to win subcontracts by requiring the transfer of at least 30 per cent of the value of the contract to the subcontracted firm upfront. A 2014 local content decree was passed to encourage foreign corporations to procure more goods and inputs through Congolese firms, and the 2018 mining code increased profit and royalty tax rates (although one might wonder at the effect of increased profit tax rates in a context where, as foregrounded in Chapter 3, domestic subsidiaries regularly declare low profits or losses).

Many African low-income-country (LIC) governments have been moving in a similar direction, seeking to strengthen the developmental benefits from a foreign corporate-led model of mining industrialization by more tightly regulating corporate activities. At the onset of the 2020s, we are living through the first generation of African mining sector reform since the 1980s focused on reversing the liberal excesses of earlier eras, carried by what is often portrayed as a rising wave of resource nationalism. As a Bloomberg article proclaimed in February 2019, 'The Fight between Miners and African Governments Is Just Getting Started' (Biesheuvel et al. 2019).

In 2017, Tanzania enacted three new laws to increase government control of mining. This included increasing state participation in mining projects, raising royalty rates, and perhaps most ambitiously, stripping foreign corporations of the right to seek international arbitration in the event of a domestic legal dispute. In 2018, Malawi passed a new mining charter seeking to strengthen domestic ownership and increase the fiscal base by addressing illicit financial flows. In 2020, Mali introduced a new mining code that eliminated foreign corporate value-added tax exemptions and shortened the period during which corporations are protected from fiscal changes. In 2022, Uganda passed a new mining and minerals act which, among other changes, established the Uganda National Mineral Company, a state-owned

---

[2] Law 17/001 of 8 February 2017.

enterprise set to take a 15 per cent equity stake in all capital-intensive mining operations and a seat on the board of directors as a shareholder. Liberia, Madagascar, and Togo were all reviewing their existing mining legislation at the time of writing, with new codes and regulatory frameworks expected in the coming years. Breathing new life into the stalled implementation of the African Union's African Mining Vision would provide further support to these country-level regulatory efforts and initiatives.

Yet, state policy in an African LIC setting, however well designed, has limited ability to address the structural constraints of price volatility, enclavity, and low labour absorption. Demand cannot be controlled, dependence upon foreign technology for capital-intensive production avoided, or levels of labour absorption at the technological frontier altered. Together, as seen by the case of South Kivu, these constraints hamper the ability of mining industrialization to stimulate broader-based processes of economic development in an African LIC setting, irrespective of ownership and management structures. This suggests that relying upon mining-led national development strategies is likely to be insufficient to achieve the African Union's (2015: 3) *Agenda 2063* aspirations that, by 2063, 'African people have a high standard of living [... and ...] economies are structurally transformed to create shared growth, decent jobs and economic opportunities for all'. Indeed, Montes (2014), Taylor (2015), and Sylla (2015) have all argued that trade liberalization in African LICs has resulted in greater export concentration and has not advanced processes of broader, non-extractive industrialization. What, then, is to be done?

In the first instance, the findings indicate the imperative for African LICs of thinking beyond leveraging comparative advantage in metals and minerals, moving away from the market-led logics underpinning the Consensus and, again grounded within Amin's (1990) notion of 'delinking' as a means to promote national sovereign projects, prioritizing the development of strategic sectors of the economy that are responsive to domestic and regional demand and needs. Here, a wealth of evidence points to the need for an active and interventionist state to guide structural change through the development and implementation of industrial policy (Amsden 1989; Wade 1990; Evans 1995; Mkandawire 2001; Chang 2004; Chang et al. 2016; Haggard 2018; Ovadia and Wolf 2018), which incorporates an appreciation of the required synchronicity between agricultural and industrial development (Kay 2002, 2009).

While there has been some recent revival of industrial policy discussions among African governments, linked to developing regional common markets and the African Continental Free Trade Area, these discussions remain heavily centred on foreign investors and investment (Behuria 2019).[3] However, the continued deference to foreign investment overlooks one of the key insights to emerge from post-colonial processes of economic transformation concerning the critical role played by domestic capitalists. State–business alliances, 'whereby the state implements a series of incentives and rewards to persuade domestic capitalists to undertake investments in targeted sectors in the economy' (Singh and Ovadia 2018: 1038), have been central to the sustained gains in social and economic development achieved during this period. Many successful industrializers, such as South Korea and Taiwan, were cautious of foreign investment during early industrialization, favouring instead the provision of supports and incentives to local business groups to develop domestic capabilities in targeted industries, including (during the initial stages) insulation from foreign competition (Evans 1995; Hauge 2020; Odijie 2020).

Continuing to favour foreign-direct-investment (FDI)-led industrialization and the very different state–TNC alliances this gives rise to could lead to any combination of the three outcomes seen through the analysis of mining reindustrialization in South Kivu, each of which would undermine the pursuit of development in the African periphery: first, the suppression of emerging domestic capitalist classes in conflict with TNC interests; second, the exclusion of domestic firms from TNC-led value chains or, for the more fortunate among them, their inclusion at, and restriction to, the lower end of value-added activities; third, low value capture and retention domestically as most of the value created by TNC-controlled production flows to overseas shareholders, senior company directors, and firms. In light of these observed tendencies, TNC dominance in key industries might prove less of a means to overcome African peripherality and more an explanatory cause.

In the mining sector itself, the evidence presented in this book suggests that the Consensus preference for foreign ownership accentuates the effects of the identified structural constraints, further eroding the space for any potentially transformative impact of mining-based development through the overseas rerouting of value towards foreign managers, directors, and shareholders alongside processes of domestic firm and capitalist class marginalization. This underscores the urgency of moving to domestic forms of ownership and management. Such a move would inevitably generate its own tensions and contradictions, creating winners and losers in the uneven and contingent

---

[3] This in a context where, as shown in section 2.2, the weight of foreign direct investment (FDI) in the national economies of African LICs has been rapidly growing and was greater in the 2010s relative to other country groups and regions. In the mid-2010s, UNCTAD (2015) forecast the possibility of FDI stock to African least-developed countries quadrupling by 2030.

process of capitalist economic development.[4] It would, nonetheless, enable an increased share of value retention within-country, including an increased share of value capture by domestic firms and capitalists, both critical elements for the advancement of national sovereign development projects in the African periphery.

The precise form and desired level of capital intensity within a shift to DOM will vary from country to country, but the evidence from the DRC provides some clues as to one possible direction such a shift might take. Looking for signs of tension and contradiction within the 1960s and 1970s Latin American development model that depended, as across African LICs in the 2010s and 2020s, upon FDI and foreign firms to drive high growth rates, Vaitsos (1973) identified the potential of social structures and local business groups not dependent on, or in conflict with, foreign interests to provide a viable alternative. In the case of South Kivu, the trader-manager class overseeing labour-intensive DOM, which had fallen into conflict with Banro since the corporation's arrival, provides just such a social structure. Within the confines of the observed structural constraints, domestically owned efforts to mechanize labour-intensive forms of local mining better meet the needs of African LIC economies for rising productivity, labour absorption, and the domestic retention of the value generated by productive activity than the TNC-led industrial model.

Arthur Lewis (1954: 184) theorized this developmental potential of peripheral labour-intensive mining economies in his open economy model of economic growth. He made the proviso to this model that wage stagnation in the tropical commercial crops export sector, on which the model was based:

> does not apply where natural resources of a particular kind are scarce. For example, the lands suitable for cultivating sugar or peanuts are very extensive. But mineral bearing lands, or lands with just the right suitability for cocoa, are relatively scarce. Hence the price of a mineral, or of cocoa, may rise to any level consistent with demand. If the lands are owned by capitalists, employing workers, this will make little difference to their wages. But if these scarce lands are owned by peasants, the peasants may of course become rich. In general, the peasants have got little out of their mineral bearing lands, especially when these have been expropriated

---

[4] As Geenen et al. (2023) have documented in the case of the DRC, for example, while productivity gains achieved via technological innovation and capital accumulation provide a solid basis for sustained processes of economic development, the impact of technological change on the organization and use of labour has been substantial.

by imperial governments (or declared to be Crown property) and sold to foreign capitalists for a song.

(Lewis 1954: 184)

His contention, supported by the findings from South Kivu, is that while labour will not necessarily benefit from the productivity growth induced by mining (re)industrialization, if scarce mineral-bearing land is owned by the peasantry, the dynamic might change.

Evidence from other African LICs provides further support to Lewis's theorization. In Liberia, Mali, and Sierra Leone, labour-intensive DOM has helped revive local agricultural production and agrarian institutions (Panella 2010; Cartier and Bürge 2011; Pijpers 2014). Bryceson and Jønsson (2010: 389) found retired labour-intensive miners in Tanzania to have 'capitalized on their earnings by investing in various kinds of local service provisioning or trading businesses'. Giving colour to these accounts, a labour-intensive shaft manager in rural southern Malawi explained:

Mining has allowed me to accomplish a number of things, I started as a digger, but eventually I have built a house, I had a car which I just sold and am involved in businesses whose capital has come from mining activities [. . .] even for the diggers, some of them have managed to buy cattle, and build houses with corrugated iron sheets. If we all save some money and invest in other activities, mining can pay off.

(Kamlongera 2011: 1135)

Furthermore, over the past decade, similar processes of mechanization to those found in South Kivu have been documented across the continent (Verbrugge and Geenen 2020; Geenen et al. 2023). This has included in LICs such as Guinea and Burkina Faso, where the use of large excavators, ball mills, metal detectors, and cyanide have become more widespread than they were a decade ago (Crawford and Botchwey 2016; Dessertine 2016; Lanzano 2020). An additional advantage of a mechanizing, labour-intensive DOM sector is its slower rate of extraction relative to capital-intensive production. Banro's Twangiza mine was around eight times more productive than SOMINKI in the 1980s, and around twenty-five times more productive than labour-intensive mining in Luhwindja. Seeking to immediately arrive at the technological frontier of highly capitalized industrial production will not only encumber the sector with the sorts of problems and constraints associated with the foreign-led model discussed earlier in this chapter but also rapidly deplete deposits, while using little labour in the process. Labour-intensive

DOM, by contrast, offers more time for the incubation of the long-term, domestically driven processes of capitalist class formation, capital accumulation, and mechanization observed across different areas of South Kivu to take place.

A longer-term perspective is warranted, which privileges technological adaptation and innovation in synchronicity with, rather than disconnected from, the surrounding economy, as was seen to be taking place organically in labour-intensive DOM at Kamituga and elsewhere in South Kivu. The aim here, rather than generating the conditions for the peaceful coexistence of domestic and foreign-owned forms of production, would be to limit the TNC-led model while nurturing the development of domestically led forms of labour-intensive mining to eventually access the deeper and more technologically complex deposits.

So, what scope might there be for the social forces driving labour-intensive DOM to emerge as a viable alternative to capital-intensive FOM? In South Kivu, the operation of MGL under Belgian colonial rule, SOMINKI under the Mobutu administration, and Banro under the Kabila administration have all been characterized by state–TNC suppression of, and hostility towards, both labour-intensive mining and the emergence of independent traders, firms, and industrialists outside of their control. This cautions against any great enthusiasm for such an emergence in the coming years and decades.

In addition, while there was evidence to suggest that the trader-manager class overseeing labour-intensive DOM in South Kivu represented both a 'class in itself' and a 'class for itself', organizing to pursue and protect its own collective interests, this organization functioned along strictly ethno-territorial logics. In Luhwindja, only Bashi from the collectivity could become shaft managers, and all traders were Bashi from Luhwindja or the neighbouring collectivity of Burinhyi. These highly localized logics underpinning class mobilization function against the development of a broader class consciousness that extends beyond the parameters of local interests.

Yet, unlike the observed structural constraints, these logics are not generalizable to other African LIC contexts. In Tanzania, Bryceson and Fisher (2014) have argued that labour-intensive DOM has promoted a collective consciousness and democratic solidarity among miners that has upended established social hierarchies, including along the marker of ethnic identity. In such a context, it is possible to imagine greater space for an alternative model of mining-based development to emerge. Indeed, towards the end of the 2010s, the Tanzanian government began to revoke several TNC concession permits, returning them to local miners (Jacob and Pedersen 2018).

However, the hoped-for global transition to low-carbon economies and societies limits the scope for such policy and the space for an alternative model of mining-based development to materialize. As Sovacool et al. (2020: 30) have noted, 'the materials and metals demanded by a low carbon economy will be immense'. More specifically, the energy transition will be highly mineral intensive for around twenty metal commodities or 'energy transition metals' (Bainton et al. 2021). These transition metals are found in abundance in at least eleven of the seventeen mineral-rich African LICs identified in section 1.1: the DRC (cobalt and copper), Eritrea (copper), Guinea (bauxite and iron ore), Liberia (iron ore), Madagascar (cobalt, nickel, and rare earths), Malawi (rare earths), Mozambique (bauxite and rare earths), Sierra Leone (bauxite and iron ore), Tanzania (bauxite, iron ore, and rare earths), Togo (iron ore), and Uganda (iron ore).

With peak global demand for energy transition metals forecast to greatly outstrip current production (by upwards of 71 per cent, 212 per cent, and to 292 per cent in the cases of nickel, cobalt, and rare earths, respectively (Bainton et al. 2021)), there will be significant external pressure for African LICs to continue prioritizing a model of capital-intensive FOM. For labour-intensive DOM to gain greater prominence in such a context, a synthesis between el-Amami's work on 'appropriate technology' and Amin's (1990) strategy of 'delinking' would be required.

As the Tunisian agronomist and dependency theorist Slaheddine el-Amami contended, and as borne out by the findings from South Kivu, local control over technological choices within a given industry provides the basis for 'accumulation from below, a widened internal market, [and] staunching the bleeding-out of value' (Ajl 2021: 93). The lower capital intensity such local control would necessitate would also lead to greater levels of labour absorption, higher levels of domestic ownership over the means of production and strategic direction, and a less enclaved industry. Such a pursuit would require embracing Amin's strategic model of 'delinking', breaking with the demands imposed by the external global economy for capital-intensive production, and reorienting strategy and policy towards serving domestic demand and promoting popular and autonomous forms of development.

Beyond Tanzania, there are few signs of such a social structure emerging in African LICs at the current juncture. In the DRC, under the presidency of Felix Tshisekedi, efforts are centring around harnessing energy transition demand for cobalt to develop a domestic and regional electric vehicle battery value chain through the continued pursuit of capital-intensive FOM. Speaking in June 2021 at the Protestant University of Congo in Kinshasa, during a panel discussion to announce a forthcoming DRC–Africa Business Forum to promote the development of this value chain, a United Nations Economic Commission for Africa (UNECA) economist commented:

> The demand for battery minerals is soaring with the most strategic of them—cobalt, lithium, and graphite—found in great quantity in the DRC and other African countries. Why not locally transform these minerals now and develop a profitable continental market for their end products, such as electric vehicle batteries in and for Africa, before the world starts looking for their alternatives with eventual tech leaps?
>
> **(UNECA 2021)**

Here, the logics underpinning the African Mining Consensus are reproduced, given renewed purpose and urgency by the supposed opportunities presented by projected demand for metals and minerals driven by the anticipated transition to low-carbon economies. Such a reproduction will lock in place, rather than move beyond, the state–corporate alliance that, in the case of South Kivu, has functioned over the long run to suppress, rather than nurture, the developmental trajectory of labour-intensive DOM.

In South Kivu itself, the retreat of Banro towards the end of the 2010s has, nonetheless, provided the breathing space labour-intensive DOM requires to develop independently from and undisturbed by TNC interference. As noted in section 3.2, Banro delisted from the Toronto Stock Exchange (TSE) in 2018, and in March 2019, the corporation split its assets and the Chinese investment fund Baiyin International Investment acquired full control of the Twangiza mine. In August 2021, its Namoya mine in neighbouring Maniema province was sold to a firm owned by Paris-listed Auplata Mining Group. At the time of writing in late 2022, production had yet to restart at either of the two mines.

In the absence of capital-intensive FOM, the mechanization of labour-intensive DOM has recovered and advanced. With Banro's withdrawal from Kamituga, the trader-manager class was authorized by the Congolese state to reinstall their mills on all sites across the mining town. By 2021, there were more than 230 ball mills across Kamituga, representing a sharp increase from the 70 or so in use back in 2012, and all under continued Congolese ownership (Bikubanya and Radley 2022). That same year, a new processing plant was opened, using a solution of hydrogen peroxide, lime, and sodium cyanide to recover a greater volume of gold particles from the extracted ore (Nkuba et al. 2022).

Based on the findings presented in this book, it is to be hoped that the recovery of domestic ownership and control over mining industrialization strategies continues to gain momentum in the years to come. This would allow for alternative models of mining-based development to step out of the long shadows cast by foreign corporations and deliver less enclaved and more inclusive development processes in the African periphery than the currently dominant but disarticulated and disruptive TNC-led model.

Banro's financing history, 1996–2018

Year	Financing
1996	Sold 460,000 common shares (C$5 per share), 400,000 units (C$5.5 per unit), and 2 million special warrants (C$9 per warrant) for gross proceeds of C$19,540,000
1998	Sold 1.25 million special warrants (C$7 per special warrant) for gross proceeds of C$8,750,000
2001	Sold 1.2 million common shares (C$0.5 per share)—of which 600,000 purchased by co-founder, Executive Vice President and Director of Banro Arnold Kondrat—for gross proceeds of C$600,000
2002	Sold 350,000 units (C$0.7 per unit)—of which 250,000 purchased by Arnold Kondrat—for gross proceeds of C$245,000
2003	Kondrat exercises warrants to purchase a further 400,000 common shares, controlling 11.6 per cent of issued and outstanding common shares of the corporation
2004	Sold 2 million common shares (C$8 per share) for total gross proceeds of C$16,000,000
2005	Raised C$18.4 million though an investment fund managed by Capital Research and Management Company and institutional accounts managed by affiliates of Capital Group International Raised C$13 million through Canada Investment Fund for Africa, a Canadian government-financed investment fund managed by Actis Capital and Cordiant Capital
2006	Completed equity financing for total gross proceeds of C$56,012,800
2008	Completed equity financing for total gross proceeds of $21,000,000
2009	Sold 10 million common shares ($1.4 per share) to complete equity financing for total gross proceeds of $14,000,000 Sold 43,479,000 common shares (C$2.3 per share) to complete equity financing for total gross proceeds of C$100,001,700
2010	Sold 67.1 million common shares (C$2.05 per share) to complete equity financing for total gross proceeds of C$137,555,000
2011	Sold 17.5 million special warrants (C$3.25 per warrant) to complete equity financing for total gross proceeds of C$56,875,000
2012	Sold 175,000 units ($1,000 per unit) for total gross proceeds of $175 million, with a 10 per cent interest rate and a maturity date of March 2017
2013	Secured $30 million credit facilities from the Congolese bank Rawbank and the Nigerian bank Ecobank ($15 million each) at interest rates of nine per cent and 8.5 per cent, respectively Sold 50.2 million common shares (C$1.35 per share), 116,000 Series A preference shares ($25 per share), and 2.4 million Series B shares ($25 per share) to BlackRock World Mining Trust for total gross proceeds of C$67,795,156 and $32,900,000 Secured $53 million in short-term loans from several lenders
2014	Sold preferred shares to Gramercy Funds Management for total gross proceeds of $40 million Signed a forward sale transaction with Gold Holding involving the prepayment by Gold Holding of $41 million in return for 40,500 ounces of gold from the Twangiza mine, deliverable over four years

Continued

Continued

Year	Financing
2015	Signed two forward sale transactions involving the prepayment by Gramercy of $40 million in return for 44,496 ounces of gold from the Twangiza mine, deliverable over three years Signed a streaming transaction involving the prepayment by Gramercy of $50 million in return for 8.33 per cent of the life-of-mine gold production from the Namoya mine at $150 per ounce Signed a forward sale transaction involving the prepayment by the purchaser of $10 million in return for 9,508 ounces of gold from the Twangiza mine, deliverable over two years Closed a $9 million loan facility with the Congolese bank Banque Commerciale du Congo at an interest rate of 9.5 per cent Signed a forward sale transaction involving the prepayment by the purchaser of $7 million in return for 8,481 ounces of gold from the Twangiza mine, deliverable over thirty-three months
2016	Signed a streaming transaction involving the prepayment by Baiyin Nonferrous Group of $67.5 million in return for 11 per cent of the life-of-mine gold production from Twangiza at $150 per ounce, reduced by 50 per cent when total production at Twangiza reaches 1.14 million ounces Secured $22.5 million loan facility from Baiyin Nonferrous Group and Gramercy at an interest rate of 8.5 per cent Sold 50 million common shares and 2.5 million purchase warrants to Baiyin Nonferrous Group for total gross proceeds of $8.75 million Entered a gold dore purchase agreement in connection with a $10 million loan facility from Baiyin International at an interest rate of 10 per cent, under which Baiyin will purchase—at market prices—50 per cent of the gold produced by Twangiza and Namoya until the loan is repaid
2017	Underwent recapitalization to refinance $207.5 million of debt Signed a forward sale transaction involving the prepayment by Baiyin and Gramercy of $45 million in return for 51,880 ounces of gold from the Namoya mine over a thirty-six-month period

Sources: Banro Annual Information Forms 1999–2016, Banro Press Releases 1998–2017, Banro Material Change Report March 2016.

Twangiza Mining suppliers by firm and nationality, 2010–2013

Company	Nationality	Company	Nationality
A&C Cosmic Solutions	South Africa	Pumptron	South Africa
AccTech Systems	South Africa	SENET	South Africa
Apex Process and Archtech	South Africa	Shaw Controls and Softline	South Africa
Aviair Cargo	South Africa	Southern Mapping Company	South Africa
Bee Refractories	South Africa	TerraSolid	South Africa
Black & White Truck	South Africa	Three6Five Network	South Africa
CBI Electric	South Africa	Turnberry Projects	South Africa
CLM Positioning Solutions	South Africa	UTI	South Africa
Club Travel	South Africa	Waterlab	South Africa
Cochrane Products	South Africa	Freight Forwarders	Kenya
Composite Boards	South Africa	Logisol	Kenya
Consolidated Water Conditioning	South Africa	Neff Auto Spares	Kenya
Control Solutions	South Africa	Union Logistics	Kenya
DoseTech	South Africa	Amic Trading Services	UAE
Drill Equip	South Africa	Intermodal Freight Limited	UAE
Engineering Top Tech	South Africa	Sheridan	UAE
FLSmidth Krebs	South Africa	Weir Solutions	UAE
G. C. Baars and Gemcom	South Africa	Far & Wide and H. Logistics	UK
Geosearch International	South Africa	Norton Rose	UK
Geowater Applications	South Africa	Nowata Limited	UK
Goldfields Technical Security	South Africa	Como Engineers	Australia
HGF Plate Heat Exchangers	South Africa	Gekko	Australia
Jachris	South Africa	Runge Limited	Australia
Karcher	South Africa	AmiCongo	DRC
Kimtrac and Klatrade	South Africa	Forrest Group and Keyprint	DRC
Leonard Light Industries	South Africa	Comexas	Belgium
LHMartinhusen	South Africa	Promulec	Belgium
Liquid8 Internet	South Africa	IntDev	Canada
Longspear	South Africa	Knight Piesold Consulting	Canada

Continued

Continued

Company	Nationality	Company	Nationality
LTG Logistics Transport	South Africa	Afriserve	Mauritius
Lumba Projects	South Africa	Resourcing for Africa	Mauritius
Macsteel Exports	South Africa	Neelkanth Lime	Tanzania
Metago Environmental Engineers	South Africa	Tata Afrique	Tanzania
Metskill	South Africa	PC World Computers	Uganda
ModelMaker Systems	South Africa	Stone Crushing	Uganda
Morgan AM&T	South Africa	Tatva Soft	India
Netsurit	South Africa	Infocus International	Malaysia
NTN Industrial	South Africa	PK Trucks	Netherlands
Onsite Services	South Africa	Easy Travel	Rwanda

Source: Twangiza Mining procurement invoices, 2010 to 2013.

Labour productivity of mining in South Kivu

To compare the labour productivity of gold mining at SOMINKI, Twangiza, and Kadumwa, two figures were needed across each of the three fields: the amount of gold produced and the units of labour directly involved in production. For SOMINKI, firm correspondence with the Congolese government in 1997 noted gold production in 1984 of 435.5 kilograms.[1] A former SOMINKI director estimated the firm's gold sector to employ 2,100 units of labour in the 1980s (1,300 at Kamituga and 800 at Lugushwa).[2]

At Twangiza, the year 2013 was used as this was the most recent year for which comprehensive production, employment, and financial data was collected, courtesy primarily of the 2013 financial accounts of Banro's subsidiary, Twangiza Mining. The calculations contain an in-built assumption of a stable workforce, although in reality there was a degree of churning. This was most pronounced, however, during mine construction in 2010. After this point, the units of labour were relatively stable.

For the exercise, production and revenue data was triangulated across three different sources. The *Centre d'expertise, evaluation et certification* (Centre of Expertise, Evaluation and Certification, CEEC) at the Congolese Ministry of Mines declared Twangiza's 2013 production of pure gold (i.e. adjusted for impurities) at 2,499.8 kilograms. This figure corresponds to the gold sales recorded in both Twangiza Mining's 2013 financial accounts and Banro's 2013 consolidated financial statement (which also adjust for impurities).

A Banro press release noted a difference of 2,094 ounces (65.13 kilograms) between the 80,497 ounces of gold sold by Twangiza in 2013 and the 82,591 ounces of gold produced.[3] It can be inferred from this that 65.13 kilograms of gold was stockpiled rather than sold. Including this stockpiled production with the declared sales of the company, it can be deduced that, in 2013, the Twangiza mine produced 2,565.9 kilograms of gold.

For the units of labour, Twangiza Mining's 2013 financial accounts record a total of 682 workers and managers contracted to the company. In the same year, 684 workers and managers worked through subcontractors providing labour or services.[4] This gives a total of 1,366 people directly involved in the mine's productive activities.[5]

Arriving at estimates for Kadumwa was a more complex exercise due to its informal and largely undocumented mode of operation. For this, between November 2016 and June 2017, thirteen monthly production and financial logbooks were collected from a convenience-selected sample of four shaft managers, representing just less than 10 per cent of the forty-four shaft managers working at the site. The logs kept daily records of shaft production and how this production was distributed between various groups (either in kind or in monetary form). Each log was tailored to correspond to the idiosyncrasies of shaft manager systems of production sharing and distribution (each one being different), based on extended conversations

---

[1] Letter from Marrio Fiocchi, SOMINKI director, to the DRC Minister of Labour, 21 February 1997.
[2] Email correspondence with Serge Lammens, former SOMINKI director, 17 November 2017.
[3] Banro, 'Banro Announces Year End 2013 Results', Banro, 31 March 2014.
[4] Email correspondence with Twangiza Mining's Senior Human Resources Officer, 28 November 2017.
[5] This figure corresponds closely to company documentation, which shows a total of 1,402 workers and managers at Twangiza Mining in 2016 (709 contracted and 693 subcontracted).

Table A3.1 Kadumwa shaft manager logbook Number 5, January–February 2017

30 January–5 February 2017	Bags of ore				Grams of gold			
	Shaft production (a)	Worker payment	Shaft expenses	Kept by shaft manager	Shaft manager	Shaft manager grams per bag (b)	Wash Basin (c)	Total shaft pro-duction (a × b + c)
Monday	30	12	7	11	0.0	–	0.0	–
Tuesday	36	13	9	14	0.0	–	0.0	–
Wednesday	29	10	6	13	0.0	–	0.0	–
Thursday	31	11	9	11	0.0	–	0.0	–
Friday	40	18	10	12	0.0	–	0.0	–
Saturday	0	0	0	0	0.0	–	0.0	–
Sunday	0	0	0	0	5.7	–	0.0	–
TOTAL	166	64	41	61	5.7	0.09	0	15.5

Source: Author calculations based on shaft manager logbook data.

with shaft managers prior to, during, and after data collection. Despite these efforts, one log-book was excluded at the post-data collection phase as bag production data was not adequately recorded.

Table A3.1 provides a one-week summary from a shaft manager monthly logbook as an example of how the logbooks were used to estimate production levels. Beginning at the far left-hand column, total shaft production was recorded as bags of ore produced, with each bag uniform in size, containing approximately 25 kilograms of ore. During the 7-day period, the shaft produced a total of 166 bags of ore. From this production, the fourteen workers received sixty-four bags as payment in kind, and forty-one bags were used to cover shaft expenses, including worker provisions, shaft extension, and shaft repair. The remaining sixty-one bags were retained by the shaft manager, from which he produced and sold 5.7 grams of gold.

By dividing the shaft manager's bag production (5.7 grams) by the number of bags he kept (sixty-one), it can be deduced that he extracted an average of 0.09 grams per bag. It is rea-sonable to assume the same ratio of gold to ore in the remaining 105 bags, given that they were produced from the same shaft during the same time frame. Thus, multiplying the shaft manager's average grams per bag by the total number of bags produced by the shaft, total shaft production for the week can be estimated at 15.5 grams.

Before presenting the data from across the twelve shafts, four issues must be noted. First, there is a possible downward bias in the productivity estimates due to the observed tendency, in the Democratic Republic of the Congo (DRC) and elsewhere for those engaged in illicit activity to underreport the levels of this activity. To ensure as great a degree of data reliability as possible, daily levels of production and trade were often directly observed or confirmed with conversations the same or the following day, and for around half of the logbooks collected, data was cross-checked directly with the written records of shaft managers (three of the four shaft managers were already recording some, but not all, of the data in notebooks).[6]

[6] These records were not for official purposes, such as tax declarations, but rather to provide a manager with recourse to a written record of past transactions should a dispute over a particular sale or purchase arise.

Second, the productivity of labour-intensive DOM varies greatly from one site to another, depending primarily upon three factors: first, the life cycle of the site, with periods of lower productivity occurring at the beginning (when workers are looking for the auriferous rock) and towards the end (when the deposit is nearing exhaustion); second, and for the same reasons, the life cycle of a mine shaft; third, the time of year, with the wet season typically less productive than the dry season due to the increased danger and difficulty of working under the heavy rains. Two measures were adopted to control, however incompletely, for these factors: the shaft sample for the study contained a range of new, mature, and ageing shafts; and data was collected across both the wet and the dry season.

Third, as with Twangiza, the data contains an in-built assumption of a stable workforce, although there was, again, a degree of churning. The impact on productivity is likely minimal, however, as generally a departing worker (e.g. leaving to harvest his agricultural production) was replaced by a new one. Fourth, shaft managers recorded their logbook activity in Congolese Francs and *renge*, the latter a measurement derived from local traders' use of hand-held scales and old coins, whereby one *renge* is equivalent to 1.423 grams. Congolese francs and the *renge* are in common usage at Kadumwa and across South Kivu. To facilitate comparison, data was converted to, and presented in, dollars, grams, and kilograms. The dollar conversion was made using the local exchange rate in Luhwindja at the time the data was collected and thus varied across the logbooks.

Following the same procedure described for the one-week sample in Table A3.1 across the twelve-monthly logbooks indicates an estimated average monthly shaft production at the site of 108.2 grams (Table A3.2). Multiplying the average monthly shaft production

Table A3.2 Kadumwa shaft manager production data, November 2016–June 2017

Monthly log number	Bags of ore		Grams of gold			
	Shaft production (a)	Kept by shaft manager	Shaft manager bags	Shaft manager grams per bag (b)	Basin production (c)	Total shaft production ((a × b) + c)
1	354	285	154.0	0.54	13.4	204.4
2	543	310	61.7	0.20	7.7	116.0
3	197	87	11.4	0.13	1.8	27.6
4	944	479	56.9	0.12	18.5	130.7
5	730	307	29.9	0.10	12.8	83.9
6	196	97	20.6	0.21	8.5	50.2
7	385	131	27.9	0.21	40.6	122.7
8	495	193	32.9	0.17	40.6	125.1
9	280	6	1.7	0.26	21.3	94.3
10	287	103	45.4	0.44	22.8	149.3
11	252	99	25.3	0.26	0.0	64.5
12	272	103	33.6	0.33	41.3	130.0
Average monthly shaft production (grams)						108.2
Total annual shaft production (grams) (108.2 grams × 44 shafts × 12 months)						57,135.8
Total annual waste production (grams) (216 grams × 12 months)						2,592.0
Total annual site production (grams)						59,727.8

Source: Author calculations based on shaft manager logbook data.

(108.2 grams) by the number of operational shafts (forty-four) and multiplying this figure by twelve months obtains an estimated annual shaft production at Kadumwa of 57,135.8 grams (or 57.1 kilograms). Finally, gold produced by ore washers from leftover ore purchased from shaft managers must be considered. There were approximately eighty ore washers at Kadumwa, and conversations with this labour group demonstrated an estimated average daily production of 0.1 gram per ore washer or approximately 2.7 grams per month (assuming that their six-day working week was followed throughout). This equates to an additional 216 grams of production per month (2.7 grams multiplied by eighty ore washers) or 2,592 grams annually, giving a total annual site production of 59,727.8 grams (or 59.7 kilograms).

For the units of labour, through a combination of a shaft census, shaft manager logbooks, and observation on site, 762 workers and managers were estimated to be working at Kadumwa in 2017 (528 shaft workers, 44 shaft managers, 80 ore carriers, 80 ore washers, and 30 water carriers). For shaft workers, the largest group, the average number of workers per shaft across the manager logbooks was eleven, ranging from nine to thirteen. From observation, shaft managers were generally managing teams of 8–15 shaft workers and so, together with the logbook data, an average of 12 workers per shaft was used to arrive at the estimated total for the site of 528 shaft workers (12 workers multiplied by 44 shafts). The number of shaft managers was taken from the shaft census, which indicated a total of forty-four operational shafts at the mine. The remaining categories of water carriers, ore carriers, and ore washers were estimated based on observation and conversations with members of each respective group.

With production and labour data from 1984 for SOMINKI, 2013 for Twangiza, and 2017 for Kadumwa, the 2017 average gold price on the London Gold Fixing of $40.42 per gram was used to facilitate comparison.[7] The resultant labour productivity data is presented in Table 5.2.

---

[7] This annual average was obtained from the World Gold Council at http://www.gold.org/research/download-the-gold-price-since-1978 (accessed 23 February 2018).

Worker wages and trader–manager profits at Kadumwa

A 'bottom-up' methodology was used to determine worker wages and trader–manager profits at Kadumwa. Beginning with site workers at the bottom of the labour hierarchy, water carriers earned 250 Congolese francs (or $0.2) per 20-litre can of water carried, with each worker carrying between four and six cans a day. Taking five cans as the average daily labour performed by a water carrier, a water carrier's daily wage can be estimated as one dollar. Ore carriers earned 500FC ($0.4) for each bag of ore carried, with each worker carrying between five and six bags a day. Taking five bags as the average daily labour performed by an ore carrier, an ore carrier's daily wage can be estimated as two dollars. Ore washer wages were more variable as it depended upon the availability and quality of the leftover ore, but interviews and conversations with this group reported daily wages of between 1,000 and 5,000 Congolese francs (around $1–4) a day per worker. From this, an average daily wage of $2.5 was taken. Based on Kadumwa's six-day working week (or twenty-seven days per month), the average monthly wages of water carriers, ore carriers, and ore washers can be estimated as $27, $54, and $67.5, respectively.

To estimate shaft worker wages, shaft manager logbooks were used. The logbooks recorded the monetary and in-kind payments made by managers to workers. Combining the data across the thirteen monthly logbooks generated an estimated average monthly wage of $163 per worker (with considerable variation from month to month) or $1,956 per year (Table A4.1).

To estimate shaft manager profits, first, the value created by each shaft can be determined by combining the shaft production data presented in Appendix 3 with the average recorded selling price obtained by shaft managers at Kadumwa of $31.21 per gram (see Table 6.4). From this figure, expenditure on worker wages, rent, and taxes were subtracted to determine profit levels. With worker wages already estimated, the rent accruing to local landowners was calculated from a combination of the monthly logbooks and extended conversations with shaft managers upon their completion. For taxes, local government authorities collected 3,600FC ($3) per shaft per week in official taxation, and analysis of Luhwindja's 2016 annual budget confirmed the entrance of this tax into the official finances of the local treasury. In addition, every Wednesday, two or three policemen came to collect 1,000FC ($0.8) per shaft for the Congolese national police division stationed in Luhwindja. Every Friday, a battalion of the Congolese national army stationed in Luhwindja came to collect 3,000FC ($2.5) per shaft, and Comité des creuseurs artisanaux de Luhwindja (CCALU)—the local miners' committee of Luhwindja—collected the same amount. The resultant calculation gives estimated average monthly profits for shaft managers of $1,379 or $16,549 per year (Table A4.2).

From here, the additional profits shaft managers generated by engaging in gold trade must be considered. Drawing on the buying and selling prices recorded in the monthly logbooks, shaft manager trading activity increased their average monthly profits by $295, from $1,379 to $1,674 per month or from $16,549 to $20,083 annually (Table A4.3).

To determine the profits made by traders, fourteen monthly financial logbooks were collected across a convenience-selected sample of eight traders. Six of these were local or small traders buying on site at Kadumwa, representing around 20 per cent of the estimated thirty or so traders operating at the site. The remaining two were from the group of seven Bukavu-based

Table A4.1 Kadumwa shaft worker monthly wages, November 2016–June 2017 (USD)

Monthly log number	Payment in kind ($)	Monetary payment ($)	Total wages ($) (a)	Workers (b)	Wages per unit ($) (a/b)
1	932	3,460	4,392	9	488
2	1,355	1,511	2,866	9	318
3	419	236	655	9	73
4	1,051	0	1,051	12	88
5	934	0	934	14	67
6	575	0	575	12	48
7	1,061	808	1,868	10	187
8	1,083	0	1,083	8	135
9	1,714	510	2,224	12	185
10	1,834	560	2,394	12	200
11	938	0	938	12	78
12	1,267	543	1,809	12	151
13	0	834	834	8	104
AVERAGE MONTHLY WAGES					163
AVERAGE ANNUAL WAGES					1,956

Notes: The far left-hand column records the value of the share of in-kind production received by the shaft workers in bags, based on the grams per bag data presented in Table A3.2 and the recorded buying price offered by the shaft manager, who buys the gold from his workers. The next column along records the monetary wages received by shaft workers, and the final column on the far right-hand side the wages received per worker (dividing the total wages by the number of workers).
Source: Author calculations based on shaft manager logbook data.

Table A4.2 Kadumwa shaft manager production profits, November 2016–June 2017 (USD)

Monthly logbook number	Value created (a)	Worker wages (b)	Rent (c)	Taxes (d)				Profits (a – b – c – d)
				Government	Army	Police	CCALU	
1	6,379	4,566	128	14	11	4	11	1,645
2	3,620	2,994	73	14	11	4	11	514
3	861	740	0	14	11	4	11	82
4	4,079	1,194	0	14	11	4	11	2,845
5	2,619	1,009	0	14	11	4	11	1,570
6	1,567	687	0	14	11	4	11	840
7	3,829	2,023	192	14	11	4	11	1,575
8	3,904	1,231	195	14	11	4	11	2,438
9	2,943	2,368	147	14	11	4	11	388
10	4,660	2,488	233	14	11	4	11	1,899
11	2,013	1,029	101	14	11	4	11	844
12	4,057	1,906	203	14	11	4	11	1,908
AVERAGE MONTHLY PROFITS								1,379
AVERAGE ANNUAL PROFITS								16,549

Notes: Wages were taken from a combination of the shaft worker wage data presented in Table A4.1 and the wages paid by shaft managers to water and ore carriers, as recorded in the monthly logbooks.
Source: Author calculations based on shaft manager logbook data.

Table A4.3 Kadumwa shaft manager trading profits, November 2016–June 2017 (USD)

Monthly log number	Shaft profits (a)	Trading profits			Total profits (a + b)
		Workers' share of production	Manager's share of production	Total (b)	
1	1,645	93	225	319	1,964
2	514	271	181	451	965
3	82	41	0	41	123
4	2,845	0	0	0	2,845
5	1,570	0	0	0	1,570
6	840	0	0	0	840
7	1,575	338	82	419	1,994
8	2,438	375	96	471	2,909
9	388	482	5	486	874
10	1,899	440	160	599	2,498
11	844	210	89	299	1,143
12	1,908	331	118	449	2,357
AVERAGE MONTHLY	1,379	–	–	295	1,674
AVERAGE ANNUAL	16,549	–	–	3,534	20,083

Notes: In monthly log number 3, no profit was made from the shaft manager's production as he sold this to a local trader due to personal circumstances preventing him from travelling to Bukavu as he had planned. In months 4, 5, and 6, no trading profits were recorded as the shaft manager in question had an oral agreement to sell all his own and his workers' gold to another manager who had helped finance his shaft construction. Many such agreements exist. In monthly logs 7–12, for example, the trading profits made by shaft managers include the purchase of other workers' production.
Source: Author calculations based on shaft manager logbook data.

traders buying most of the gold produced at Kadumwa (and across Luhwindja). Kadumwa traders provided eleven of the fourteen logs and Bukavu traders the remaining three. The logs kept daily records of how much gold a trader bought and sold and the corresponding buying and selling price.

For the Kadumwa traders, conversations prior to data collection revealed gold trading transactions to be more uniform and less complex than the distribution of production overseen by shaft managers, and so each trader completed a standardized log template based on these transactions. For the Bukavu traders, data was taken directly from their bookkeeping, which kept daily records of the weight and price per gram of each purchase and sale. As with shaft managers and traders, conversations were held at the end of each month of collected data to check for inconsistencies and clarify any ambiguities. The monthly profits recorded by six local traders at Kadumwa were similar to those made by shaft managers from their trade, with an average of $395 recorded across the eleven monthly trader logbooks (Table A4.4).

While only three logbooks were collected from the big traders in Bukavu, both the logbooks and conversations and interviews with the group suggested that each month they traded anything from one to several kilograms of gold, making up to several thousand dollars of monthly profits. In addition, and as mentioned in the main text, most Bukavu-based traders also owned and managed several shafts in Luhwindja or the surrounding area, providing them with a further source of profit.

Table A4.4 Kadumwa local trader profits, November 2016–June 2017 (USD)

Monthly log number	Grams bought	Profits ($)
1	44.6	161
2	29.0	141
3	30.4	160
4	92.8	246
5	39.5	121
6	52.0	296
7	88.0	423
8	35.7	322
9	21.4	254
10	409.0	1,811
11	229.5	407
AVERAGE	97.4	395

Notes: To determining profits, transport and accommodation costs incurred travelling to and from Bukavu have been deducted.
Source: Author calculations based on trader logbook data.

The wage data for site and shaft workers are presented in Table 5.3 as a point of comparison against worker wages at Twangiza, while all wage and profit data for workers, managers, and traders are presented in Table 6.3.

Twangiza wage distribution, 2017

To determine the distribution of wages to labour at Twangiza, employment at the mine was divided into three main categories: hired labour, subcontractor workers, and Twangiza Mining employees. The first category of hired labour comprised three Congolese labour hire firms: Cinamula, Diphil, and Zuki. The second category of subcontractor workers comprised eleven subcontractor firms, two of which were domestic (Premium, providing sand, and Group Rubuye, providing drilling activities) and nine foreign: Société Générale de Surveillance (gold certification), Savannah (aviation), COMEXAS Group (customs), Aggreko (power), Tsebo Outsourcing Group (catering), Civicon (road maintenance), G4S (security), Rubuye (drilling), and Simba Logistics (transportation).[1] The third category comprised Banro's subsidiary, Twangiza Mining.

For Twangiza Mining, the subsidiary's 2013 financial accounts provided a detailed breakdown of the number of employees by category. For hired labour and subcontractor workers, a subcontractor survey and subcontractor manager and director interviews determined the total units of labour working across the fourteen firms, along with the relative weighting between different groups (workers, managers, and directors). Taken together, the survey and interviews gave an estimated total of 724 employed as hired labour or subcontracted workers or managers at Twangiza Mining in 2017. This aligns with the 693 subcontracted workers and managers documented by Banro at Twangiza Mining in 2016,[2] but is 40 more than the 684 recorded in the subsidiary's 2013 financials and used to determine the site's productivity in Appendix 3. To equate the two sets of data, the figure of 724 employed in 2017 was revised down proportionally across each firm and group to reflect the 684 recorded in 2013 (Table A5.1).

Next, with the employment data determined, the wages received by each group within and across the three categories was assessed. Twangiza Mining payrolls and worker and manager payslips from 2012 and 2013 corresponded precisely to an internal corporate document listing worker and manager classification and wages for 2016, and so this corporate document was used for assessing wage distribution. The classification included multiple wage levels within each worker or manager group.[3] As the exact distribution of employees across these sub-groupings was unknown, the median wage within each group was taken. Wages for foreign Twangiza Mining managers were doubled to reflect the fact that these groups received their salary payment twice, once in-country and once to a foreign bank account, most often in their home country (as explained in section 5.2). For director wages, which weren't included in the corporate document, the publicly available annual wage earned by the equivalent position of a director of the subsidiary Banro Congo was taken.[4] For hired labour and subcontracted employment, in the absence of company documentation, wage data was collected through a firm survey, firm manager and director interviews, a labour survey, and interviews and conversations with workers. The data was then collated and triangulated to produce an average group wage for each category. The resultant data is presented in Table 5.4.

[1] The subcontracting firms Rand Refinery and Engen, presented in the subcontractor overview in section 4.3, are not included here as neither had staff assigned specifically to the Twangiza mine.
[2] Banro, 'Banro Employment Creation, Direct and Indirect', internal company documentation, 2016.
[3] For instance, there were nine levels of manager and director classification and wage remuneration.
[4] Morning Star, http://www.morningstar.com (accessed 13 January 2017).

Table A5.1 Twangiza Mining subcontractor employment, 2013

Category	Company	Group			TOTAL
		Workers	Managers	Directors	
Hired labour	Cinamula	108	6	1	115
	Zuki	104	5	1	110
	Diphil	99	5	1	104
Subtotal hired labour		311	15	3	329
Subcontractor	G4S	125	13	1	139
	Tsebo Outsourcing Group	60	9	1	70
	Simba Logistics	48	11	1	60
	Civicon	20	3	1	24
	Groupe Rubuye	10	4	1	15
	Premium	12	2	1	15
	Société Générale de Surveillance	11	3	0	14
	COMEXAS Group	8	3	1	12
	Aggreko	3	1	1	5
	Savannah	0	1	0	1
Subcontractor total		297	50	8	355
TOTAL		608	65	11	684

Source: Subcontractor survey, subcontractor manager, and director interviews.

Estimating the buying price at Luhwindja, 2017

Estimations of the buying price of gold within South Kivu's value chain, from the local level of the Kadumwa mine through to the near-final buyers in Dubai, were generated through interviews and conversations with gold traders and refineries, alongside trader bookkeeping records and financial logbooks. The results of this exercise, using the 2017 average gold price of $40.42 per gram, are presented in Figure A6.1.[1] The appearance of the tola in this figure requires explanation. As Geenen (2014: 233) has detailed, the tola:

> was in use in British India, as well as in Zanzibar, from where it spread over the whole of eastern Africa to measure gold and silver. In Bukavu, the tola is the measure of reference and prices are usually expressed in USD per tola, which is equal to 11.664 grams (rounded).

Here, buying prices have been converted into grams to facilitate comparison.

While the data presented in Figure A6.1 are representative of gold trade calculations in Kadumwa's production network and present the formulas in most common usage, they fail to capture the nuances and variations inherent to this trade. Other, often less convoluted, formulas were used in Bukavu, but the final buying price arrived at only varies from the formula presented by a few percentage points (although, of course, this is still significant when trading in large volumes).[2]

At Kadumwa, however, there is more variation, for three reasons. First, some local traders didn't follow the London Gold Fixing at all but rather the buying price they heard others using. Second, after running calculations based on the London Gold Fixing, some made a further reduction to account for expenses, where the basis for determining the amount to be reduced was unspecified and variable. Third, many described the commonly used system at Kadumwa known as 'the lottery', whereby the gold was bought from workers in such small quantities that it wasn't measured at all, but an offer of a few or several dollars was made by a trader based on a visual assessment alone.

At this most local level of purchase, then, the general tendency was to arrive at a non-formulaic and non-standardized buying price. This suggested, first, the possibility for variance in the site-level buying price offered by different traders on the same day and, second, the possibility for a lower buying price than the one indicated by the calculation presented in Figure A6.1. Looking at the eleven monthly logs provided by Kadumwa traders confirms these impressions as the average buying price was 14.6 per cent lower than the average selling price at Bukavu (Table A6.1). This difference is significantly greater than the 5.1 per cent difference resulting from the formula presented in Figure A6.1 (between a buying price of $34.71 and a selling price of $36.55).

---

[1] This figure owes a debt of gratitude to Geenen's (2014: 232) doctoral thesis, for which she conducted a similar exercise based on a generic example of South Kivu's gold value chain.

[2] For instance, one Bukavu trader explained that to calculate his buying price for Luhwindja gold, which he knew to be of approximately 97 per cent purity, he simply divided the London Fixing by 24 and then divided again by 1.423 (to convert the price from renge to grams). Based on the 2017 gold price of $40.42 per gram (or $1,257 per troy ounce), this gave a buying price of $36.81, $0.22 higher than the more commonly used formulas.

Group	Buying Price (per gram)		Explanation
Golden and Jewellery Refinery, UAE	$1,257–6	= $1,251	Convention using London Gold Fixing
	$1,251/31.1035	= $40.22	1 troy ounce = 31.1035 grams
	$40.22 × 0.97	= **$39.01 buying price**	Luhwindja gold = 97% purity
Mines Propres Refinery, DRC	$1,257/2.845	= $441.83	Convention using London Gold Fixing
	$441.83/95.5	= $4.63	Convention
	$4.63 × 97	= $448.77	Luhwindja gold = 97% purity
	$448.77/11.664	= **$38.47 buying price**	1 tola = 11.664 grams
Bukavu Traders, DRC	$1,257/2.845	= $441.83	Convention using London Gold Fixing
	$441.83/95.5	= $4.63	Convention
	$4.63 × 97	= $448.77	Luhwindja gold = 97% purity
	$44.77–5%	= $426.33	Factoring weight loss on sale
	$426.33/11.664	= **$36.55 buying price**	1 tola = 11.664 grams
Luhwindja Traders, DRC	$1,257/25.45	= $49.39	Convention using London Gold Fixing
	$49.39/1.423	= **$34.71 buying price**	1 renge = 1.423 grams

Figure A6.1 Kadumwa production network, buying price formulas

Note: Prices based on London Gold Fixing of $1,257 per troy ounce/$40.42 per gram.
Source: Author calculations based on refinery and trader interviews, trader bookkeeping records, and trader financial logs.

Table A6.1 Kadumwa gold trader buying and selling
prices, November 2016–June 2017 (USD)

Monthly logbook number	Difference between buying and selling price	
	$	%
1	4.75	14.7
2	5.80	16.5
3	2.87	9.1
4	3.33	10.3
5	7.82	20.7
6	6.73	17.1
7	7.39	18.4
8	4.03	11.5
9	3.51	10.0
10	6.25	17.7
11	5.26	15.0
AVERAGE	5.25	14.6

Source: Trader financial logbooks and bookkeeping records.

The buying price offered to miners by Kadumwa traders should, then, be adjusted down
to reflect the average 14.6 per cent difference recorded by the financial logs, which are more
sensitive to the variation and nuances of site-level buying price practices than the formulaic
expression. This gives the revised buying price of $31.21 per gram used in Table 6.4. Support-
ing the downward adjustment, this revised price correlates more closely than the formulaic
buying price of $34.71 per gram to the average buying price recorded across the eleven Kad-
umwa trader logs (collected across a similar period from November 2016 to June 2017) of
$30.11 per gram.

Bibliography

Addison, T. and A. Roe (2018) *The Management of Resources as a Driver of Sustainable Development*. Oxford: Oxford University Press.

AfDB (African Development Bank) (2013) *African Economic Outlook 2013: Structural Transformation and Natural Resources*. Paris: African Development Bank.

AfDB (2016) *Creating Local Content for Human Development in Africa's New Natural Resource-Rich Countries*. Flagship Report Paper Series No. 6. Paris: African Development Bank.

Ajl, M. (2021) 'The Hidden Legacy of Samir Amin: Delinking's Ecological Foundation', *Review of African Political Economy* 48(167): 82–101.

Akyüz, Y. (2017) *Playing with Fire: Deepened Financial Integration and Changing Vulnerabilities of the Global South*. Oxford: Oxford University Press.

AllAfrica (2017) 'Uganda: Mines Director Katto Orders All Illegal Artisanal Miners Out of Mines', 3 November, http://allafrica.com/stories/201711040012.html (accessed 15 December 2017).

Alobo Loison, S. (2015) 'Rural Livelihood Diversification in Sub-Saharan Africa: A Literature Review', *Journal of Development Studies* 51(9): 1125–1138.

Amin, S. (1972) 'Underdevelopment and Dependence in Black Africa: Origins and Contemporary Forms', *Journal of Modern African Studies* 10(4): 503–524.

Amin, S. (1990) *Delinking: Towards a Polycentric World*. London: Zed Books.

Amin, S. (2011) *Global History: A View from the South*. London: Pambazuka.

Amsden, A. (1989) *Asia's Next Giant: South Korea and Late Industrialisation*. Oxford: Oxford University Press.

Andreasson, S. (2015) 'Varieties of Resource Nationalism in Sub-Saharan Africa's Energy and Minerals Markets', *The Extractive Industries and Society* 2: 310–319.

Andreoni, A. and F. Sial (2020) 'Not Business as Usual: The Development of Tanzanian Diversified Business Groups (DBGs) under Different Regimes of Capitalist Accumulation', Anti-Corruption Evidence (ACE) Research Consortium Working Paper No. 22. London: School of Oriental and African Studies.

AU (African Union) (2009) *Africa Mining Vision*. Addis Ababa: African Union.

AU (African Union) (2015) *Agenda 2063: The Africa We Want*. Addis Ababa: African Union.

Bafilemba, F. and S. Lezhnev (2015) *Congo's Conflict Gold Rush: Bringing Gold into the Legal Trade in the Democratic Republic of Congo*. Washington, DC: The Enough Project.

Bainton, N., D. Kemp, E. Lèbrel, J.R. Owen, and G. Marston (2021) 'The Energy-Extractives Nexus and the Just Transition', *Sustainable Development* 29(4): 624–634.

Banchirigah, S.M. (2006) 'How Have Reforms Fuelled the Expansion of Artisanal Mining? Evidence from Sub-Saharan Africa', *Resources Policy* 31: 165–171.

Banchirigah, S.M. and G. Hilson (2010) 'De-agrarianization, Re-agrarianization and Local Economic Development: Re-orientating Livelihoods in African Artisanal Mining Communities', *Policy Sciences* 43(2): 157–180.

Banro (2009) 'Banro Acquires Refurbished Process Plant to Fast Track Gold Production at Its Twangiza Project', press release, 13 August.

Banro (2010a) 'Banro Ships Gold Plant from Australia and Signs Milestone Agreements with Luhwindja Community and the Artisanal Miners at Twangizza', press release, 16 June.

Banro (2010b) *Twangiza Mining Policy and Procedures Manuel: Procurement & Stores*. Toronto: Banro Corporation.

Banro (2014) *'Banro Announces Year End 2013 Results'*, 31 March. Toronto: Banro Corporation.

Banro (2016a) *Annual Information Form*. Toronto: Banro Corporation.

Banro (2016b) *'Banro Employment Creation, Direct and Indirect'*, internal company documentation. Toronto: Banro Corporation.

Banro (2018a) *'Banro Announces Intention to Proceed with Recapitalization Plan'*, press release, March, http://sedar.com (accessed 27 June 2023); https://www.newswire.ca/news-releases/banro-announces-intention-to-proceed-with-recapitalization-plan-675809993.html.

Banro (2018b) *'Banro Announces Effectiveness of Its Recapitalization Plan'*, press release, May, http://sedar.com (accessed 27 June 2023); https://www.newswire.ca/news-releases/banro-announces-effectiveness-of-its-recapitalization-plan-and-intent-to-terminate-registration-under-securities-exchange-act-of-1934-with-the-us-securities-and-exchange-commission-681676581.html.

Bates, R. (1981) *Markets and States in Tropical Africa: The Political Basis of Agricultural Policies*. Berkeley and Los Angeles, CA: University of California.

Behuria, P. (2019) *'African Development and the Marginalisation of Domestic Capitalists'*, Working Paper No. 115. Manchester: Global Development Institute.

Bernstein, H. (2007) 'Capitalism and Moral Economy: Land Questions for Sub-Saharan Africa', Global Poverty Research Group and Brooks World Poverty Institute Conference Paper. Manchester: University of Manchester.

Bezuidenhout, A. and S. Buhlungu (2011) 'From Compounded to Fragmented Labour: Mineworkers and the Demise of Compounds in South Africa', *Antipode* 43(2): 237–263.

Bezy, F. (1957) *Problèmes structurels de l'économie Congolaise*. Louvain: Editions E. Nauwelaerts.

Bezy, F., J.P. Peemans, and J.M. Wautelet (1981) *Accumulation et sous-dévéloppement au Zaire 1960–1980*. Louvain-la-Neuve: Presses Universitaires de Louvain.

Biesheuvel, T., W. Clowes, and F. Njini (2019) 'The Fight between African Governments is Just Getting Started', *Bloomberg*, 14 February, https://www.bloomberg.com/news/articles/2019-02-14/the-fight-between-miners-and-african-governments-is-just-getting-started (accessed 15 August 2022).

Bikubanya, D. and B. Radley (2022) 'Productivity and Profitability: Investigating the Economic Impact of Gold Mining Mechanisation in Kamituga', *DR Congo, The Extractive Industries and Society* 12. https://doi.org/10.1016/j.exis.2022.101162.

Bishakabalya, K.B.P. (1995) 'La commercialisation de l'or à Bukavu et l'économie du Sud-Kivu', Masters thesis. Bukavu: Université Catholique de Bukavu.

Bisharhwa, M. (1982) 'Luhwindja, une chefferie agitée (1903–1969)', Masters thesis. Bukavu: Institut superieur pedagogique de Bukavu.

Blair, E. (2016) 'Eritrea Looks to Bild Mining Sector to Kickstart Economy', 26 February, http://www.reuters.com/article/us-eritrea-mining/eritrea-looks-to-build-mining-sector-to-kick-start-economy-idUSKCN0VZ13S (accessed 12 August 2021).

Bloch, R. and G. Owusu (2012) 'Linkages in Ghana's Gold Mining Industry: Challenging the Enclave Thesis', *Resources Policy* 37(4): 434–442.

Blomstrom, M. and A. Kokko (2007) 'From Natural Resources to High-Tech Production: The Evolution of Industrial Competitiveness in Sweden and Finland', in D. Lederman and W.F. Maloney (eds) *Natural Resources: Neither Curse nor Destiny*. Washington, DC: World Bank, pp. 213–256.

Boianovsky, M. (2013) 'The Economic Commission for Latin America and the 1950s' Debate on Choice of Techniques', *Review of Political Economy* 25(3): 373–398.

Bokondu, G., J. Mpolesha, and D. Tshimena (2015) *Analyse et potential de croissance des revenus du secteur minier en RDC*. Kinshasa: Deutsche Gesellschaft fur Internationale Zusammenarbeit.

Bolt, M. and D. Rajak (2016) 'Introduction: Labour, Insecurity and Violence in South Africa', *Journal of Southern African Studies* 42(5): 797–813.

Botin, J.A. (2009) *Sustainable Management of Mining Operations*. Littleton: Society for Mining, Metallurgy, and Exploration.

Bryceson, D.F. (1996) 'Deagrarianisation and Rural Employment in Sub-Saharan Africa: A Sectoral Perspective', *World Development* 24(1): 97–111.

Bryceson, D.F. (1999) 'African Rural Labour, Income Diversification and Livelihood Approaches: A Long-Term Development Perspective', *Review of African Political Economy* 26(80): 171–189.

Bryceson, D.F. and E. Fisher (2014) 'Artisanal Mining's Democratising Directions and Deviations', in D.F. Bryceson, E. Fisher, J.B. Jønsson, and R. Mwaipopo (eds) *Mining and Social Transformation in Africa: Mineralising and Democratising Trends in Artisanal Production*. London: Routledge, pp. 179–206.

Bryceson, D.F. and J.B. Jønsson (2010) 'Gold Digging Careers in Rural East Africa: Small-Scale Miners' Livelihood Choices', *World Development* 38(3): 379–392.

Bryceson, D.F. and J.B. Jønsson (2014) 'Mineralising Africa and Artisanal Mining's Democratising Influence', in D.F. Bryceson, E. Fisher, J.B. Jønsson, and R. Mwaipopo (eds) *Mining and Social Transformation in Africa: Mineralising and Democratising Trends in Artisanal Production*. London: Routledge, pp. 1–22.

Buraye, J.K., N. Stoop, and M. Verpoorten (2017) 'Defusing the Social Minefield of Gold Sites in Kamituga, South Kivu: From Legal Pluralism to the Re-making of Institutions?', *Resources Policy* 53: 356–368.

Bush, R. (2010) 'Conclusion: Mining, Dispossession and Transformation in Africa', in A. Fraser and M. Larmer (eds) *Zambia, Mining and Neoliberalism*. New York: Palgrave Macmillan, pp. 237–268.

Byres, T.J. (1996) *Capitalism from Above and Capitalism from Below: An Essay in Comparative Political Economy*. Basingstoke: Macmillan.

Calvo, G., A. Valero, and A. Valero (2019) 'How Can Strategic Metals Drive the Economy? Tungsten and Tin Production in Spain during Periods of War', *The Extractive Industries and Society* 6: 8–14.

Campbell, B. (2008) 'Regulation and Legitimacy in the Mining Industry in Africa: Where Does Canada Stand?', *Review of African Political Economy* 35(117): 367–385.

Cardoso, F.H. (1977) 'The Consumption of Dependency Theory in the United States', *Latin American Research Review* 12(3): 7–24.

Cardoso, F.H. and E. Faletto (1979) *Dependency and Development in Latin America*. Los Angeles, CA: University of California Press.

Carisch, E. (2014) *Congo's Golden Web: Countries That Profit from the Illegal Trade in Congolese Gold*. Johannesburg: Southern Africa Resource Watch.

The Carter Center (2017) *Improving Governance of Revenues from the Mining Industry*. Kinshasa: The Carter Center.

Cartier, L.E. and M. Bürge (2011) 'Agriculture and Artisanal Gold Mining in Sierra Leone: Alternatives or Complements?', *Journal of International Development* 23: 1080–1099.

Chachage, C.S. (1995) 'The Meek Shall Inherit the Earth But Not the Mining Rights: Mining and Accumulation in Tanzania', in P. Gibbon (ed.) *Liberalised Development in Tanzania*. Uppsala: Institute for African Studies, pp. 37–108.

Chang, H.J. (2004) 'The Market, the State and Institutions in Economic Development', in H.J. Chang (ed.) *Rethinking Development Economics*. London: Anthem Press, pp. 41–60.

Chang, H.J., J. Løhr, and M. Irfan (2016) *Transformative Industrial Policy for Africa*. Addis Ababa: United Nations Economic Commission for Africa.

Cheru, F. (1992) 'Structural Adjustment, Primary Resource Trade and Sustainable Development in Sub-Saharan Africa', *World Development* 20(4): 497–512.

Chirishungu Chiza, D. (2008) *Renaissance de la Republique Democratique du Congo et métamorphose économique et social du Sud-Kivu*. Kinshasa: Bushiru.

CIFA (2005) 'Actis and Cordiant Make Their First Investment in Democratic Republic of the Congo', press release, 7 November.

CIFA (2006) 'Final Closing of US$212 Million Canada Investment Fund for Africa', press release, 28 July.

Collier, P. and A. Hoeffler (2002) 'Greed and Grievance in Civil War', World Bank Policy Research Working Paper No. 2355. Washington, DC: World Bank.

Congo Research Group (2019) *The CNPSC Rebellion: Social Marginalization and State Complicity in South Kivu*. New York: Congo Research Group.

Cornish, F. (2020) 'Communicative Generalisation: Dialogical Means of Advancing Knowledge through a Case Study of an "Unprecedented" Disaster', *Culture & Psychology* 26(1): 78–95.

Cramer, C., J. Sender, and A. Oqubay (2020) *African Economic Development: Evidence, Theory, Policy*. Oxford: Oxford University Press.

Crawford, G. and G. Botchwey (2016) 'Foreign Involvement in Small-Scale Mining in Ghana and its Impact on Resource Fairness', in M. Pichler, C. Staritz, K. Küblböck, C. Plank, W. Raza, F.R. Peyré (eds) *Fairness and Justice in Natural Resource Politics*. Routledge: London and New York, pp. 181–199.

Cuvelier, J. and T. Raeymaekers (2002) *Supporting the War Economy in the DRC: European Companies and the Coltan Trade*. Antwerp: International Peace Information Service.

De Failly, D. (2001) 'Coltan: Pour Comprendre . . .', in S. Marysse and F. Reyntjens (eds) *L'Afrique des Grands Lacs. Annuaire 2000–2001*. Paris: L'Harmattan, pp. 279–306.

Deneault, A., D. Abadie and W. Sacher (2008) *Noir Canada: Pillage, corruption et criminalité en Afrique*. Montreal: Editions Ecosociété.

De Putter, T. and S. Decrée (2013) 'Le potential minier de la RDC: Mythes et composantes d'une dynamique minière', in S. Marysse and J. Omasombo Tshonda (eds) *Conjonctures Congolaises 2012: Politique, secteur minier et gestion des ressources naturelles en RD Congo*. Paris: L'Harmattan, pp. 47–62.

Dessertine, A. (2016) 'From Pickaxes to Metal Detectors: Gold Mining Mobility and Space in Upper Guinea, Guinea Conakry', *The Extractive Industries and Society* 3: 435–441.

Domenech, J. (2008) 'Mineral Resource Abundance and Regional Growth in Spain, 1860–2000', *Journal of International Development* 20(8): 1122–1135.

Dunning, J.H. and S.M. Lundan (2008) *Multinational Enterprises and the Global Economy*. Cheltenham and Northampton: Edward Elgar Publishing.

Dziwornu, A. (2018) 'Scale, Local Content and the Challenges of Ghanaians Employment in the Oil and Gas Industry', *Geoforum* 96: 181–189.

Edwards, Z. (2020) 'Applying the Black Radical Tradition: Class, Race, and a New Foundation for Studies of Development', in B. Eiden and M. McCarthy (eds) *Rethinking Class and Social Difference*. Bingley: Emerald Publishing, pp. 155–183.

EITI (Extractive Industries Transparency Initiative) (2011) 'Tanzania Extractive Industries Transparency Initiative', Final Report. Thame: EITI.

EITI (2015) 'Rapport de réconciliation des paiements effectués par les industries extractives à l'Etat Malagasy et des recettes perçues par l'Etat Malagasy Exercice 2012', Thame: EITI.

Empain Group (n.d.) 'Archives Summary', Tervuren Museum, http://www.africamuseum.be/sites/default/files/media/docs/research/collections/archives/archives-empain-bck.pdf (accessed 17 August 2021).

Engels, B. (2022) 'Income Opportunities for Many or Development through State Revenues? Contested Narratives on Mining', *Critical African Studies*. https://doi.org/10.1080/
21681392.2022.2133732.

Engels, B. and K. Dietz (2017) *Contested Extractivism, Society and the State: Struggles over
Mining and Land*. London: Palgrave Macmillan.

Englebert, P. (2014) 'Democratic Republic of Congo: Growth for All? Challenges and Opportunities for a New Economic Future', Working Paper No. 6. Johannesburg: The Brenthurst
Foundation.

Esteves, A.M., B. Coyne, and A. Moreno (2013) *Local Content Initiatives: Enhancing the Subna-
tional Benefits of the Oil, Gas and Mining Sectors*. New York: Natural Resource Governance
Institute Briefing.

Evans, P. (1995) *Embedded Autonomy: States and Industrial Transformation*. Chichester:
Princeton University Press.

Farole, T. and D. Winkler (2014) *Making Foreign Direct Investment Work for Sub-Saharan
Africa: Local Spillovers and Competitiveness in Global Value Chains*. Washington, DC:
World Bank.

Fine, B. (2008) 'The Minerals–Energy Complex is Dead: Long Live the MEC?', Paper presented to Amandla Colloquium. Cape Town: Amandla Colloquium.

Fischer, A.M. (2014) *The Disempowered Development of Tibet in China: A Study in the
Economics of Marginalization*. Plymouth: Lexington Books.

Fischer, A.M. (2015) 'The End of Peripheries? On the Enduring Relevance of Structuralism
for Understanding Contemporary Global Development', *Development and Change* 46(4):
700–732.

Flyvbjerg, B. (2006) 'Five Misunderstandings about Case-Study Research', *Qualitative Inquiry*
12(2): 219–245.

Fritz, M., J. McQuilken, N. Collins, and F. Weldegiorgis (2018) *Global Trends in Artisanal and
Small-Scale Mining (ASM): A Review of Key Numbers and Issues*. Winnipeg: International
Institute for Sustainable Development.

Furtado, C. (1983) *Accumulation and Development: The Logic of Industrial Civilization*.
Oxford: Martin Robertson.

Garrett, N. and M. Lintzer (2010) 'Can Katanga's Mining Sector Drive Growth and Development in the DRC?', *Journal of Eastern African Studies* 4(3): 400–424.

Garrett, N. and H. Mitchell (2009) *Trading Conflict for Development: Utilising the Trade
in Minerals from Eastern DR Congo for Development*. London: Resource Consulting
Services.

Geenen, S. (2011) 'Local Livelihoods, Global Interests and the State in the Congolese Mining
Sector', in A. Ansoms and S. Marysse (eds) *Natural Resources and Local Livelihoods in the
Great Lakes Region of Africa: A Political Economy Perspective*. London: Palgrave Macmillan,
pp. 149–169.

Geenen, S. (2014) 'The Political Economy of Access to Gold Mining and Trade in South Kivu,
DRC', PhD thesis. Antwerp: University of Antwerp.

Geenen, S. (2015) *African Artisanal Mining from the Inside Out*. London: Routledge.

Geenen, S. and B. Radley (2014) 'In the Face of Reform: What Future for ASM in the Eastern
DRC?', *Futures* 62(A): 58–66.

Geenen, S. and J. Verweijen (2017) 'Explaining Fragmented and Fluid Mobilization in Gold
Mining Concessions in Eastern Democratic Republic of the Congo', *The Extractive Industries and Society* 4(4): 758–765.

Geenen, S., D. Fahey, and F.I. Mukotanyi (2013) 'The Future of Artisanal Gold Mining
and Miners under an Increasing Industrial Presence in South Kivu and Ituri, Eastern
Democratic Republic of Congo', Discussion Paper No. 2013.03. Antwerp: Institute of
Development Policy and Management, University of Antwerp.

Geenen, S., B. Nkuba, and B. Radley (2023) 'Technologies and Transformations. Traces from a Collective Research Project', *The Extractive Industries and Society* 12. https://doi.org/10.1016/j.exis.2022.101184.

Gereffi, G. (2014) 'Global Value Chains in a Post-Washington Consensus World', *Review of International Political Economy* 21(1): 9–37.

Gereffi, G., J. Humphrey, and T. Sturgeon (2005) 'The Governance of Global Value Chains', *Review of International Political Economy* 12(1): 78–104.

Ghai, D. (1972) 'Perspectives on Future Economic Prospects and Problems in Africa', in J. Bhagwati (ed.) *Economics and World Order: From the 1970s to the 1990s.* New York: Macmillan, pp. 257–286.

Girvan, N. (1970) 'Multinational Corporations and Dependent Underdevelopment in Mineral-Export Economies', *Social and Economic Studies* 19(4): 490–526.

Girvan, N. (2006) 'Caribbean Dependency Thought Revisited', *Canadian Journal of Development Studies* 27(3): 328–352.

Global Witness (2009) *Face à un fusil, que peut-on faire?: La guerre et la militarisation du secteur minier dans l'est du Congo.* London: Global Witness.

Global Witness (2016) *River of Gold: How the State Lost Out in an Eastern Congo Gold Boom, While Armed Groups, a Foreign Mining Company and Provincial Authorities Pocketed Millions.* London: Global Witness.

Graham, Y. (2022) 'Reflections on the African Mining Vision: The Fragmented Terrain of Mineral Governance in Africa', *New Agenda* 83: 15–18.

Greco, E. (2020) 'Africa, Extractivism and the Crisis This Time', *Review of African Political Economy* 47(166): 511–521.

Group of Experts on the DRC (2011) *Final Report of the Group of Experts on the Democratic Republic of the Congo.* New York: United Nations Security Council.

Haggard, S. (2018) *Developmental States.* Cambridge: Cambridge University Press.

Hanlin, R. and C. Hanlin (2012) 'The View from Below: Lock-In and Local Procurement in the African Gold Mining Sector', *Resources Policy* 37(4): 468–474.

Hansen M.W., L. Buur, A.M. Kjær, and O. Therkildsen (2016) 'The Economics and Politics of Local Content in African Extractives: Lessons From Tanzania, Uganda and Mozambique', *Forum for Development Studies* 43(2): 201–228.

Harvey, D. (2004) 'The "New" Imperialism: Accumulation by Dispossession', *Socialist Register* 40: 63–87.

Hauge, J. (2020) 'Industrial Policy in the Era of Global Value Chains: Towards a Developmentalist Framework Drawing on the Industrialisation Experiences of South Korea and Taiwan', *World Economy* 43(8): 2070–2092.

Hesselbein, G. (2007) 'The Rise and Decline of the Congolese State: An Analytical Narrative on State-Making', Working Paper No. 21. London: Crisis States Research Centre.

Hesselbein, G. (2009) 'The Economic Foundations of State-Building and State-Failure: A Political Economy of Sub-Saharan African States', PhD thesis. Zurich: University of Zurich.

Hirschman, A. (1977) 'A Generalised Approach to Development, with Special Reference to Staples', *Economic Development and Cultural Change* 25: 67–80.

Hilson, A.E. and J.S. Ovadia (2020) 'Local Content in Developing and Middle-Income Countries: Towards a More Holistic Strategy', *The Extractive Industries and Society* 7: 253–262.

Hilson, G. (2002) 'An Overview of Land Use Conflicts in Mining Communities', *Land Use Policy* 19: 65–73.

Hilson, G. (2009) 'Small-Scale Mining, Poverty and Economic Development in Sub-Saharan Africa: An Overview', *Resources Policy* 34: 1–5.

Hilson, G. (2019) 'Why Is There a Large-Scale Mining "Bias" in Sub-Saharan Africa?', *Land Use Policy* 81: 852–861.

Hilson, G. and N. Yakovleva (2007) 'Strained Relations: A Critical Analysis of the Mining Conflict in Prestea, Ghana', *Political Geography* 26: 98–119.

Hoffman, K. (2021) 'Ethnogovernmentality: The Making of Ethnic Territories and Subjects in Eastern DR Congo', *Geoforum* 119: 251–267.

Hormeku-Ajei, T. and C. Goetz (2022) 'A History of Resource Plunder', *New Agenda* 83: 10–15.

Horner, R. and D. Hulme (2019) 'From International to Global Development: New Geographies of 21st Century Development', *Development and Change* 50(2): 347–378.

Ietto-Gillies, G. (2013) *The Theory of the Transnational Corporation at 50+*. London: London South Bank University and Birkbeck University of London.

International Council on Mining and Metals (2016) *Role of Mining in National Economies*. London: International Council on Mining and Metals.

Itaman, R. and C. Wolf (2021) 'Industrial Policy and Monopoly Capitalism in Nigeria: Lessons from the Dangote Business Conglomerate', *Development and Change* 52(6): 1473–1502.

Jacob, T. and R.H. Pedersen (2018) 'New Resource Nationalism? Continuity and Change in Tanzania's Extractive Industries', *The Extractive Industries and Society* 5(2): 287–292.

Kamlongera, P.J. (2011) 'Making the Poor "Poorer" or Alleviating Poverty? Artisanal Mining Livelihoods in Rural Malawi', *Journal of International Development* 23: 1128–1139.

Kamundala, G. (2012) *Exploitation minière industrielle et artisanale au Sud-Kivu: Possibilités d'une cohabitation pacifique?*. Antwerp: International Peace Information Service.

Kamundala, G., S. Marysse, and F.M. Iragi (2015) 'Viabilité économique de l'exploitation artisanale de l'or au Sud-Kivu face à la compétition des entreprises minières internationales', in S. Marysse and J. Omasombo Tshonda (eds) *Conjonctures Congolaises 2014. Politiques, territoires et ressources naturelles: Changements et continuités*. Paris: L'Harmattan, pp. 167–195.

Kaplinsky, R., M. Morris, and D. Kaplan (2011) *A Conceptual Overview to Understand Commodities, Linkages and Industrial Development in Africa*. London: Africa Export Import Bank.

Kavanagh, M. (2022) 'UN Experts Want Better Gold Data as Trade Fuels Congo Violence', *Bloomberg*, 18 June, https://www.bloomberg.com/news/articles/2022-06-18/un-experts-want-better-gold-data-as-trade-fuels-congo-violence (accessed 29 July 2022).

Kay, C. (2002) 'Why East Asia Overtook Latin America: Agrarian Reform, Industrialisation and Development', *Third World Quarterly* 23(6): 1073–1102.

Kay, C. (2009) 'Development Strategies and Rural Development: Exploring Synergies, Eradicating Poverty', *Journal of Peasant Studies* 36(1): 103–137.

Kennes, E. (2005) 'The Mining Sector in Congo: The Victim or the Orphan of Globalization?', in S. Marysse and F. Reyntjens (eds) *The Political Economy of the Great Lakes Region in Africa: The Pitfalls of Enforced Democracy and Globalization*. Basingtsoke: Palgrave Macmillan, pp. 152–189.

Kibwe-Kasongo, V. (1994) 'Analyse financiere de la société minière et industrielle du Kivu (SOMINKI) 1986–1990', Masters thesis. Bukavu: Université Catholique de Bukavu.

Kinyonde, A. and C. Huggins (2019) 'Resource Nationalism in Tanzania: Implications for Artisanal and Small-Scale Mining', *The Extractive Industries and Society* 6: 181–189.

Kvangraven, I.H., M.D. Styve, and U. Kufakurinani (2021) 'Samir Amin and Beyond: The Enduring Relevance of Amin's Approach to Political Economy', *Review of African Political Economy* 48(167): 1–7.

Kyanga, W.A. (2013) 'SOMINKI en liquidation: Aide-memoire sur l'evolution de la société à Kamituga', unpublished report, Bukavu.

Lanzano, C. (2020) 'Guinea Conakry and Burkina Faso: Innovations at the Periphery', in B. Verbrugge and S. Geenen (eds) *Global Gold Production Touching Ground*. London: Palgrave Macmillan, pp. 245–262.

Laudati, A. (2013) 'Beyond Minerals: Broadening "Economies of Violence" in Eastern Democratic Republic of Congo', *Review of African Political Economy* 40(135): 32–50.

Lewis, A. (1954) 'Economic Development with Unlimited Supplies of Labour', *Manchester School of Economic and Social Studies* 22(2): 139–191.

Lujala, P., N.P. Gleditsch, and E. Gilmore (2005) 'A Diamond Curse?: Civil War and a Lootable Resource', *Journal of Conflict Resolution* 49(4): 538–562.

Lukusa, G. (2016) *L'économie congolaise de 2007 à 2016: Persistance des facteurs d'enlisement en RDC*. Paris: L'Harmattan.

Luning, S. (2008) 'Liberalisation of the Gold Mining Sector in Burkina Faso', *Review of African Political Economy* 35(117): 387–401.

MacGaffey, J. (1986) 'Fending-for-Yourself: The Organization of the Second Economy in Zaire', in G. Nzongola-Ntalaja (ed.) *The Crisis in Zaire: Myths and Realities*. Trenton, NJ: Africa World Press, pp. 141–156.

MacGaffey, J. (1991) *Entrepreneurs and Parasites: The Struggle for Indigenous Capitalism in Zaire*. Cambridge: Cambridge University Press.

MacGaffey, J. (1992) 'Initiatives From Below: Zaire's Other Path to Social and Economic Restructuring', in G. Hyden and M. Bratton (eds) *Governance and Politics in Africa*. London: Lynne Rienner Publishers, pp. 243–261.

Manky, O. (2018) 'Part-Time Miners: Labor Segmentation and Collective Action in the Peruvian Mining Industry', *Latin American Perspectives* 45(5): 120–135.

Marysse, S. and C. Tshimanga (2013) 'La renaissance spectaculaire du secteur minier en RDC: Ou va la rente minière?', in S. Marysse and J. Omasombo Tshonda (eds) *Conjonctures Congolaises 2012: Politique, secteur minier et gestion des ressources naturelles en RD Congo*. Paris: L'Harmattan, pp. 11–46.

Marysse, S. and C. Tshimanga (2014) 'Les "trous noirs" de la rente minière en RDC', in S. Marysse and J. O. Tshonda (eds) *Conjonctures Congolaises 2013: Percée sécuritaire, flottements politiques et essor économique*. Paris: L'Harmattan, pp. 131–168.

Matata Ponyo, M. (2017) 'Qualité de l'ajustement budgétaire et croissance économique: Le cas de la RDC 1974–2015', PhD thesis. Kinshasa: University of the Congo.

Mayer Brown (2015) *Main Legal Issues Regarding Financing of Mining Projects in Eritrea*. London: Mayer Brown.

Mazalto, M. (2008) 'La réforme du secteur minier en République Démocratique du Congo: Enjeux de gouvernance et perspectives de reconstruction', *Afrique contemporaine* 3(227): 53–80.

McGee, N. (2018) 'Banro Debut-for-Equity Restructuring Approved by Court', *The Globe and Mail*, 28 March, http://www.theglobeandmail.com/business/industry-news/energy-and-resources/article-banro-debt-for-equity-restructuring-approved-by-court (accessed 18 August 2021).

Melber, H. (2016) 'The African Middle Class(es)—In the Middle of What?', *Review of African Political Economy* 44(151): 142–154.

Mkandawire, T. (1988) 'The Road to Crisis, Adjustment and Deindustrialisation: The African Case', *Africa Development* 13(1): 5–31.

Mkandawire, T. (2001) 'Thinking about Developmental States in Africa', *Cambridge Journal of Economics* 25(3): 289–314.

Mkandawire, T. and C.C. Soludo (1999) *Our Continent Our Future: African Perspectives on Structural Adjustment*. Dakar: CODESRIA.

Money, D., H.O. Frøland, and T. Gwatiwa (2020) 'Africa–EU Relations and Natural Resource Governance: Understanding African Agency in Historical and Contemporary Perspective', *Review of African Political Economy* 47(166): 585–603.

Montes, M. (2014) *Obstacles to Development in the Global Economic System*. Geneva: South Centre.

Morris, M., R. Kaplinsky, and D. Kaplan (2012) '"One Thing Leads to Another": Commodities, Linkages and Industrial Development', *Resources Policy* 37(4): 408–416.

Mosley, P. and J. Weeks (1993) 'Has Recovery Begun?: Africa's Adjustment in the 1980s Revisited', *World Development* 21(10): 1583–1606.

Maphanga, T. (2022) 'The African Mining Vision: Prospects and Challenges', *New Agenda* 83: 19–22.

Mthembu-Salter, G. (2009) 'Social and Economic Dynamics of Mining in Kalima', DRC, Working Paper No. 185. Pretoria: Institute for Security Studies.

Mupepele Monti, L. (2012) *L'industrie minérale Congolaise*. Kinshasa: L'Harmattan RDC.

Mushagalusa, A. (2018) 'Etude portant sur le régime de protection des travailleurs prestant dans les entreprises de sous–traitance', unpublished report. Bukavu, DRC.

Ndikumana, L. (2015) 'Integrated Yet Marginalized: Implications of Globalization for African Development', Working Paper No. 381. Amherst, MA: Political Economy Research Institute.

Newman, S. (2012) *Financialisation and Transnational Supply Chains: Implications for Developing Countries*. Geneva: United Nations Conference on Trade and Development.

Nkuba, B., A.G. Muhanzi, and M.F. Zahinda (2022) 'How Do Technological Changes in Artisanal and Small-Scale Gold Mining Affect the Environment and Communities' Health?', *The Extractive Industries and Society* 12. https://doi.org/10.1016/j.exis.2022.101178.

Ntampaka, K. (1978) 'De la legislation sur le travail: Un essai d'interpretation des conditions des travailleurs sous le régime syndical au Kivu (1946–1960)', Masters thesis. Bukavu: Institut superier pedagogique de Bukavu.

Nyame, F.K. and J. Blocher (2010) 'Influence of Land Tenure Practices on Artisanal Mining Activity in Ghana', *Resources Policy* 35(1): 47–53.

OGP (*Observatoire gouvernance et paix*) (2008) *Potentialités des entités administratives decentralisés: Collectivité chefferie de Luhwinja*. Bukavu: Observatoire gouvernance et paix.

OGP (2010) *Resources minières et développement de la RD Congo: La gouvernance minière au Sud-Kivu*. Bukavu: Observatoire gouvernance et paix.

Ocampo, J.A., C. Rada, and L. Taylor (2009) *Growth and Policy in Developing Countries: A Structuralist Approach*. New York: Columbia University Press.

Odijie, M.E. (2020) 'Is Traditional Industrial Policy Defunct? Evidence from the Nigerian Cement Industry', *Review of International Political Economy* 27(3): 686–708.

Olsson, O. (2006) 'Diamonds are a Rebel's Best Friend', *World Economy* 29(8): 1133–1150.

Ovadia, J.S. (2016) 'Local Content Policies and Petro-development in Sub-Saharan Africa: A Comparative Analysis', *Resources Policy* 49: 20–30.

Ovadia, J.S. and C. Wolf (2018) 'Studying the Developmental State: Theory and Method in Research on Industrial Policy and State-Led Development in Africa', *Third World Quarterly* 39(6): 1056–1076.

Owenga Odinga, E.L. (2014) *Droit minier, tome 1: Régime minier général pour les mines et les carrières*. Kinshasa: Publications pour la promotion du droit congolais.

Panella, C. (2010) 'Orpaillage artisanal et cotoniculture: Economie, oecuménique et éthique sociale dans le basidibé (Mali)', in C. Panella *Worlds of Debts: Interdisciplinary Perspectives on Gold Mining in West-Africa*. Amsterdam: Rozenberg Publishers, pp. 49–78.

Pederson, R.H., W. Mutagwaba, J.B. Jønsson, G. Schoneveld, T. Jacobe, M. Chacha, X. Weng, and M.G. Njau (2019) 'Mining-Sector Dynamics in an Era of Resurgent Resource Nationalism: Changing Relations between Large-Scale Mining and Artisanal and Small-Scale Mining in Tanzania', *Resources Policy* 62: 339–346.

Peemans, J. (1975) 'The Social and Economic Development of Zaire since Independence: An Historical Outline', *African Affairs* 74(295): 148–179.

Pegg, S. (2006) 'Mining and Poverty Reduction: Transforming Rhetoric into Reality', *Journal of Cleaner Production* 14(3–4): 376–387.

Perks, R. (2011) '"Can I Go?" Exiting the Artisanal Mining Sector in the Democratic Republic of the Congo', *Journal of International Development* 23: 1115–1127.

Peyer, C., P. Feeney, and F. Mercier (2014) *PR or Progress? Glencore's Corporate Responsibility in the DRC.* Oxford: Bread for All, Rights and Accountability in Development, and Fastenopfer.

Pierre, J. (2020) 'The Racial Vernaculars of Development: A View from West Africa', *American Anthropologist* 122(1): 86–98.

Pijpers, R. (2014) 'Crops and Carats: Exploring the Interconnectedness of Mining and Agriculture in Sub-Saharan Africa', *Futures* 62: 32–39.

Pozzebon, M. and I.A. Fontenell (2018) 'Fostering the Post-Development Debate: The Latin American Concept of Tecnologia Social', *Third World Quarterly* 39(9): 1750–1769.

Prebisch, R. (1950) *The Economic Development of Latin America and Its Principal Problems.* New York: UN Economic Commission for Latin America.

Putzel, J., S. Lindemann, and C. Schouten (2008) 'Drivers of Change in the Democratic Republic of Congo: The Rise and Decline of the State and Challenges for Reconstruction', Working Paper No. 26. London: Crisis States Research Centre.

Radley, B. and C. Vogel (2015) 'Fighting Windmills in Eastern Congo? The Ambiguous Impact of the "Conflict Minerals" Movement', *The Extractive Industries and Society* 2: 406–410.

Raeymaekers, T. (2014) *Violent Capitalism and Hybrid Identity in the Eastern Congo: Power to the Margins.* Cambridge: Cambridge University Press.

Ramdoo, I. (2016) 'Local Content Policies in Mineral-Rich Countries: An Overview', Discussion Paper 193. Maastricht: European Centre for Development Policy Management.

Randgold Resources (2018) 'Commissioning of Automated Underground Mind drives Production Growth at Kibali', 23 April, http://www.randgoldresources.com/commissioning-automated-underground-mine-drives-production-growth-kibali (accessed 4 October 2018).

Reuters (2018) 'Banro Gold Mind Trucks Attacked in Eastern Congo, Two Dead', 11 August, https://www.reuters.com/article/us-banro-congo-violence-idUSKBN1KW0IY (accessed 28 June 2023).

Richards, J.P. (2009) *Mining, Society and a Sustainable World.* New York: Springer.

Rio Tinto (2018) 'Pioneering Progress: 2018 Sustainable Development Report', London: Rio Tinto.

Rodgers, E. (2006) 'Conflict Diamonds: Certification and Corruption: A Case Study of Sierra Leone', *Journal of Financial Crime* 13(3): 267–276.

Rothenberg, D. (2014) *Selected Oral Histories from the Artisanal Mining Industry in North Kivu and South Kivu.* Tempe, AZ: Arizona State University.

Rustad, S.A., G. Østby, and R. Nordås (2016) 'Artisanal Mining, Conflict, and Sexual Violence in Eastern DRC', *The Extractive Industries and Society* 3: 475–484.

Schatzberg, M. (1980) *Politics and Class in Zaire: Bureaucracy, Business, and Beer in Lisala.* New York: Africana Publishing Company.

Scheck, J. and S. Patterson (2015) 'How a BlackRock Bet on African Gold Lost Its Luster', *Wall Street Journal*, updated 3 November, https://www.wsj.com/articles/how-a-blackrock-bet-on-african-gold-lost-its-luster-1446602000?mod=videorelated (accessed 16 February 2019).

Sematumba, O. (2011) *Economie minière à l'est de la RDC: Apres le marteau de Joseph Kabila, l'enclume de Barack Obama?* Goma: Pole Institute.

Sensoy, A., E. Hacihasanoglu, and D.K. Nguyen (2015) 'Dynamic Convergence of Commodity Futures: Not All Types of Commodities are Alike', *Resources Policy* 44: 150–160.

Shafiee, S. and E. Topal (2010) 'An Overview of Global Gold Market and Gold Price Forecasting', *Resources Policy* 35(3): 178–189.

Sharife, K. (2016) 'Panama Papers Reveal Dubious Behaviour by DRCs Gold Traders', 4 April, https://panamapapers.investigativecenters.org/drc/# (accessed 21 February 2018).

Singh, J.N. and J.S. Ovadia (2018) 'The Theory and Practice of Building Developmental States in the Global South', *Third World Quarterly* 39(6): 1033–1054.

Sovacool, B.K., S.H. Ali, M. Bazilian, B. Radley, B. Nemery, J. Okatz, and D. Mulvaney (2020) 'Sustainable Minerals and Metals for a Low-Carbon Future', *Science* 367(6473): 30–33.

Spittaels, S., K. Matthysen, Y. Weyns, F. Hilgert, and A. Bulzomi (2014) *'Analysis of the Interactive Map of Artisanal Mining Areas in Eastern DR Congo: May 2014 Update'*, Antwerp: International Peace Information Service.

Stoop, N., J.K. Buraye, and M. Verpoorten (2016) 'Relocation, Reorientation, or Confrontation? Insights from a Representative Survey among Artisanal Miners in Kamituga, South-Kivu', Working Paper No. 2016.09. Antwerp: University of Antwerp.

Storm, S. (2015) 'Structural Change', *Development and Change* 46(4): 666–699.

Sunkel, O. (1972) 'Big Business and "Dependencia": A Latin American View', *Foreign Affairs* 50: 517–531.

Sunkel, O. (1973) 'Transnational Capitalism and National Disintegration in Latin America', *Social and Economic Studies* 22(1): 132–176.

Suwandi, I. (2015) 'Behind the Veil of Globalization', *Monthly Review* 67(3): 37–53.

Sylla, N.S. (2015) 'From a Marginalised to an Emerging Africa? A Critical Analysis', *Review of African Political Economy* 41(1): 7–25.

Taylor, I. (2015) 'Dependency Redux: Why Africa is Not Rising', *Review of African Political Economy* 43(147): 1–18.

Tegera, A. (2011) *Réouverture des activités minières à l'est de la RD Congo: Enjeux et défis.* Goma: Pole Institute.

Toye, J. (1994) 'Structural Adjustment: Context, Assumptions, Origin and Diversity', in R.V.D. Hoeven and F.V.D. Kraaij (eds) *Structural Adjustment and Beyond in Sub-Saharan Africa.* London: James Currey, pp. 18–35.

Tshibambe, G.N. (2018) 'De la théorie de la dependencia: De l'importation à la réception locale à Lubumbashi', in M.K. Badi and C. Ross (eds) *Transitos materiales e inmateriales entre Africa, Latinoamérica y El Caribe.* Santiago: Ariadna Ediciones, pp. 193–205.

UNCTAD (United Nations Conference on Trade and Development) (2005) *Economic Development in Africa: Rethinking the Role of Foreign Direct Investment.* New York and Geneva: UNCTAD.

UNCTAD (2007) *The Least Developed Countries Report 2007: Knowledge, Technological Learning and Innovation for Development.* New York and Geneva: UNCTAD.

UNCTAD (2010) *The Least Developed Countries Report 2010: Towards a New International Development Architecture for LDCs.* New York and Geneva: UNCTAD.

UNCTAD (2013) *World Investment Report 2013: Global Value Chains, Investment and Trade for Development.* New York and Geneva: UNCTAD.

UNCTAD (2015) *World Investment Report 2015: Reforming International Investment Governance.* New York and Geneva: UNCTAD.

UNCTAD (2019) *World Investment Report 2019: Special Economic Zones.* New York and Geneva: UNCTAD.

UNDP (United Nations Development Programme) (2016) *Mapping Mining to the SDGs: An Atlas.* Geneva: UNDP.

UNECA (United Nations Economic Commission for Africa) (2011) *Minerals and Africa's Development*. Addis Ababa: UN Economic Commission for Africa.

UNECA (2021) 'Experts Unveil Fortunes Awaiting DRC, Africa in the Battery-Electric Vehicle Value Chain', 30 June, https://www.uneca.org/stories/experts-unveil-fortunes-awaiting-drc,-africa-in-the-battery-electric-vehicle-value-chain (accessed 31 August 2022).

UNEP (United Nations Environment Programme) (2015) *Experts' Background Report on Illegal Exploitation and Trade in Natural Resources Benefitting Organized Criminal Groups and Recommendations on MONUSCO's Role in Fostering Stability and Peace in Eastern DR Congo*. Kinshasa: UNEP.

UNIDO (United Nations Industrial Development Organization) (2012) *Promoting Industrial Diversification in Resource Intensive Economies: The Experiences of Sub-Saharan Africa and Central Asia Regions*. Geneva: UNIDO.

Van Acker, F. (2005) 'Where Did All the Land Go? Enclosure & Social Struggle in Kivu (D.R. Congo)', *Review of African Political Economy* 32(103): 79–98.

Vaitsos, C. (1973) '*Foreign Investment Policies and Economic Development in Latin America*', *Journal of World Trade* 7(6): 619–665.

Verbrugge, G. and S. Geenen (eds) (2020) *Global Gold Production Touching Ground*. London: Palgrave Macmillan.

Verbrugge, G. and R. Thiers (2021) 'Artisanal and Small-Scale Mining', in A.H. Akram-Lodhi, D. Kristin, B. Engels, and B.M. McKay (eds) *Handbook on Critical Agrarian Studies*. Cheltenham: Edward Elgar, pp. 401–409.

Verweijen, J. (2017) 'Luddites in the Congo?', *City* 21: 466–482.

Verweijen, J., P. Schouten, F.O. Simpson, and C.Z. Pascal (2022) 'Conservation, Conflict and Semi-Industrial Mining: The Case of Eastern DRC', Institute of Development Policy Analysis and Policy Brief No. 49. Antwerp: University of Antwerp.

Vlassenroot, K. and T. Raeymaekers (2004) *Conflict and Social Transformation in Eastern DR Congo*. Gent: Academia Press Scientific.

Vogel, C. (2022) *Conflict Minerals Inc.: War, Profit and White Saviourism in Eastern Congo*. London: Hurst Publishers.

Wade, R. (1990) *Governing the Market: Economic Theory and the Role of the Government in East Asian Industrialization*. Princeton, NJ: Princeton University Press.

Werner, M., J. Bair, and V.R. Fernàndez (2014) 'Linking Up to Development? Global Value Chains and the Making of a Post-Washington Consensus', *Development and Change* 45(6): 1219–1247.

Weyns, Y., L. Hoex, and K. Matthysen (2016) 'Analysis of the Interactive Map of Artisanal Mining Areas in Eastern DR Congo, 2015 Update', Antwerp: International Peace Information Service.

Wilburn, D.R. and K.A. Stanley (2013) *Exploration Review*. Reston, VA: United States Geological Survey.

Williamson, J. (1993) 'Democracy and the "Washington Consensus"', *World Development* 21(8): 1329–1336.

Wilson, T. (2016) 'Banro Trucks Targeted in Attack Kidnappings in Eastern Congo', *Bloomberg*, 19 September, https://www.bloomberg.com/news/articles/2016-09-19/banro-trucks-targeted-in-attack-kidnappings-in-eastern-congo (accessed 10 August 2018).

Witangila bin-Mubya, D. (1982) 'La question salariale au Kivu (1945–1960)', Masters thesis. Bukavu: Institut superieur pedagogique de Bukavu.

World Bank (1957) *The Economy of the Belgian Congo*. Washington, DC: World Bank.

World Bank (1970) *The Congo's Economy: Evolution and Prospects, Volume I: Main Report*. Washington, DC: World Bank.

World Bank (1973) *Recent Economic Development and Prospects of the Republic of Zaire, Volume II: Annexes and Statistical Appendix*. Washington, DC: World Bank.

World Bank (1975) *The Economy of Zaire, Volume III: Annexes and Statistical Appendix*. Washington, DC: World Bank.

World Bank (1981) *Accelerated Development in Sub-Saharan Africa: An Agenda for Action*. Washington, DC: World Bank.

World Bank (1984) *Zaire: Problèmes de développement région du Kivu*. Washington, DC: World Bank.

World Bank (1985) *Zaire Economic Memorandum Economic Change and External Assistance*. Washington, DC: World Bank.

World Bank (1992) *A Strategy for African Mining*. Washington, DC: World Bank.

World Bank (2010) *The World Bank's Evolutionary Approach to Mining Sector Reform*. Washington, DC: World Bank.

World Bank (2015) *The Power of the Mine: A Transformative Opportunity for Sub-Saharan Africa*. Washington, DC: World Bank.

World Bank (2020) *2020 State of the Artisanal and Small-Scale Mining Sector*. Washington, DC: World Bank.

World Gold Council (2011) *The Social and Economic Impacts of Gold Mining*. London: World Gold Council.

Wright, G. and J. Czelusta (2007) 'Resource-Based Growth Past and Present', in D. Lederman and W. F. Maloney (eds) *Natural Resources: Neither Curse nor Destiny*. Washington, DC: World Bank, pp. 183–212.

Young, C. and T. Turner (1985) *The Rise & Decline of the Zairian State*. Maddison, WI: The University of Wisconsin Press.

Publishers' acknowledgements

I would like to thank the following publishers for permission to reproduce some of my material from across these four papers:

Radley, B. 'A Distributional Analysis of Artisanal and Industrial Wage Levels and Expenditure in the Congolese Mining Sector', *Journal of Development Studies*, copyright © Taylor & Francis Ltd, reprinted by permission of Taylor & Francis Ltd, http://www.tandfonline.com.

Radley, B. 'Class Formation and Capital Accumulation in the Countryside: Artisanal and Small-Scale Gold Mining in South Kivu, DR Congo', *Journal of Agrarian Change*, copyright © John Wiley & Sons Ltd, reprinted by permission of John Wiley & Sons Ltd, http://www.wiley.com.

Radley, B. and S. Geenen. 'Struggles over Value: Corporate-State Suppression of Locally Led Mining Mechanisation in the Democratic Republic of the Congo', *Review of African Political Economy*, copyright © ROAPE Publications Ltd, reprinted by permission of Taylor & Francis Ltd, http://www.tandfonline.com on behalf of ROAPE Publications Ltd.

Radley, B. 'The End of the African Mining Enclave? Domestic Marginalization and Labour Fragmentation in the Democratic Republic of Congo', *Development and Change*, copyright © International Institute of Social Studies, reprinted by permission of John Wiley & Sons Ltd, http://www.wiley.com.

Index

For the benefit of digital users, indexed terms that span two pages (e.g., 52–53) may, on occasion, appear on only one of those pages.